THE HANDBOOK OF
SUSTAINABILITY LITERACY

The Handbook of
SUSTAINABILITY
LITERACY

Skills for a changing world

Edited by Arran Stibbe

green books

First published in the UK in 2009
by Green Books Ltd,
Dartington Space, Dartington Hall,
Totnes, Devon TQ9 6EN

Reprinted 2011

Cover design by Stephen Prior

ISBN 978 1 900322 60 7

Text printed on 100% recycled paper
by TJ International, Padstow, Cornwall, UK

Contents

Acknowledgements 8

Introduction *by Arran Stibbe and Heather Luna* 9

PART 1: SKILLS FOR A CHANGING WORLD

1 **Ecocriticism:** the ability to investigate cultural artefacts 19
from an ecological perspective *by Greg Garrard*

2 **Optimisation:** the art of personal sufficiency *by John Naish* 25

3 **Grounded Economic Awareness:** economic awareness 30
based on ecological and ethical values *by Satish Kumar*

4 **Advertising Awareness:** the ability to expose advertising 37
discourses that undermine sustainability, and resist them
by Arran Stibbe

5 **Transition Skills:** skills for transition to a post-fossil-fuel age 43
by Stephen Quilley

6 **Commons Thinking:** the ability to envisage and enable 51
a viable future through connected action *by Justin Kenrick*

7 **Effortless Action:** the ability to fulfil human needs 58
effortlessly through working with nature *by Ling Feng*

8 **Permaculture Design:** designing our lives with nature 64
as the model *by Patrick Whitefield*

9 **Community Gardening:** skills for building community 70
and working within environmental limits *by Alma Clavin*

10 **Ecological Intelligence:** viewing the world relationally 77
by Stephen Sterling

Contents

11 **Systems Thinking:** the ability to recognise and analyse the interconnections within and between systems *by Glenn Strachan*   84

12 **Gaia Awareness:** awareness of the animate qualities of the Earth *by Stephan Harding*   89

13 **Futures Thinking:** the ability to envision scenarios of a more desirable future *by Sue Wayman*   94

14 **Values Reflection and the Earth Charter:** the ability to critique the values of an unsustainable society and consider alternatives *by Jeffrey Newman*   99

15 **Social Conscience:** the ability to reflect on deeply-held opinions about social justice and sustainability *by Myshele Goldberg*   105

16 **New Media Literacy:** communication skills for sustainability *by John Blewitt*   111

17 **Cultural Literacy:** understanding and respect for the cultural aspects of sustainability *by Kim Polistina*   117

18 **Carbon Capability:** understanding climate change and reducing emissions *by Lorraine Whitmarsh, Saffron O'Neill, Gill Seyfang and Irene Lorenzoni*   124

19 **Greening Business:** the ability to drive environmental and sustainability improvements in the workplace *by Zoe Robinson*   130

20 **Materials Awareness:** the ability to expose the hidden impact of materials on sustainability *by Melinda Watson*   137

21 **Appropriate Technology and Appropriate Design:** the ability to design systems, technologies and equipment in an appropriate way *by Mike Clifford*   144

22 **Technology Appraisal:** the ability to evaluate technological innovations *by Gavin Harper*   150

23 **Complexity, Systems Thinking and Practice:** skills and   156
techniques for managing complex systems
by Dick Morris and Stephen Martin

24 **Coping with Complexity:** the ability to manage complex   165
sustainability problems *by Bland Tomkinson*

25 **Emotional Well-being:** the ability to research and reflect   171
on the roots of emotional well-being *by Morgan Phillips*

26 **Finding Meaning without Consuming:** the ability to experience   178
meaning, purpose and satisfaction through non-material wealth
by Paul Maiteny

27 **Being-in-the-World:** the ability to think about the self in   185
interconnection and interdependence with the surrounding world
by John Danvers

28 **Beauty as a Way of Knowing:** the redemption of knowing   191
through the experience of beauty *by Barry Bignell*

PART 2: EDUCATIONAL TRANSFORMATION
FOR SUSTAINABILITY LITERACY

29 **Citizen Engagement** *by Geoff Fagan*   199

30 **Re-educating the Person** *by Karen Blincoe*   204

31 **Institutional Transformation** *by Anne Phillips*   209

32 **A Learning Society** *by Kate Davies*   215

Acknowledgements

The Handbook of Sustainability Literacy: skills for a changing world arises from a larger project, *Soundings in Sustainability Literacy,* which is funded by the Higher Education Academy's Education for Sustainable Development Project and the University of Gloucestershire Centre for Active Learning. The project is undertaken in partnership with the Environmental Association of Universities and Colleges, the United Nations Regional Centre of Expertise in Education for Sustainable Development (Severn Region), and the University of Brighton. Many thanks to authors for attending events and workshops, contributing chapters and working on multiple drafts, as well as to all the peer reviewers and proofreaders. The editing of the book and communication with authors was done entirely with open source software (using the Ubuntu operating system), which is developed by groups of programmers working voluntarily to fulfil the needs of the wider community rather than for profit. The software proved very suitable for the task. Although printed on recycled paper with vegetable inks, the book does have an environmental cost, so appreciation is due to all those affected by its manufacture; it is hoped that the harm caused will be compensated for to some extent by the impact of the content of the book. Final thanks go to Ryoko, Kaya and Sen for providing a warm, friendly, and lively atmosphere for editing the book in.

Introduction

Arran Stibbe

Humanities Department and Centre for Active Learning,
University of Gloucestershire

Heather Luna

Higher Education Academy
Education for Sustainable Development Project

It has long been recognised that the social and physical worlds we inhabit are in a state of rapid change; within this turmoil, the only place that we can find continuity is in the certainty of change itself. The twentieth century saw astounding changes in population, in technology, in urbanisation, in industrialisation, in globalisation – facilitated mainly by the availability of cheap and abundant fossil fuels and the drive to use them to produce more and more food and material goods. Over the course of the twentieth century, world population increased 3.5 times to reach six billion; the number of cars in the UK rose from 8000 to 21 million; and in 1999 more people were living in cities than the entire world population of 1950.

The premise of this book is that the twenty-first century will be a time of change no less dramatic than that of the twentieth century, but that the changes will be of an entirely different nature. The reason for this is a convergence of trends which are individually subject to uncertainty, but collectively give a clear indication of the trajectory of society. The world population is continuing to expand, consumption in the larger developing countries is increasing rapidly, and the consequential demands for energy, water and biological resources are rising. At the same time, we can no longer depend on the input of energy from cheap fossil fuels, partly because of restrictions imposed by climate change legislation, but also because oil production is set to peak and start its inevitable decline, threatening everything that depends on it, from transportation and plastics to agriculture. These trends, combined with the now inevitable impact of climate change, ecosystem degradation, and the exhaustion of a wide range of resources, mean that the Earth is becoming a less hospitable place for human life, and the lives of countless other species.

There is, therefore, an increasingly important facet to the already multifaceted concept of sustainability. In 1987, the Bruntland report wrote of the importance of meeting the needs of the present without compromising the ability of future generations to meet their own needs. Since then, efforts to build more sustainable societies have failed dramatically. Those born in 1987 are now in their twenties; they are members of the future generations Bruntland was referring to, and their ability to meet their own needs in the future *has* been compromised. Increasingly, sustainability becomes a struggle not only to ensure that future generations have the means to survive, but also to meet the needs of the present in the deteriorating conditions of the world.

As the Transition Movement (Hopkins 2008) has shown so well, combining the ideal of allowing future generations to meet their needs with the far more practical task of preparing for difficult times ahead in the near future can galvanise communities into action, with immediate and multiple benefits. If carefully planned, the transition toward a society which relies far less on fossil fuels and physical materials has the potential to satisfy a wide range of human needs which are not being effectively met by the present consumerism-based society. The transition could help people escape from the addiction and isolation of consumerism, gain a sense of belonging to a community, improve their mental and physical health through time spent working in and with nature, reduce the risk of obesity and the many illnesses associated with a sedentary lifestyle, live in a cleaner environment, and find meaningful employment – while still benefiting from advances in medicine and appropriate technology. The improvements may, of course, be short-lived and overtaken by external changes that are simply too large to adapt to, such as resource conflicts, extreme weather events and ecological breakdown. But even if short-lived, the benefits are nonetheless real for those enjoying them, and the self / community / business / society in transition provides a model of sustainability for those in power who are well-placed for influencing the trajectory of society. Transition, then, is an emerging aspect of sustainability that is well covered in this book, and complements other important aspects such as global social justice. Social justice is only possible if developed countries massively reduce their consumption and provide aspirational models based on fulfilling people's needs rather than on competitive material accumulation.

The ability to take steps towards building a more sustainable self and society requires far more than knowledge *about* sustainability – it requires *sustainability literacy*. This book uses the term *sustainability literacy* to indicate the skills, attitudes, competencies, dispositions and values that are necessary for surviving and thriving in the declining conditions of the world in ways which slow down that decline as far as possible. Gaining practical skills requires a form of learning which goes beyond memorising and repeating facts. It requires *active learning*, a broad term used to refer to self-reflection, self-directed enquiry, learning by doing, engagement with real life issues, and learning within communities of practice.

The metaphorical use of the term 'literacy' in *sustainability literacy* stretches it from its literal use within the area of reading and writing. However, in linguistic theory, *literacy* refers to far more than a binary category 'can/cannot read and write'. Instead, it refers to a wide range of *practices* people are empowered to participate in, through having skills in using language in particular ways. For example, being influential and successful in the commercial world requires the ability to read and write business plans, reports and formal letters. Literacy, then, is a collection of skills that allow for effective participation and influence in diverse areas of social life. As people gain *sustainability literacy* skills, they become empowered to read society critically, discovering insights into the unsustainable trajectory that the society is on and the social structures that underpin this trajectory. But more than this, they become empowered to engage with those social structures and contribute to the re-writing of self and society along more sustainable lines.

Ray Anderson, former CEO of Interface Carpets, provides an example of someone who had very little in the way of sustainability literacy, but started reading society and his own role within it critically, and began to re-write himself and his business in more sustainable ways. The change was triggered when Anderson experienced a sudden epiphany while reading Paul Hawken's (1994) *The Ecology of Commerce*. He came across the term 'the death of birth' and, in his own words:

> It was E.O. Wilson's expression for species extinction, the death of birth, and it was the point of a spear into my chest, and I read on and the spear became deeper, and it was an epiphanous experience, a total change of mindset for myself, and a change of paradigm. (Anderson 2005).

He realised that the company he was leading, Interface Carpets, was acting in an entirely unsustainable way:

> . . . it dawned on me that the way I was running Interface was the way of the plunderer. Plundering something that's not mine. Something that belongs to every creature on earth. [I realised that] someday people like me will end up in jail. . . . (Anderson 2005)

At this point we could say that Anderson had gained, at a deep reflective level, *knowledge about sustainability*. Sustainability literacy, however, is more than that – it is the ability to act on that knowledge. Anderson managed to transform his company from one selling carpets to be disposed of after use to one which provided a carpet covering *service*. His company started renting out carpet tiles, reusing them when no longer required, replacing only those that had worn out, and even then recycling the discards using energy generated from wind and sun. Transforming corporations in this way requires skills in *ecological intelligence*, to understand the impact of actions on the ecosystems which support life, *systems thinking*, to gain a holistic picture of inputs, outputs and waste to maximise reuse and recycling, *appropriate technology* and *appropriate design* to minimise the adverse impacts of the technologies employed, *cultural literacy* to adapt solutions to specific cultures, and a wide range of other sustainability literacy skills described in this book.

The initial impetus for the book was the realisation that educational policy tends, even now, to revolve around twentieth-century skills – skills for commercial innovation, further industrialisation of society, economic growth, international competitiveness, and financial prosperity. The further we proceed in the twenty-first century, the more short-term these goals seem – a temporary bubble of financial prosperity existing on paper only, already partially burst by the 'credit crunch', and about to be burst on a much larger scale by the 'ecological crunch', the 'peak oil crunch', and the 'climate change crunch'.

In order to explore what skills would be more suitable for life in the twenty-first century, the book brings leading sustainability educators together with specialists from a wide range of areas, including engineering, art, permaculture, outdoor education, anthropology, literature, mathematics, business studies, climatology, ecology, and linguistics. Interaction and discussion among authors was encouraged through a series of workshops and symposia, including the national conference *Soundings in Sustainability Literacy*, as well as through a peer review process. In the first section of the book, *Skills for a Changing World*, the authors of twenty-eight chapters explore a particular skill, attribute or disposition, such as *Materials Awareness*, *Permaculture Design*, or *Futures Thinking*. The chapters show why the skill in question is important for life in the changing world of the twenty-first century, and give active learning exercises for development of the skill. They each close with a list of resources for gaining a deeper insight into the skill described. In the second section, *Educational Transformation for Sustainability Literacy*, four chapters explore the question of how educational systems and institutions will need to adapt if they are to help learners gain the sustainability literacy skills described in the first section.

The book is intended to be a *handbook* in the sense of containing practical ideas that can be adapted and applied by a wide range of educators, from parents to professors, but not as a rigid guide to the 'one right way'. There is no simple, empirical way of determining whether a particular skill will help learners survive and thrive in the future conditions of the world, not least because those conditions are uncertain. Instead, the book aims to bring together multiple, carefully thought-out perspectives which can shift the debate away from the narrow focus in main-stream educational policy on 'skill sets' for employability. These skill sets often fail to take into consideration environmental limits, social justice, or adaptation to the deteriorating ability of the Earth to support human life. They are, therefore, unlikely to serve the long-term interests of learners, businesses, societies, the human species or the wider community of life. Alternative possibilities, more grounded in the realities of the changing world, need to be articulated, but without reproducing the same 'tick-box' approach to skills associated both with dominant discourses and with some efforts to define sustainability literacy in the past.

The aim of the book is, therefore, to open up a range of previously un-thought-of paths, some of which will no doubt be rejected, but some considered worthy of further exploration. There may well be parts that are contentious or refutable, but given the conditions of the world this was considered preferable to something that was so blandly abstract that it was beyond debate. To borrow words from Rachel Carson (1962:16), 'I would ask those who find parts of this book not to their taste or consider that they can refute some of the arguments to see the picture as a whole. We are dealing with dangerous things and it may be too late to wait for positive evidence of danger'.

To help convey the picture as a whole, the layout of the book is designed to facilitate reading from cover to cover, with chapters exploring similar themes placed in proximity, and chapters which build on each other placed in sequence. The remainder of this introduction provides a brief overview of the book, mentioning all the chapters in the order they appear (the titles of the chapters are in italics).

* * *

The starting point of the book is not the environmental problems which are undermining the ability of the Earth to support human life, but instead the social, cultural and economic systems that give rise to those problems. Without considering this deeper level we will, to use Allen's (1951:19) expression, be 'fighting against circumstances':

> . . . what, then, is the meaning of 'fighting against circumstances'? It means that a man is continuously revolting against an effect without, while all the time he is nourishing and preserving its cause in his heart

Of particular concern in the opening chapters are the economic and social forces which encourage unnecessary consumption, debt and environmental destruc-tion, and the ability of learners to critique and resist these forces (chapters: *Ecocriticism, Optimisation, Grounded Economic Awareness* and *Advertising Awareness*). Critique by itself, however, is not enough. Learners also need practical skills to equip them for the transition away from consumerist societies – which are entirely dependent on fossil fuels – towards strong, resilient communities capable of fulfilling human needs with minimal use of energy and resources (chapters: *Transition Skills* and *Commons Thinking*). One path for moving beyond fossil fuels is to develop skills for working with nature to make the best possible use of 'ecosystem services' – the services which fulfilled basic and higher human needs long before the discovery of fossil fuel (chapters: *Effortless Action, Permaculture Design* and *Community Gardening*).

The transition to a more sustainable society requires thinking in fundamentally different ways from those that set society on a trajectory towards collapse in the first place. New ways of thinking (which are often revivals of older ways that have become marginalised) include the ability to think of the world relationally, as consisting of interconnected systems, and as having animate qualities itself (chapters: *Ecological Intelligence, Systems Thinking* and *Gaia Awareness*). Unless underpinned by ethics and values, however, new ways of thinking can be appropriated by political and commercial forces to serve narrow industrial goals. The ability to think in new ways, therefore, needs to be complemented by the ability to reflect on what kind of society or world is desirable, on what is important and worth protecting, and what, deep down, there is an ethical obligation to do (chapters: *Futures Thinking, Values Reflection and the Earth Charter* and *Social Conscience*).

The vision that emerges requires expression, not because reflection necessarily results in a 'better' vision, but because there are too many visions expressed by dominant forces in society that have not yet been updated to respond to the changed and changing context of the twenty-first century. Effectively and persuasively expressing a vision for the future involves skills in oral presentation, writing, and skilful use of new media, as well as the ability to communicate in ways which are culturally appropriate and sensitive to different perspectives (chapters: *New Media Literacy* and *Cultural Literacy*).

The concept of sustainability goes far beyond environmental concerns, including aspects such as social justice; intergenerational justice; mental and physical well-being; social, economic and cultural transformation; and the flourishing of the diversity of life. However, none of these is possible within a degraded and unliveable environment, so skills in reducing environmental footprints are an essential part of sustainability literacy (chapters: *Carbon Capability, Greening Business* and *Materials Awareness*). Technological issues are also highly relevant, primarily because it is technology which enables fossil fuel energy and environmental resources to be converted, on an immense and unsustainable scale, into material goods and then waste. As energy use becomes increasingly constrained and environmental resources depleted, it will be necessary for people to develop skills in rethinking and redesigning the role that technology plays in society (chapters: *Appropriate Technology and Appropriate Design* and *Technology Appraisal*). Technology, however, is only one aspect of the highly complex task of building a society along sustainable lines, and technological solutions have to be considered within the web of other factors that influence sustainability (chapters: *Complexity, Systems Thinking and Practice* and *Coping with Complexity*).

The deepest level of sustainability literacy is the psychological level, since problems which manifest themselves outwardly in injustice or destruction of the environment arise from social and cultural systems which are, in turn, located in individual psychology and social cognition. One important psychological aspect is awareness of what, deep down, gives people a sense of well-being. Only with this awareness can we find ways to gain life satisfaction without the over-consumption of resources (chapters: *Emotional Well-being* and *Finding Meaning without Consuming*). One psychological problem that is frequently blamed for both a lack of emotional well-being and for the kind of self-centred behaviour which leads to environmental destruction is *ecological alienation*. Ecological alienation is the feeling that human beings exist independently and separately from an external 'environment'; that our lives are not entwined with the lives of other organisms within the web of interconnection that is life. The ability to reconnect and feel a part of the world rather than apart from it may be an important factor in the ability to live sustainably (chapters: *Being-in-the-World* and *Beauty as a Way of Knowing*).

The final four chapters form a separate section entitled *Educational Transformation for Sustainability Literacy*, and move on from questions of the skills themselves to the next logical question: how can the educational system and educational institutions be transformed to enable learners to gain those skills? The suggestions are radical and thought-provoking, including rethinking not only the physical campus and curriculum, but also who the learners are and whose interests educational institutions serve (chapters: *Citizen Engagement, Re-educating the Person, Institutional Transformation* and *A Learning Society*).

* * *

From the many perspectives expressed in the chapters, a complex picture emerges of the skills, attributes and dispositions that the authors feel are necessary for life in the twenty-first century. It is, however, a picture which is far from complete and one which needs continuous updating and expanding on as the conditions of the world change. The project, therefore, continues with a multi-media version of *The Handbook of Sustainability Literacy* available at www.sustainability-literacy.org which includes additional chapters, video interviews with authors, discussion groups and further resources.

One final point is that, given the trajectory of society and the seeming lack of political will to make changes significant enough to change that trajectory, it is easy to lose hope or cling to highly unlikely 'solutions', such as electric cars for solving the energy crisis, genetic engineering to solve the food crisis, or planetary engineering to solve climate change. Finding well-grounded hope lies instead in taking a stark and honest look at the changing conditions of the world, developing the skills necessary for responding to those conditions, and building a better future in whatever ways remain realistic and possible.

References and resources

Allen, James (1951) *As a Man Thinketh*. New York: Peter Pauper Press.

Anderson, Ray (2005) in Achbar, Mark; Abbott, Jennifer and Bakan, Joel (2005) *The Corporation*. Vancouver: Big Picture Media.

Carson, Rachel (1962) *Silent Spring*. Boston: Houghton Mifflin.

Hawken, Paul (1994) *The Ecology of Commerce*. London: Collins.

Hopkins, Rob (2008) *The Transition Handbook: From oil dependency to local resilience*. Dartington: Green Books.

Villiers-Stuart, Poppy and Arran Stibbe (eds.) (2009) *The Handbook of Sustainability Literacy (multimedia version)*. www.sustainability-literacy.org.

Part 1

Skills for a Changing World

Chapter 1

Ecocriticism

*The ability to investigate cultural artefacts
from an ecological perspective*

Greg Garrard

Bath Spa University

A recent TV advertisement for a self-storage company shows a tidal flow of ordinary household junk – CD and DVD cases, surplus clothes, shoes and the like – furling and lapping in a bedroom like waves on a shoreline. Most people can probably identify with the predicament, but what interests an ecocritic is a critical absence: a human being with money, by whose agency all that overwhelming *stuff* ended up there.

Ecocritics, who analyse literary and other texts from an environmentalist standpoint, observe that our environmental crisis poses not only technical, scientific and political questions, but also *cultural* ones. Our habits of representation affect and reciprocally reflect our actions, but the enormous temporal and spatial scale of phenomena such as climate change and mass extinction, and the complex moral questions inherent in them, pose challenges for our existing artistic forms. A feeble effort like the film *The Day After Tomorrow* is an object lesson: it compresses decades of real but insensible climatic change into a few days of climactic drama, vilifies an individual – the US Vice-President – for the whole problem, and reduces global warming to a silly spectacle like *Independence Day* or *Volcano*.

At the same time, our language is packed with seldom-examined assumptions about sustainability, such as the notion of the 'consumer', a strange but ubiquitous creature described by Raymond Williams as "a very specialised variety of human being with no brain, no eyes, no senses, but who can gulp" (Williams 1989:216). Ecocriticism, then, is the ability to critique existing discourses, cultural artefacts, forms and genres, and explore alternatives. There is extensive published material on ecocritical research and pedagogy; what follows is a compressed and simplified example of how its first principles might be taught.

Three Hours to Save the Planet!

Hour One: Infosphere

The exercise was inspired by Bill McKibben's *The Age of Missing Information*, which contrasts two versions of May 3, 1990: his own experience of camping and walking in the countryside of upstate New York, and the thousands of hours of cable TV recorded for him in Fairfax, Virginia, that day: drama, sports, infomercials, Christian programming, soaps, adverts, nature documentaries – everything. Having collected the tapes, he watched *all* of them, concluding that:

> We believe we live in the 'age of information', that there has been an information 'explosion', an information 'revolution'. While in a certain narrow sense this is the case, in many important ways just the opposite is true. We also live at a moment of deep ignorance, when vital knowledge that humans have always possessed about who we are and where we live seems out of reach. An Unenlightenment. An age of missing information. (McKibben 2006:9)

Rather than recount his insights to learners – who hate to be preached at as much as anyone – the educator can see what observations they make on their own in just one hour of channel surfing. They must avoid stopping for more than a few minutes to watch any one programme; it is the cumulative *effect* that matters here: what is shown and what is not shown, and the implicit values communicated. It is not simply a case of 'rejecting' TV – as if anyone could – but of exposing its constitutive assumptions for discussion.

The learner needs some questions to be getting on with, although more may well occur to her. She needs to surf *all* the channels to get a real sense of scope – the looping repetition of 'TV Gold' and the music channels, the cheery bullying of the shopping channels, the portentous banality of most of the news, and the particularities of what are called 'nature' and 'history'. She needs to make notes of what she sees, what it says to her, what seems to be *missing* – not just accidentally absent (which is everything it does not show), but excluded necessarily by the exigencies of the medium and its commercial demands. So:

- What sorts of *places* are represented on TV? Which countries and on what sorts of scales (i.e. inside houses, underneath rocks, from space, etc.)?
- What is the *good life*, as seen on TV? What makes us happy? What is valuable? What about death?
- Where does *history* begin and end, and what sorts of things happen in it?
- What about *pace*? Are there implications about whether faster or slower is better?
- What counts as *nature*? What sorts of creatures, doing what sorts of things, in what locations?

- What is *news* – and what is not?

More generally, the questions can be about when and why we watch TV, what it feels like to watch for a long time, and what it does to our range of emotions and experiences.

My own immediate – and pretty obvious – responses would be that history seems to be mainly populated by Nazis, nature is full of medium-sized animals eating and having sex, faster is always better – as in the tedious frenzy of 24-hour news – and the good life is about managing your body ('You're worth it'), admiring other people's, and accumulating stuff that, at the same time, you don't really care about because you're above that sort of thing: "Some things in life are priceless. For everything else, there's Mastercard." The preoccupation in recent years is *transformation* – of your body, home or 'lifestyle'. Good things come to those who can't wait, whereas the dedicated practice using patiently-acquired skills is at best unrepresentable and at worst just *sad*.

Hour Two: Biosphere
Bill McKibben spent a day on a mountaintop, but our learners are going to spend just one hour out of doors, either sitting still quietly somewhere, or wandering around aimlessly. The further away from each other and human habitation they can get, the better – although that's a tall order in most parts of the UK. Even just being in the garden alone will do. Crucially, all electronic devices must be switched off. For some, this will be like going cold turkey, and of course that's part of the lesson. Getting dressed properly may be a challenge too: learners may not have any appropriate clothes. You might ask them to write down their thoughts and feelings, or wait until they return. Bringing back found objects feels like primary school, but can be surprisingly exciting.

So, again, here are some questions. This exercise is harder, because the conclusions are in some ways paradoxical or elusive. The mere sensation of *decompression* will be bewildering for many; I have had students tell me they have never been silent for so long.

- Do you know what things around you are called – the names of trees, birds, clouds? Does it matter?
- What sort of 'information' could you glean – and what do you need to know – out here?
- Is it uncomfortable? Is discomfort bad? Why?
- Is it boring? What do we mean by 'boredom'?
- Focus on each of your senses one at a time – sight, smell and taste, hearing, touch, temperature, inner physical sensations (tiredness, hunger, desire, muscular tension). What's going on?

- Vary the scale a bit – try to take a long view, then get as close up as you can, turning over rocks or bits of rotten wood, looking behind things. What happens to your sense of time and space? What about death?

Not many will experience some Romantic epiphany, but most will be surprised. Silence, boredom, discomfort and non-competitive, unpaid exertion – anathema in TV world – turn out to yield strange insights.

Hour Three: Poetry

Poetry confuses many students because it is at once visceral and intellectual: it pounds like a heartbeat or ululates like a mourner, yet can seem a fiendish cipher to which the educator alone has the key. From the childish pleasures of rhyming to the synoptic allusiveness of 'The Waste Land', poetry seems somehow to straddle nature and culture. In fact, an ecocritic will ultimately want to use poetry to question that familiar dichotomy.

There are several anthologies of 'ecopoetry' of varying quality and character, such as Neil Astley's useful but finger-wagging *Earth Shattering* and Alice Oswald's marvellously estranging *The Thunder Mutters*. Romantic poetry inspired some of the first ecocritical studies, but contemporary poets engage with nature in ways that go beyond encomia to beauty or sublimity. Try the widely-anthologised 'Corson's Inlet' by A.R. Ammons (Astley 2007:99), inviting learners to contrast it with Wordsworth's 'Lines Composed a Few Miles Above Tintern Abbey'. Some questions to ask:

- The most striking difference is surely formal: Wordsworth's blank verse and Ammons's jagged free verse lineation; and, correspondingly, iambic pentameter versus shifting, pulsating 'eddies of meaning' and rhythm. What difference does this make?
- How does the poetic persona relate to the environment? How is he physically situated in it? What sorts of lessons does he find in it?
- What do the poems have to say about memory, beauty, fragility, danger, constancy and change?
- Characterise the diction: the kinds of nouns, verbs and adjectives you find in each poem. What do these say about the poem?
- Which do you like the most? Why?

A simple way of contrasting the poems is to say that Wordsworth's is a poem *about nature* – its (rather general) aesthetic allure and the sustenance it offers the human spirit – while Ammons has written an *ecological* poem that is attentive to the detail of a specific environment in the process of a particular encounter.

'Tintern Abbey' reflects upon the speaker's "sense sublime of something far more deeply interfused" than the phenomenal world of animals and plants, while Ammons roams amongst myriad creatures struggling for survival – but epitomising beauty nonetheless. Wordsworth's happiness depends upon the "cheerful faith, that all which we behold is full of blessings", whereas Ammons resolves only to "try / to fasten into order enlarging grasps of disorder", always acknowledging "that there is no finality of vision." The advent of evolutionary biology and ecology marks a fundamental breach between Wordsworth and Ammons: the first decentres the human subject from the pinnacle of creation, and the second foregrounds a notion of *fragility* unavailable to most Romantic poets (although see Bate 2000:153-75).

Conclusion

Criticising telly, looking under rocks and reading poetry will not save the planet, but not because ecocriticism is simply ineffectual: culture and its values will need to be understood, critiqued and transformed if a sustainable society is to be achieved. It will not save the planet because that phrase – like the very idea that you could do anything of ecological significance in three hours (besides perhaps making a baby) – is part of the problem. First of all, 'the planet', in any meaningfully complete sense, is well beyond our capacity to 'destroy'. We can disrupt the climate, wrecking large-scale human civilisations and annihilating thousands of other species, but life – the vast majority of it microscopic – will go on. And even if we really mean 'our planet' – the habitats and food species favoured by humans, the creatures we love, need and are fascinated by – saving is a religious concept, not an ecological one. As Rebecca Solnit (2007) has pointed out:

> Saving is the wrong word. Jesus saves and so do banks [sic!]: they set things aside from the flux of earthly change. We never did save the whales, though we might've prevented them from becoming extinct. We will have to continue to prevent that as long as they continue not to be extinct.

Just as there's no such thing as bad weather, only inappropriate clothing, there's no such thing as 'saving the planet', only keeping on thinking and working for a sustainable society forever. No environmentalist wants to leave behind anaesthetic dentistry, safe obstetrics, clean drinking water or even just Gore-Tex and mountain bikes; still better technologies than these will be required. Yet, as Big Yellow Self-Storage recognise, we are already drowning in stuff, and we need better ideas, feelings and values even more urgently than scientific breakthroughs. As the nature writer Aldo Leopold concluded in his seminal *A Sand County Almanac* in 1949:

We are remodeling the Alhambra [desert] with a steam-shovel, and we are proud of our yardage. We shall hardly relinquish the shovel, which after all has many good points, but we are in need of gentler and more objective criteria for its successful use. (Leopold 1968/1949: 226)

In the face of a lethal compact of ignorance, economic self-interest and the legacy of anthropocentric values, we shall paradoxically have to define and assert such 'gentler' criteria – what Leopold calls a 'land ethic' – with all the vigour, wit and critical insight of which an alternative culture is capable. Ecocriticism is a part of that struggle.

Notes

Visit www.asle.org.uk and www.asle.org for definitions, discussions and bibliographies of ecocriticism.

References and resources

Astley, Neil (ed.) (2007) *Earth Shattering: Ecopoems*. Tarset: Bloodaxe.

Bate, Jonathan (2000) *The Song of the Earth*. London: Picador.

Buell, Lawrence (2005) *The Future of Environmental Criticism*. Oxford: Blackwell.

Garrard, Greg (2004) *Ecocriticism*. London: Routledge.

Leopold, Aldo (1968/1949) *A Sand County Almanac, and Sketches Here and There*. Oxford: Oxford University Press.

McKibben, Bill (2006) *The Age of Missing Information* (2nd edn.). New York: Random House.

Oswald, Alice (ed.) (2005) *The Thunder Mutters: 101 poems for the planet*. London: Faber.

Solnit, Rebecca (2007) *Acts of Hope: Challenging empire on the world stage*. Massachusetts: Orion Society.

Williams, Raymond (1989) *Resources of Hope: Culture, democracy and socialism*. London: Verso.

Chapter 2

Optimisation

The art of personal sufficiency

John Naish

Author of *Enough: Breaking free from the world of excess*

In the modern developed world, the vast majority of us can be supplied with the things we need as a basis for living contented and fulfilled lives, such as food, heating, health care, safe transport and security. But our society tells us that we should always pursue 'more' – whether it be more money, possessions, choices, work or growth . . . and ultimately more of a commodity called 'happiness'.

But this approach is increasingly backfiring, with the Western world now suffering growing epidemics of depression, stress and anxiety – along with a range of stress-related physical diseases such as cardiovascular disease. This population-wide pursuit of 'always more' has also set consumer culture on a course towards ecological collapse. Thus, our constant striving appears to make us increasingly miserable as well as physically endangered (see de Graaf 2005).

The constant, all-consuming pursuit of 'more' is only a recent phenomenon. From the dawn of civilisation until shortly after the Second World War, it was considered admirable in Western culture to know when you had enough of any particular thing, and to understand where having more would actually prompt less satisfaction, because your pursuit had taken you into the world of diminishing returns where you have to put more effort into attaining something, but the rewards get increasingly smaller. The rewards can also rapidly turn into negatives: too much work robs us of time we might spend enjoying the fruits of that labour; and consuming excess food lies behind the West's 'obesity epidemic'. The old art of knowing when you had enjoyed the optimum amount of anything is encapsulated in the Edwardian table saying: 'Thank you, I have had an elegant sufficiency, and any more would be superfluous.'

This Western philosophy stretches back to Aristotle, who devised the idea of the Golden Mean, where the path to contentment lies between the 'twin evils' of having too much or too little. This idea is also in the Chinese *Tao Te Ching* written in 260BC by Lao Tsu, which declares, "He who knows he has enough is rich" (see Maurer 1982). In 18th-century Europe, frugal living was considered the cool lifestyle choice: outside royal courts, luxury goods were often spurned, thanks to the practice of 'worldly asceticism', a Calvinist idea that offered hope of salvation through diligent use of God's gifts (e.g. Planet Earth). Puritans and Quakers promoted the 'Christianity writ plain' ideal, where it was considered good to produce, but bad to consume more than necessity required. Those who lived luxuriously were criticised for squandering resources that might support others.

It might seem odd that humans have had to develop social conventions for knowing when they have had enough, rather than being able to perceive this instinctively. But the basic difficulty lies in our ancient instincts: through millions of years of early evolution, humankind's great success as a species lay in its ravenous, dissatisfied striving for 'always more'. The humans who made it through the frequent famines, plagues and natural disasters of the Pleistocene era were the ones who always stockpiled, always grabbed the most land and possessions, always gorged when food was available. They never had to develop an instinct that said 'enough'. They never had to learn how to deal with abundance. And they survived to pass us their genes.

When humans began to organise themselves into civilisations capable of creating regular material abundances as well as surviving shortages, it became necessary to develop a philosophy of enoughness, of personal sufficiency, so that resources could be shared and enjoyed, optimised rather than squandered. This approach, pioneered by the likes of Aristotle and Lao Tsu, remained broadly accepted until the aftermath of the Second World War, when the vastly expanded wartime industrial power of America faced shrinkage and depression unless consumers could be persuaded to want ever more and more new things, and to take out credit to buy them.

The American marketing guru Victor Lebow, a former director of Fabergé, described this trend in the *Journal of Retailing* in 1950: "We need things consumed, burned up, worn out, replaced, and discarded at an ever-increasing rate," he wrote. "Our enormously productive economy demands that we make consumption a way of life, that we convert the buying and use of goods into rituals, that we seek our spiritual satisfaction, our ego satisfaction, in consumption."

Lebow's clarion call was amply answered. The rapidly expanding power of post-war marketing, sales and advertising helped to ensure that personal consumption grew at an exponential rate across the developed world. Vast industrial growth also precipitated revolutions in technology that brought leaps in the realms of communications, healthcare, transport and construction – sufficient to make our lives comfortable and potentially sustainable . . . so long as we learn to live within the planet's capacity to support our activity.

For while the post-war period of rapidly spiralling consumption was great for manufacturers, it became apparent that it wasn't so beneficial for the planet. By the 1970s a welter of ideas had emerged about the need to say 'enough growth'. The most famous examples are two books: E. F. Schumacher's *Small Is Beautiful: A Study of Economics as if People Mattered*, and the high-powered Club of Rome think-tank's *The Limits to Growth*.

Since the 1970s we have lived with the growing awareness that our ecosystem is fragile, that perpetual economic growth is impossible and that every time we earn or consume, we may make the world potentially worse for our children. By the late 1980s, even *The Sun* newspaper had appointed its own green correspondent. Today the most bullish Western consumers' consciences are regularly punctured by shards of eco-understanding. But our culture and economy remain centred on the idea that there is no alternative to continuing to produce and consume ever more, even when we know that it may prove calamitous. So why hasn't our behaviour changed?

One reason is that our marketing culture has become extremely effective at targeting our subconscious brains. We may consciously know that chasing and consuming more and more is bad for us and bad for the planet, but subconsciously, we still feel driven to do so. We are like the 60-a-day man who knows that smoking will kill him, but still he can't stop (see Marshall 2007).

One of the most effective tools used by advertisers is the cult of celebrity (see Evans and Hesmondhalgh 2005). All the new 'even better' products that advertisers dangle in front of us seem to be owned by beautiful people. There's Liz Hurley in perfumed ecstasies over a new cosmetics range; Daniel Craig manfully tapping on a product-placed laptop while pretending to be James Bond. Our subconscious minds tend to over-identify with celebrities because we evolved in small tribal groups. In Neolithic times, if you knew someone, then they knew you, too. If you didn't attack each other, you were probably friends. Our minds still work this way – and give us the false idea that the celebrities we see so much are somehow our acquaintances.

Humans are also born imitators: this talent underlies much of our species' success, as it enabled us to adapt to changing environments far quicker than our competitors could via biological evolution alone. What gets us far ahead of other primates is our attention to detail. A chimp can watch another chimp poking a stick into an ant-hill and then mimic the basic idea, but only humans can replicate a clever technique exactly. As a result, we need to choose with great care whom we copy. We have evolved to emulate the habits of the most successful people we see, in the hope that imitation will elevate us to their rank. This helps to explain why many of us feel compelled to keep up materially with celebrities, the mythical alpha-people in our global village.

There's a dark side to the celebrity effect, too. We so want to be part of our tribe's top clique that we're perpetually anxious about being snubbed by it.

Feeling left out makes us so mad that our ability to act intelligently plummets. This was shown by a series of tests that involved making students feel sorely excluded. Roy Baumeister, a psychologist at Case Western Reserve University, invited undergraduates to meet a group of impressive strangers and then asked them to name two of the group that they would like to work with on a project.

But next the students were told that, sorry, the strangers did not rate them. The rebuffed students' IQs plunged by about a quarter for several hours. Their aggressiveness rose. Baumeister says his tests reveal that tribal rejection interferes with our self-control: "It strikes a blow that seems to interfere with our ability for complex reasoning," he says. "You may do stupid things" (Baumeister et al. 2002). Thus our perpetual exclusion from the celebrity clique makes us more likely to dumbly, impulsively buy stuff – just because it is endorsed by people we desperately want to love us.

Celebrities are only one weapon in the marketeers' broad battery of highly sophisticated subconscious persuaders which constantly make us feel compelled to pursue more new things and to feel bad about the things that we already possess. But although this constant pursuit of 'more' is having increasingly toxic social and environmental effects, no one in power would dare to suggest that we curb the advertisers' activities – unless they are advertising products that actively harm health, such as tobacco and alcohol.

In fact, the very idea of creating a culture that encourages us to live sustainably balanced lives by rediscovering the lost art of sufficiency is currently taboo. There is a distinct lack of high-level discussions on alternative ways to organise our society. For the sake of personal and planetary balance, we urgently need to develop an economic system that is effectively zero-growth, to stop putting any more strain on our systems. But this is not up for discussion in the corridors of power, says Tim Jackson, a Green economist who sits on the Sustainable Development Commission, a UK government watchdog.

I asked him what would happen if we were to wave a magic wand, so that one morning we woke to find that suddenly everyone in Britain was living a personally and planetarily sustainable existence, he said: "This is the hardest question of all. I've just raised this at our commission and was told by a Treasury official that switching to true sustainable development might mean that we have to go back to living in caves. The government has a split personality on this. It keeps telling people to get out of their cars and consume less. But we would be up the creek without a paddle if everyone did. As it currently exists, our economy relies strictly on increases in consumption."

The credit crunch has clearly shown that our postwar culture of more-more-more cannot be sustained, but the lack of government action means that we have to achieve change from the grass roots, by learning as individuals the lost art of sufficiency – the art of being highly wary of marketing tricks and knowing when to say, "That's enough for me, I have the optimum amount of this, and I want to leave space and time for other bounties in my life." It is a challenge for all of us.

Example discussion questions to stimulate reflection on optimisation

- Discuss what 'enough' means to you. When is excess permissible? When is it enjoyable? How do you put limits on your own actions?
- Can governments pass effective laws to make people consume only enough of certain things? Which items can be limited and how? Which items can never be limited, and have to be left to individuals' own discretion?
- Can you ever have too much of the following: friendship, gratitude, social connection, rewarding leisure time, contentment? Discuss ways in which consumer society can prevent us from enjoying these qualities to the full.

References and resources

Baumeister, Roy; Twenge, Jean and Nuss, Christopher (2002) 'Effects of social exclusion on cognitive processes: anticipated aloneness reduces intelligent thought'. *Journal of Personality and Social Psychology*, 83:4, 817-27.

de Graaf, John; Wann, David and Naylor, Thomas (2005) *Affluenza: The all-consuming epidemic.* San Francisco: Berrett-Koehler.

Evans, Jessica and Hesmondhalgh, David (2005) *Understanding Media: Inside celebrity.* Milton Keynes: Open University Press.

Lebow, Victor (1992) Quoted in Alan Durning's *How Much is Enough? The consumer society and the future of the Earth.* London: Norton.

Marshall, George (2007) *Carbon Detox: Your step-by-step guide to getting real about climate change.* London: Gaia.

Maurer, Herrymon (1982) *Tao, The Way of the Ways.* Cambridge: Cambridge University Press (includes a translation of the *Tao Te Ching*).

Schumacher, Ernst F. (1993/1974) *Small is Beautiful: A Study of Economics as if People Mattered.* London: Vintage.

Chapter 3

Grounded Economic Awareness

Economic awareness based on ecological and ethical values

Satish Kumar

Editor of *Resurgence*

The banks, stock-markets and all of our financial transactions are supposed to be in the hands of highly educated, intelligent people. Then how have they managed to bring the system so close to the brink of disaster that they have to go to the government with cap in hand, begging to be bailed out?

The answer is staggeringly simple. They have confused money with wealth; they have failed to follow the fundamental truth that money is not wealth: money is only a measure of wealth and a means to exchange wealth. Real wealth is good land, pristine forests, clean rivers, healthy animals, vibrant communities, nourishing food and human creativity. But the leaders of money markets have turned the land, forests, rivers, animals and human creativity into commodities to be bought and sold, and even the money itself has become a commodity – speculators trade in money to make more money.

Money is a good invention as a means to an end, but now money itself has become an end. We buy and sell houses, forests, foods and land to make money. Almost everything has become a commodity – it is acceptable to engage in any kind of trading as long as it makes money. Eighty to ninety percent of the money whirling around the world, day and night, is unrelated to any goods or services or any kind of real wealth. Money which was a means to trade has been turned into a status symbol, a source of power and prestige. This false philosophy of money is the root cause of the credit crunch and it will lead to what Monbiot (2008) calls the "nature crunch".

The nature crunch is not something in the distant future – melting icecaps and climate chaos are already with us, and that is because of our obsession with making money at all costs. We are over-fishing our oceans to make money, clear-cutting the rainforests, poisoning the land with chemical fertilisers, putting animals in factory farms, manipulating seeds with genetic engineering, the list goes on – and all this is to maximise money. We are prepared to let the natural systems that life depends on suffer, but are not prepared to slow down the pace of money growth. Of course, money has a place within the broad context of sustainability and a harmonious relationship with the natural world, but we have to put it in its place and keep it there, rather than allow it to dominate our lives to such an extent that the human community, as well as the earth community, is endangered.

If learners are to contribute in their future personal and professional lives to a more sustainable society, they will need to gain an awareness of economics that goes beyond considerations of money in isolation, to an awareness of the larger systems which support life – the systems that economies, as well as people, are embedded within. They need to gain what could be called place-based economic awareness. This chapter explores the relationship between economics and ecology using images which could help plant the seeds of place-based, grounded economic awareness in minds of learners.

* * *

In the great botanical garden of Kolkata (formerly Calcutta) there is the thousand-year-old Great Banyan Tree. It has one thousand branches. Each branch forks into two branches – one moves upwards and embraces the sky, the other drops down to put roots in the earth, thus creating a new trunk to support the skyward branch.

Looking at this ancient tree it is difficult to distinguish which is the original trunk or the original branch. Each new trunk is grounded in the place by putting down new roots. This is one of the most amazing examples of sustainable growth – while branches spread in the sky looking up to the sun and the stars, the trunks and the roots remain firmly fixed in place.

There is another great tree which is in England. It is a yew tree in a churchyard in Dartington, Devon. Botanists believe that this yew is between 1,800 and 2,000 years old. In other words it is almost as old as Christianity itself, and the tree was there long before the church.

"What is the secret of the sustainability of this great yew?" I asked Dartington's Head Gardener.

"The roots of this tree are as broadly and deeply embedded in the place as the branches are spread wide and high in the sky. Of course, you don't see the roots, but they take as much space as the trunk and the branches you can see," the gardener answered.

"Is this true of most trees?" I enquired.

"Yes, it is. The great oak, the birch, the beech, the Lebanese cedar you see here in the garden are all embedded in their place. They have extensive networks of roots underground. If the trees did not have a sense of place, they would not survive."

What a perfect illustration of balance, harmony and wholeness: outward growth complemented with inward growth. If only the globalisers of the economy learned from the trees; if only the bankers, hedge-fund holders, stock-market managers, financial experts and economists could see this relationship between inner growth and outer growth; if only manufacturers and retailers could realise that the economics of the planet has to be built on the economics of place. Economics without a sense of place has no place in a sustainable society. The breadth of the economy has to be in balance with its depth.

We cannot save the planet and destroy the place. We cannot serve the interest of the global community and undermine the interest of the local community. Large is lovely only if it is balanced by the beauty of the small; if we allow the small to diminish, then one day the large, too, will perish. Large banks are in a sorry state of affairs because they have swallowed the small savings banks and mutual societies; we sowed the seeds of the credit crunch when we abolished the credit unions; we laid the foundation of the economic downturn when we blindly pursued the path of unlimited economic growth. What goes up comes down.

Economy and ecology are made of three Greek words: *oikos, logos, nomos*. 'Oikos' means home, a place of relationships where all of life shares and participates in the evolution of the earth community. 'Logos' means knowledge of our planet home; and 'nomos' means management of our home. Together with knowledge of ecology and economics, learners need skills in reflecting on a third 'e', ethics. If they gain these skills, then they can help contribute to building 'oikos', our planet home, on the firm foundation of ethical and spiritual values without which it will be unstable and unsustainable. They need to help the economy stay within the parameters of ecology, ethics and equity.

But day and night we chant the mantra of 'economy', while our ecology is in ruins, our ethics have been shelved, our principles of justice and equity are put on the back burner. We blindly follow the religion of materialism, we worship the god of money, and we sacrifice everything at the altar of the economy. We indulge in consumerism as if there was no tomorrow. As a result, in the short term, banks are running out of money, consumers are short of cash, house prices are tumbling and unemployment is rising. In the longer term, we face global warming, global terrorism, global poverty and population explosion.

The cause of all these multiple crises is our disconnection with the place to which we belong. Wherever we live, we need to be rooted in our place. If each and every one of us took care of our place, our home, our community, the soil by which we are sustained and the biosphere of which we are an integral part, then the whole planet would be taken care of. Being embedded in a place is a prerequisite for being free to look up at the sky and embrace the world. Love of place

Photograph by Francesca Zunino.

and love of planet are two sides of the same coin – when we belong to a place, we belong to the planet. When we lose our place, we lose our planet.

I wish everyone would join the NIMBY (Not In My Back Yard) movement. If every backyard is saved from motorways, airports, industrial estates, business parks and superstores, then the whole country will be saved from them.

Great economists, industrialists, business leaders and politicians, despite their years in education, seem to have forgotten even the true meaning of economy. They only think in terms of profit maximisation and increased money supply; whereas the true economy means good housekeeping, proper management of all aspects of the home. The criterion of good house management is to ensure that all the members of the household are living in harmony with each other and the place. And, of course, home is always a particular place. So in order to address the root causes of both economic turbulence and unsustainability, learners will need to reflect on the foundations of economic theory and revise them.

The present financial crash and market meltdown offer learners an opportunity to look deeply at current systems and consider designs for a new paradigm of sustainability. The economics of debts and derivatives has been exposed as fake and fragile. The bottom-up economics of people and place, like trees, is clearly resilient and reliable. What booms can only bust; to avoid bust we also have to avoid boom.

Days begin to grow after the equinox until they reach the summer solstice. Then we enjoy the balmy summer mornings and warm evenings – but we cannot have such long summer days forever. After the solstice, days have to decline and we have to accept the dark winter nights. Only near the Equator can we have days and nights in equilibrium. The challenge for learners in the future, when they become politicians, economists and business leaders, is to find an economic equator and market equilibrium for a steady-state economy.

People talk about making poverty history, but to do that we also have to make wealth history. The very wealthy are the other side of the very poor; higher mountains are bound to create deep valleys. A culture of equilibrium requires a shift in values towards balance, harmony, proportionality, and a sense of place.

The way that the current economic recession is being dealt with is to bail out the banks and fuel consumerism, put more money in mortgages and hope to get back to business as usual. This shows a great lack of ethical, ecological, and economic awareness among politicians and business leaders. If learners, the leaders of the future, are to contribute to a more sustainable world, then they will need to gain skills in grounded economic awareness. They will then be able to follow a different path, thinking holistically, and investing in land and agriculture, in renewable energy and practical skills. The earth is our true bank. We are at a crossroads. Let us equip learners with a deep awareness of place so that they can choose the right path and build a rooted, resilient economy in equilibrium with its surroundings.

Activity

The following activity is adapted from *The Transition Handbook* (Hopkins 2008:60). It is based on a permaculture exercise where participants sit in a circle and model the interconnections between elements of a woodland ecosystem. Participants each have a label such as *chestnut tree, owl, mouse, soil, rain, bluebell, sun, bee* or *nettle,* and pass the end of a large ball of string backwards and forwards to illustrate relationships. The bee passes the string to the bluebell, mentioning the relationship of pollination, the bluebell to the rain, and so on until what results is a complex web of interrelationships. This represents a natural, grounded economy, based entirely on entities which have a real existence in the world, and on relationships which support the sustainable continuation of the ecosystem. If disturbed (a participant disappears and the string is cut), then the system shows resilience, reforming in new patterns to let life go on, although the system is also fragile, and loss of a key element such as rain will cause collapse.

In the next stage, Hopkins suggests relabelling the participants, using roles from a traditional town (greengrocers, carpenters, butchers, clothes makers, teachers, basket weavers, coppicers, etc.). Again, the ball is passed around to show relationships, and a complex and resilient web emerges. A traditional town economy is based on individual people trading real goods that are related to sustaining the well-being of the community, and can reorganise itself, up to a point, to cope with change. If disturbed too much, however, for example by the encroachment of out-of-town supermarkets, the community will collapse, leading people to depend on the world of transnational capital for their survival.

A final stage can be added to this activity. In this stage, participants are bankers, hedge-fund managers, money traders, transnational corporations and abstract entities such as debt, liquidity, and capital. Included too can be concrete participants such as forests, exploited workers, the oceans, consumers up to their necks in debt, and so on. The relationships revealed in this exercise show how flows of transnational capital emanating from the casino culture of global finance can have huge and unpredictable impacts on people's lives and on natural systems. The exercise can reveal how arbitrary and fragile the relationships are, and hint at the scale of the consequences if key elements of the global web are disturbed (e.g. disruption to interbank lending, or the end of cheap oil). Or the exercise could lead to total confusion, as participants realise that they have no idea how the economic system their society is based on influences the lives of the people around them and the ecological systems they depend on for life. Either way, the activity introduces learners to the importance of grounded economic awareness – awareness that is crucial for the task ahead of building an economic system rooted in reality and in place.

References and resources

Daly, Herman (2000) *Ecological Economics and the Ecology of Economics*. London: Edward Elgar.

Hopkins, Rob (2008) *The Transition Handbook: From oil dependency to local resilience*. Dartington: Green Books.

Monbiot, George (2008) 'The stock market crunch is petty compared to the nature crunch'. *The Guardian*, 14 October 2008.

Resurgence. www.resurgence.org (publishes articles promoting creativity, ecology, spirituality and frugality).

Schumacher, Ernst F. (1993/1973) *Small is Beautiful: A Study of Economics as if People Mattered*. London: Vintage. (This book, and E. F. Schumacher's well-known essay on Buddhist Economics within it, should be read again and again. Schumacher provides a vision of economics where people and planet matter and where spiritual values underpin economic values.)

Schumacher, Ernst F. (1993) *This I Believe and other essays*. Dartington: Green Books.

Chapter 4

Advertising Awareness

The ability to expose advertising discourses
that undermine sustainability, and resist them

Arran Stibbe

University of Gloucestershire

Catching a glimpse into the deep insights about human needs that modern psychology has revealed requires little more than picking up the nearest magazine and critically analysing the advertisements within it. Since Edward Bernays, the nephew of Sigmund Freud, first started applying his uncle's psychological theories to public relations and advertising in the 1920s, a significant proportion of the effort of modern psychology has been applied to the task of convincing people to consume. A magazine advertisement for a vacuum cleaner reads:

> Life isn't always neat and tidy. It's about laughing, crying, loving, dancing, maybe even shouting. So we've developed the new QuickClick tool change system and the ComfoGlide floor tool, to save you energy and time to enjoy what we've all been put into the world to actually do. Live. (Kärcher advertisement 2006).

Bernays' vision was of harnessing humans' dangerous and irrational desires and instinctive biological drives – like the desire to laugh, cry, love, dance and shout, perhaps – and channelling them into something safer and more economically productive, like consuming and producing vacuum cleaners (see Curtis 2002). It is easy to see how Bernays' ideas could arise in his historical context: a deep suspicion of human emotional drives following the rise of the Nazis, and, after the war, a massive over-production capacity that needed to be met with increased consumption. The idea was to divert dangerous libidinal energy into the harmless and economically beneficial pursuit of consumerism. The context now, though, is very different, as over-consumption and the ecological damage it causes threaten the future ability of the Earth to support human life and the life of countless other species.

Despite the change in context, the legacy of Bernays exists in a clearly identifiable discourse of modern advertising. This discourse calls on deep human desires and needs to sell people unnecessary things which will not, in the end, come close to satisfying those needs. A vitamin advertisement shows a woman deeply peaceful in a yoga posture, but suggests "For the inner journey, take an alternative route." The question is: why buy a product which is unlikely to lead to a deep state of peace, with money that needs to be earned in a stressful job, when all that is necessary is some time out and a few stretches to actually feel more peaceful. Another advertisement, for a bathroom cleaner, shows a glorious picture of nature but then suggests "Enjoy the freshness of the outdoors in the safety of your own home", as if the synthetic aromas of bathroom cleaners are a convenient substitute for the freshness of nature. A mobile phone advertisement shows people enjoying a moment of real connection and joy as they dance together on a platform in Liverpool Street Station, followed by the message "Life's for sharing" superimposed on someone who is not dancing at all but instead talking on a mobile phone, as if it was somehow equivalent.

Countless advertisements use images of happy times spent with friends, exercise in the fresh air, explorations of nature, dancing, peaceful moments, romance, and other aspects of life which in themselves require very little or no consumption of resources or production of waste. They then use these images to sell material products which are often not only unnecessary but ecologically damaging to produce and dispose of. Advertisements can therefore be useful for stimulating reflection on ways of genuinely fulfilling higher human needs and the forces which distract people away from these needs towards unnecessary material consumption.

The particular discourse described above could be called the *pseudo-satisfier* discourse since the advertisements unrealistically represent a material product as a substitute for, or path towards gaining, something that will satisfy deep human needs. Learners can actively explore the discourse for themselves by searching though magazines (particularly the kind of magazines they typically read), and selecting advertisements which depict experiences they consider to be life-enhancing. This is a valuable process in itself because it requires reflection on higher human needs and their fulfilment (see *Emotional Well-being*, p.171). Learners can expose the model behind the discourse and express it in their own way (e.g., "material consumption is the path to deep fulfilment"). The validity of the model can be investigated at a personal level through visualisation exercises such as imagining the feelings that arise from being in the places depicted in the advertisements (in nature, spending happy times with friends, close moments with family, dancing, being physically active, discovering romance etc.), compared with what the products themselves (toilet cleaner, sugary drink, junk food, mobile phone, trainers, perfume) can actually deliver.

Central to sustainability literacy is awareness of the *consequences* of discourses for the sustainability of society (Stibbe 2008). In the case of the *pseudo-satisfier* discourse, the consequences are not only in terms of the ecological impact of the products, but also on the social sustainability of generating material aspirations that are unfulfillable for all, and the personal sustainability of a life of over-consumption, debt, clutter and stressful work to pay for it all. Awareness is only the first step, however. The next step, and an essential one for sustainability literacy, is the ability to take *action*, in this case the ability to resist the *pseudo-satisfier* discourse. Resistance could be at a personal level by avoiding products which are unlikely to satisfy higher needs, and searching for genuine satisfiers instead (see *Finding Meaning without Consuming*, p.178). Or it could be at a social level, raising public awareness of the negative impact of advertising, or campaigning against certain forms of advertising such as those which try to associate junk food with family love in the minds of children.

One activity which involves learners in learning-through-action (i.e. learning through actual awareness-raising activities, rather than just 'exercises') is the creation of a public exhibition of counter-advertisements along the lines of *Adbusters:*

Figure 1: Image adapted and reproduced with permission
from Adbusters (www.adbusters.org/gallery/spoofads).

Activity

- Carefully analyse a range of spoof advertisements from the Adbusters website (see Figure 1 as an example). Describe the discourses that are being resisted, the reasons for resistance, and the visual and linguistic techniques used to create the spoofs.
- Now look through ordinary magazines to find an advertising discourse that you feel needs to be resisted from a sustainability perspective. Discuss what it is about the discourse which potentially undermines sustainability.
- Create a spoof advertisement for public display which resists the discourse.

For the *pseudo-satisfier* discourse, spoof advertisements could be created by simply altering slogans of actual advertisements so that they promote the life-enhancing, low-consumption activities that the advertisements actually depict, rather than the product. A cola advertisement which shows friends having fun together could be changed from "Coke is it!" to "Time with friends is it!"; "Enjoy the freshness of the outdoors in the safety of your own home" could become "Enjoy the freshness of the outdoors"; "For the inner journey, take an alternative route" could become "For the inner journey, stretch your body and relax deeply." In general, there are many genuinely satisfying and completely free experiences which could be promoted for general health, well-being and sustainability, but it is exactly these which are excluded from being advertised directly because no-one profits in an immediate financial sense. This is clearly one of the forces behind the unsustainability of society, but one that learners can become actively involved in resisting through exercises such as this.

The *pseudo-satisfier* discourse is, of course, just one of the discourses within the world of advertising with potential implications for sustainability. There are many others, such as the *dissatisfaction-manufacturing* discourse ("Discoloured toenails? Now there's no need to hide them"), the *convenience-constructing* discourse ("Royal Grass [artificial grass] makes gardening a pleasure"), the *greenwash* discourse ("Exploration of space has changed how we live and think from global communications to a better understanding of climate change" – from a space tourism advertisement), and even a *climate change* discourse ("HOPE – Hummer Owners Prepared for Emergencies", from an advertisement which implies that the best way to prepare for climate catastrophe is to buy a Hummer). All of these discourses have particular models of the world behind them. The *convenience-constructing* discourse reproduces a model where physical activity (mowing the grass) is 'inconvenient' but stress and ill-health from sedentary work in order to afford a life of over-consumption is not. The *greenwash* discourse implies a model where environmentally damaging pursuits (like car driving or space tourism) are 'green' because of irrelevant factors such as improved fuel efficiency or a vague connection to climate change research.

It would not be possible for learners to be 'taught' the many discourses of advertising and the models behind them because they are in a continual state of change, and each learner will have their own evolving model of sustainability to gauge discourses against. Instead, learners can prepare themselves to engage with any discourse they come across in the future through gaining skills in critical discourse analysis and the ability to resist discourses which they feel could potentially damage them personally and undermine the sustainability of the society they live in.

To summarise, then, this chapter looked at the *pseudo-satisfier* discourse in advertising, and described some forms of active learning for investigating and resisting it. Exploring this particular discourse is valuable in itself because learners can go beyond awareness of how advertising promotes ecologically damaging over-consumption, to reflection on genuine, non-consumptive ways to fulfil higher human needs. It also provides a starting point for gaining broader skills in engagement with discourses through four main steps: *recognising patterns, exposing underlying models, reflecting on the consequences of models for sustainability* and *taking action*. The final stage, *taking action*, includes resistance of negative discourses but can also include the creation or promotion of positive discourses, ones which learners feel are more likely to contribute to a more sustainable society. Overall, a discursive approach like this is intended to involve learners in critical awareness of, and active engagement in, the social structures around them that ultimately determine whether the society they are part of is sustainable.

References and resources

Achbar, Mark; Abbott, Jennifer and Baker, Joel (2005) *The Corporation*. Vancouver: Big Picture Media (this inspiring documentary film explores the psychology of corporations as well as psychological techniques used in advertising).

Adbusters. www.adbusters.org (includes spoof advertisements and the *Journal of the Mental Environment*).

Curtis, Adam (2002) *Century of the Self*. www.bbc.co.uk/bbcfour/documentaries/features/century_of_the_self.shtml (this acclaimed BBC documentary examines the rise of the all-consuming self against the backdrop of the Freud dynasty).

Fairclough, Norman (2001) *Language and Power*. London: Longman (includes a useful Critical Discourse Analysis approach to advertising).

Language and Ecology Research Forum. www.ecoling.net (the forum includes a wide range of resources for analysing discourses from a sustainability perspective, including the online journal *Language & Ecology*).

Stibbe, Arran (2008) 'Reading and writing society: the role of English subjects in education for sustainability'. *The Higher Education Academy English Subject Centre Newsletter*, 14. www.english.heacademy.ac.uk/explore/publications/newsletters/newsissue14 (a more detailed exploration of the relationship between sustainability literacy and Critical Discourse Analysis).

Chapter 5

Transition Skills

Skills for transition to a post-fossil-fuel age

Stephen Quilley

Keele University

Production of cheap, abundant fossil fuels is peaking and will soon be withering away. . . . Around the world, numerous sovereign governments are close to becoming dysfunctional – likely with very bad consequences. We are pumping so much of the wrong kinds of gases into the atmosphere that the poles are melting, the seas are rising, the land is drying out and some day soon this planet is going to be very tough to live on. (Whipple 2009)

The twenty-first century is going to be different – perhaps more so than most of us had realised. Official commentaries habitually focus on progress – the challenge of matching our increasing scientific understanding of the natural world and the continuing flow of new technologies, with corresponding improvements in our social and political arrangements. But what if change involves systemic failures and geopolitical conflict? What if the techno-economic escalator of development runs into the sand? What if change involves a *decrease* in the complexity of societies and economies? What if globalisation falters and is replaced by a more visceral relocalisation of human activity? What if the sum of human knowledge, represented by the institutions of modern science, actually begins to shrink? This is the scenario underpinning the peak oil movement and which James Kunstler, in *The Long Emergency* and his recent novel *World Made by Hand*, has elaborated most cogently.

In this chapter I explore this vista of serious rupture and discontinuity and its implications for sustainability education. I provide an overview of the kind of 'transition skills' that may become relevant to the survival and well-being of our children and their communities over the coming decades. I conclude by suggesting ways in which such skills might be taught alongside traditional academic disciplines in a variety of learning contexts.

Transition implies radical discontinuity and upheaval

There have always been tensions at the heart of the concept of sustainability: between the ecological limits to growth and the irrefutable demands for social development in the global south; between optimistic Cornucopians trumpeting the possibilities of ecological modernisation and pessimistic Malthusians warning of overshoot. Teachers and lecturers attempting to green their institutions and push the issue of sustainability into both curricula and institutional practice, constantly brush up against these ambiguities and the diverging scenarios that they engender.

Advocates of 'weak' sustainability and most non-ecological economists tend to assume that the sustainable readjustment of the relationship between human economics and global ecology can take place over a relatively long time period. They share an optimistic faith in technology and assume that, with the appropriate regulatory reforms and institutional innovations, the sustainable re-orientation of national and global economies can be achieved with a minimum of disruption. The assumption is that 'ecological modernisation' is *continuous* with the trajectory of twentieth-century industrialism and consumerism.

In contrast, the Transition movement (see Hopkins 2008) is predicated on abrupt discontinuity arising from two factors:

- The reality of rapid and potentially catastrophic **climate change**.
- The reality of **peak oil** – an imminent, permanent short fall in oil supply, increasing year on year with massive geo-political, economic and social consequences.

From a 'peak oil' perspective, the coming energy crunch will send globalisation spiralling into reverse, resulting in a massive reduction in global and national flows of people, goods and information (see Kunstler 2005, 2008). In the long term, the effect of this will be to re-create much more localised, 'bio-regional' patterns of economic production and consumption. Anticipating global systemic failures, and taking profound socio-economic upheaval, state-failure and (implicitly) conflict as likely, the movement focuses on enhancing the **resilience** of local communities (see Barry & Quilley 2008). Although clearly supportive of mainstream efforts to reduce emissions and to develop more eco-cyclical business models, Transition eschews party politics. Although avoiding the survivalist discourse of many peak oil forums, *The Transition Handbook* does refer to "burn-out", "collapse" and "overshoot" as scenarios that are likely to play out in the absence of a "planned and urgent energy descent" (Hopkins 2008: 48-9). And whether the end of the current global order takes the form of a planned energy descent or a chaotic implosion, "The time for seeing globalisation as an invincible and unassailable behemoth, or localisation as some kind of lifestyle choice, is over" (p.15), and "Small is inevitable" (p.68). But at the same time, Transition transforms the survivalist discourse of the North American peak oil movement, arguing that positive, uplifting visions of a more convivial post-oil future are more likely to induce active participation and behavioural change: "The Transition approach [demonstrates that] the future with less oil could be preferable to the present" (p. 53); "Our best chance of a successful collective transition will not come from presenting people with the possibility of [collapse/disintegration] scenarios" (p. 49).

So Transition is less about politics per se than enabling community self-reliance through relocalisation – initiatives which 'prefigure' or anticipate what is seen to be an inevitable reversal of globalisation. Awareness of peak oil, climate change and now the global economic crisis is driving 'solutions-oriented' experiments in sustainable community. Focusing as it does on very practical issues such as skills/re-skilling, food, energy, transport, land use, cultivation and above all community building, Transition is a form of D.I.Y. geared towards the bottom-up transformation of local communities, preparing them for 'the long emergency'.

Education for upheaval

For those who are happy to take the continuity in economic and political life as an article of faith, the agenda of sustainable education is relatively unproblematic. Advances are being made, year on year, with dozens of new sustainability-related courses, impressive green buildings and sustainable campus management systems. However, after the rollercoaster year of 2008, the spectre of *discontinuity* – geo-political conflict, social upheaval and systemic failure – seems suddenly plausible and for seasoned peak oil pundits, more than likely. Transition educators working within mainstream institutions find themselves in an odd and sometimes awkward position. We find ourselves wearing two hats, and operating with two partially incompatible discourses – one of continuity and development and the other of rupture, discontinuity and survival.

So if we do need to hedge our bets, then what kind of skills should we be thinking about for the long emergency? How do we educate for upheaval? Moreover, how do we combine Transition skills with mainstream sustainability education?

Two central and related features of the post-petroleum age will be the reversal of twentieth-century mechanisation and automation and the collapse of energy-intensive farming and food provisioning systems. The brave new world of localised production and consumption will be, as Kunstler puts it, a "world

Sunset on the era of fossil fuels: view of Ratcliffe-on-Trent Power Station, Nottinghamshire. *Photo by Malcolm Plant.*

made by hand" – craft operations dependent on skilled artisans using hand tools combined with a resurgence of animal power (draught-horses, oxen etc.) and the intensive use of unskilled human labour. Losing our fossil-fuel slaves will certainly make life harder in many ways. But Kunstler, Heinberg and Hopkins are not alone in discerning the possibility of a new era of human dignity and self-worth rooted in vibrant, participative and self-sufficient local communities.

Taken seriously, this scenario suggests that we need to develop a completely different kind of education. The system that we have developed over the last hundred years is designed to develop abstract, cognitive skills and forms of theoretical understanding which equip students to take up ever more specialised functional niches in the economy. Developments in education have run parallel to the steadily advancing complexity of economy and society – what sociologists refer to as the 'division of labour'. Workers in all areas of the economy have become ever smaller and more dedicated cogs in an increasingly complex economic machine. Underlying these changes in classical engineering and manufacturing employment as well as the proliferating service economy, has been the rapid and totally pervasive tendency towards automation and mechanisation. And driving the entire process has been access to unlimited, cheap fossil-fuel energy.

The downside of this economic-educational regime has been the systematic downgrading of artisanal and craft skills in manufacturing, in agriculture and even in the service, leisure and domestic sectors. With the reliance on black box technologies and expert systems there has been a corresponding erosion of folk knowledge and expertise. Individuals and communities have lost the power to repair and maintain the material artifacts upon which they depend; they have forgotten horticultural and domestic skills and 'know-how' built up and passed down between generations over decades, centuries and millennia. And in adapting to the complexity and hyper-mobility of the modern world, individuals have become cut adrift from extended family and community, depending to an ever greater extent on the complex systems of state and society to guarantee health and well-being.

So what kind of skills and aptitudes should we try to incorporate into a Transitional education system? New Zealand Transitioner Michael O'Brien (2009) came up with a list of 200 artisan skills that were required to make a Victorian town function effectively. The few that I list here give some indication of the range.

Woodland crafts. Coppicers, hurdle makers, rake makers, fork makers, besom makers, handle makers, hoop makers, ladder makers, crib makers, broaches and peg makers, clog sole cutters, bodgers, charcoal burners, oak basket makers, trug makers, stick and staff makers, field gate makers, willow basket makers, net makers.

Building crafts. Stone masons, joiners, roofers, floor layers, wallers, thatchers, slaters, lime burners, paint makers, glass blowers, glaziers, stained glass artists, mud brick makers, tile makers, chimney sweeps, plumbers, decorators, bridge builders, French polishers, sign writers.

Field crafts. Hedge layers, dry stone wallers, stile makers, well diggers, peat cutters, gardeners, horticulturists, vintners, arborists, tree surgeons, foresters, farmers, shepherds, shearers, bee keepers, millers, fishermen, orchardists, veterinarians.

Workshop crafts. Chair makers, iron founders, blacksmiths, wheelwrights, coopers, coppersmiths, tinsmiths, wood turners, coach builders, boat builders, sail makers, rope makers, wainwrights, block makers, leather tanners, harness makers, saddlers, horse collar makers, boot and shoe makers, cobblers, clog makers, knife makers, cutters, millstone dressers, potters, printers, typographers, calligraphers, bookbinders, paper makers, furniture makers, jewellers, mechanics, boiler makers, boiler men, soap makers, gunsmiths, sword smiths, brush makers, candle makers, artists, sculptors, firework makers, cycle builders, bone carvers, musical instrument makers, clay pipe makers, tool makers.

Textile crafts. Spinners, weavers, dyers, silk growers, tailors, seamstresses, milliners, hatters, lace makers, button makers, mat and rug makers, crochet workers, tatting and macramé workers, knitters, quilters, smock workers, embroiderers, leather workers, felt makers.

Domestic crafts. Fish smokers, bacon curers, butter makers, cheese makers, brewers, cider makers, wine makers, distillers, herbalists, ice cream makers, butchers, fishmongers, pie makers, pickle makers, bakers, barristers and coffee roasters, homeopaths, reflexologists, osteopaths, naturopaths, storytellers, teacher naturalists, historians, jesters, actors, administrators, philosophers, labourers, poets, writers, midwives, publicans, booksellers, librarians.

To these we might add a new sector – *Repair, Maintenance and Salvage* – that we might expect to feature in any imploding post-carbon economy. During the 1970s radical educationalists such as Ivan Illich often remarked on the fact that in developing countries one could always find untutored, practical and effective know-how – people who could repair radios, keep an old engine running, make, mend and salvage. As the expert systems upon which we have relied break down, we will need to rediscover this confident, practical, experimental attitude to machinery and technology – not least because for many decades we may be dependent on salvaging and reconditioning the technological detritus of the petroleum age.

Hedging our bets

My wife and I have two young boys who are just coming up to school age. Clearly we want them to have the same educational opportunities as we have had. And I am certainly not going to deny them the chance of a university education just because Jim Kunstler has speculated that industrial civilisation might crash and burn. On the other hand, I am worried. I worry about whether they will be able to avoid being conscripted into someone else's army or militia, about whether they will be tough enough to survive in a chaotic and possibly violent world, about whether they will have the skills and independence of mind to enable them to thrive in a simpler and more self-sufficient world.

Our own strategy will, I think, be to find somewhere where we can home educate the boys and so, hopefully, combine the pursuit of academic qualifications with the development of an ambitious array of craft and artisanal skills and aptitudes. But this is a personal solution. As a professional educator, I am also aware of the opportunities and benefits that might arise – in schools, universities, colleges, hospitals, prisons – from combining traditional forms of learning, with a resurgence of craft and artisanal skills, from wainwrighting and cooperage to home brewing and saddlery. As a university lecturer it occurs to me that we need to re-invent the notion of apprenticeship – and find a way of making education bifocal, such that academic degrees and secondary school diplomas are consistently combined with the learning of practical craft skills.

With regard to institutions, one obvious point of entry is the food provisioning system. In the UK, Jamie Oliver and Hugh Fearnley-Whittingstall have paved the way. Schools, universities and colleges are now ripe for experiments in permaculture and self-provisioning. Many campus universities and some schools have sufficient land and student labour to move in the direction of food self-sufficiency, with the growing and processing of food at the core of the student experience.

Finally, we might think of more ambitious educational experiments, specifically designed to promote an array of Transition-related self-sufficiency skills. I am developing my own ideas for a post-graduate *One Planet Institute* in this mould (see p.50). However, outside of formal education we might think in terms of developing short courses, perhaps building on what people are already doing in areas such as bushcraft and appropriate technology. What matters is not so much what we learn individually, but the range of skills and experience available within communities – the social stock of knowledge. In the context of Transition, we must all become apprentices – to each other and to master craftsmen and women – as well as reflexive observers of the ecological and material patterns of our lives.

References and resources

Barry, John and Quilley, Stephen (2008) 'Transition towns: "survival", "resilience" and the elusive paradigm shift in sustainable living'. *Eco-Politics Online*, 1:2, 12-31.

The Energy Bulletin. www.energybulletin.net (the main clearing house for peak oil- and transition-related news items – a brilliant and comprehensive resource).

Future Scenarios: mapping the cultural implications of peak oil and climate change. www.futurescenarios.org.

Hopkins, Rob (2008) *The Transition Handbook: From oil dependency to local resilience.* Dartington: Green Books.

Kunstler, James (2005) *The Long Emergency: Surviving the converging catastrophes of the 21st century.* London: Atlantic Books.

Kunstler, James (2008) *World Made by Hand.* New York: Atlantic Monthly Press.

Life after the oil crash. www.lifeaftertheoilcrash.net (one of the most influential peak oil sites and forums).

O'Brien, Michael (2009) *Victorian Oamar: A vision for the future.* Extract reproduced online at http://transitionculture.org/category/localisation.

One Planet Institute. www.oneplanetinstitute.com (my own take on combining academic study with bushcraft and artisanal craft).

Whipple, Tom (2009) 'The peak oil crisis: what of 2009?' *Falls Church News Press*, 22 January 2009.

The Wolf at the Door: A beginner's guide to peak oil. http://wolf.readinglitho.co.uk.

Chapter 6

Commons Thinking

*The ability to envisage and enable a viable future
through connected action*

Justin Kenrick

University of Glasgow, and PEDAL – Portobello Transition Town

What is Commons thinking?

The further we move into this century, the more urgently we realise that we need to relearn the political and personal skills of envisaging and enabling a viable future. This skill is not new: it is at the heart of Commons regimes the world over. Commons regimes manage socio-environmental relations in ways that attend to the *finite* nature of human and natural systems in a way which – paradoxically – ensures their *infinite* abundance continues.

The Commons are life-sustaining or life-enhancing resources and services that have not been divided up and assigned a monetary value in the global economy but instead are shared – according to evolving arrangements and agreements – among members of a community or group. They range from the air we breathe, pollination provided by bees, land that provides dwelling and food for gathering, cultivating and sharing rather than selling, to allotments, libraries, public parks, pavements and on to childcare, care for the elderly and words of comfort given freely and willingly rather than at an hourly rate. Pitted against the Commons, however, are the forces of Enclosure, which attempt to appropriate, own and sell resources that were once accessible not through the power of money but through the rights and responsibilities gained by being a member of a community. The processes of Enclosure spread from England to the rest of the British Isles: dispossessing people of their land, displacing them, and using these same people to colonise and appropriate the land of peoples in Commons regimes the world over. However, Commons regimes continue all over the world. These range from place-based communities agreeing how to use and share resources for the well-being of all their members (whether amongst forest peoples of Central Africa, community buy-outs on the west coast of Scotland, or transition towns in the UK) to emerging communities of practice – such as groups of educators working together towards sustainability and empowerment. Wherever and whenever people find ways to ensure that our well-being ensures the well-being of others – and to refuse the logic that asserts that our well-being depends on exploiting others (both other people and the environment) – then we are re-asserting Commons processes and resisting the processes of Enclosure which now threaten the systems that support human life.

This chapter aims to describe one important skill for rebuilding political, community and personal resilience: the ability to think in a Commons way. This way of thinking is crucial to tackling the root causes of economic and ecological meltdown, to restoring the local, national and global Commons, and so recovering a future that can often – to say the least – seem precarious. Commons regimes persist and re-emerge wherever people retain the political space to concern themselves with maintaining social and ecological resilience. They persist in the face of pressure from more powerful outside forces which seek to exploit, in a short-sighted way, the social and ecological resources upon which the community depends.

Commons thinking involves identifying the way one is complicit in the Enclosure or destruction of the Commons, in order to extricate oneself from such processes and instead identify with and strengthen the processes that maintain abundance for all. In essence, Commons approaches assume a world of abundant relations from which individual entities emerge and are sustained, whereas the Western dominance perspective assumes a world of scarcity where discreet entities are brought into relationship through processes of control and competition.

Putting it bluntly, these contrasting problem-solving approaches can be thought of in terms of:

A **Commons approach** which assumes that:

- we live in a common life-world upon which we all depend,
- any problems stem from a breakdown in relationships, and
- solutions are primarily about restoring these relationships

and a **dominance approach** which assumes that:

- one's well-being ultimately depends on controlling the devalued other (whether other life forms, other humans, or other aspects of oneself),
- problems are about the lack of such control, and
- the solution involves the dominant realm (the mind, the 'developed' world,

the adult, the expert, or humans in general) imposing control on the supposedly inferior realm.

How dominance thinking misrepresents the Commons

When the 'Commons' is referred to at all in dominant thinking, it is usually in terms of the so-called 'Tragedy of the Commons', and this term is used to argue that left to ourselves (without the market and government to control our behaviour) we would each choose to exploit our ecological context for our own individual benefit even though this would inevitably lead to the destruction of the ecosystems (the Commons) on which we all depend. In fact, the opposite is the case. Even Garrett Hardin, the inventor of the term, later admitted that the phrase describes, not a Tragedy of 'Commons regimes', but a Tragedy of 'Open Access regimes' (Kirkby et al. 1995).

The irony here is that an excellent example of an 'Open Access regime' is that of capitalism, where the only understanding of being 'rational' is of acting in one's own immediate, narrow self-interest. 'Open Access regimes' describe situations where people are persuaded to act in a way that has no consideration for the longer term of themselves, their children or others. Commons regimes, in sharp contrast, always have unwritten or written rules about who can use what resource when and for how long, in order to ensure everyone's well-being over the longer term (Kirkby et al. 1995, Kenrick 2005). Some may be wealthier than others, and there is always negotiation, argument or conflict as the rules are changed, kept, or broken; but the basic principle is that you don't get a free lunch (and getting a free lunch is exactly what advertisers, political parties and any other open access regime pundit try to persuade us we can get). Commons regimes are how humans have effectively self-organised for millennia; and it is somehow typical (in an Orwellian 1984 kind of way) that the term is then used to denote a 'tragedy' in order to assert that our only hope is a market system regulated by government, when it would be blindingly obvious to a Martian anthropologist that such a system has brought us to the brink of extinction, and that we need to change it fast.

Commons systems have recently re-emerged in the UK – both through the land reform movement and community buy-outs that have swept through rural Scotland since the mid-1990s, and through the proliferation of Transition initiatives (see *Transition Skills*, p.43) in Ireland, Scotland, England and Wales since 2007. These are recent examples of Commons regimes re-emerging because people realise that it is more rational to base their well-being on collectively caring about those around them, than to believe they can – over the long term – improve their own lives at the expense of their neighbours. The Transition approach embodies Commons thinking and is a creative, empowering, and immediately gratifying proof that – if we come at problems from a Commons perspective – our solutions will improve life for us all, rather than deal with symptoms in ways that exacerbate the original problem.

Naming the problem: ecological collapse, or why it is rational to be *scared*

The first step in bringing Commons thinking to bear is to recognise the problem, and the way in which all aspects of it are related. In today's *Sunday Herald* newspaper (2009.03.29) under the headline: 'Two Months to Save the World', Professor Jacqueline McGlade, the European Environment Agency's executive director, states that:

> Even if all the current promises to cut greenhouse gas emissions are honoured, the world will still see global temperatures rise by an average of four degrees centigrade by the end of the century. . . This is hot enough to make most of the world uninhabitable.

Climate change demonstrates that it is short-sighted in the extreme to base our well-being on destroying the life support system upon which we depend, and hoping that imposing technological or political solutions can protect us from the consequences. Climate change is a consequence of a system in which companies are legally obliged to maximise profits for shareholders; profits are made by externalising the social and environmental costs; and if companies aren't willing to externalise these costs to make these profits, then they are simply swallowed up by those who will. Ongoing destruction of the Earth's life support system ensues. From a Commons perspective, climate change is as much a reason to be hopeful as a reason to be fearful, since it is an urgent wake-up call to stop this socio-ecological devastation which will destroy us sooner rather than later if we don't act now.

To take a brief snapshot of the current ecological situation, we can see that accelerating climate change feedback loops are evident in the Arctic, which – as recently as 2007 – was predicted by the UN's IPCC to be ice-free in summer by 2100, but is now predicted to be ice-free by 2011-2015. Accelerating climate change feedback loops are also evident in the Amazon, southern Europe and Australia, where drying-out forests and bush are vulnerable to devastating fires; and in the weakening of the planet's carbon sinks – especially the Southern Ocean – to absorb our carbon pollution (Climate Safety 2008). Meanwhile we are persuaded that only economic growth can meet our needs. The responses to climate change by corporate-compliant governments focus on carbon trading, which does not directly reduce the CO_2 going into the atmosphere, but turns it into a tradable commodity. The focus is also on maintaining the so-called 'carbon sink' forests of the global South so that economic growth can continue unchecked, while justifying global players' appropriation of local peoples' forests and livelihoods (Griffiths 2007).

Recovering a Commons way of thinking, or why it is rational to be *hopeful*

Moving towards a society based on Commons sufficiency requires recovering a *Commons way of thinking* and relinquishing dominance thinking, the dualistic problem-solving approach underpinning non-egalitarian and unsustainable social systems. Several questions follow from this:

- How do we make the transition from a system in which problems are made worse by the way solutions are imposed – imposed by a supposedly superior realm on a supposedly inferior realm – to a system that no longer divides the world into superior and inferior realms?

- How do we move towards a recognition that – in the current system – development workers, police, doctors, social workers and teachers are entirely dependent on others' poverty, criminal acts, ill-health, social problems and supposed lack of education? For example, how do we recognise that ending poverty in Africa does not require the supposedly 'superior' wealthy and educated 'West' to intervene with charity, but requires the 'West' to stop building its wealth on forces of extraction and domination that impoverish Africa?

- How do we move to a Commons society in which sufficiency and security are grounded in the ability to respond to fear and lack by continually rebuilding relationships of trust? How do we create a society in which the other's problem is recognised as arising from a mutual world, and in which solutions are sought through dialogue and engagement?

Commons thinking recognises the rich resources available to us by starting from ensuring the well-being of locality, and the well-being of others in their localities, rather than from a system of competition over resources made scarce by that very competition. Resources are assumed to be abundant, and are made abundant by ensuring that all people and other species (all ecosystems) have sufficient to meet their needs and to ensure their flourishing. This is predicated on the notion that my well-being depends on your well-being, and on the assumption that solving problems involves working to restore relationships of trust rather than seeking to impose solutions on others.

As Lohmann (2005:20) points out, "Communal use adapts land, water and work to local needs rather than transforming them for trade and accumulation." In the sustenance economy, "Satisfying basic needs and ensuring long-term sustainability are the organising principles for natural resource use" (Shiva 2005: 18). Such Commons approaches can perhaps best be understood as Life Projects:

> Life Projects are about living a purposeful and meaningful life. In this sense, their political horizons cannot be located in the future, just as living in the present cannot be put on hold in pursuit of a future goal. . . . Life Projects have no political horizon; they are the political horizon. They are not points of arrival, utopian places, narratives of salvation or returns to paradise. They are the very act of maintaining open-endedness as a politics of resilience. (Blaser 2004: 48)

Life Projects are coming into focus not only through standing out as a force to be reckoned with in the Global South and North, but also through their ability to build alliances through which to wrest political space from governments controlled by corporations. This is evident in the way indigenous people have moved to take control of national governments in places like Bolivia, to secure degrees of autonomy through legal means in places like Canada, or through creative modes of resistance in places like Mexico. In the UK, it is evident in crofting communities' successful campaigns to take back collective control of their communities, which led to the Scottish Land Reform Act securing that right for a whole range of rural communities. It is also evident in the emerging movement of Transition Initiatives in villages, towns and cities where local people are seeking to enable their communities to make the transition from an oil-based economy to a local economy where local decision-making can ensure sufficiency for all.

Activity

In small groups, in pairs or by yourself try bringing a Commons way of thinking to problem-solving. As you attempt the exercise, notice if your response persistently seeks to revert to a habitual dominant, dualistic problem-solving approach:

> Think of a political problem that is bothering you (an example given above is that of poverty in Africa – others could be the role of air travel in generating carbon emissions; population growth and poverty; ways of ensuring well-being while reducing carbon emissions to zero; supporting an ageing population; the lack of affordable childcare; or 'ghost-town' high streets due to out-of-town supermarkets).

Instead of thinking about how this problem can be solved by the wealthy/ powerful/ intelligent/ experts imposing a solution on those deemed poor/ powerless/ stupid/ non-experts, *imagine* that the problem does not lie in the devalued lacking something but in the powerful imposing something; imagine that the solution lies in supporting connections rather than controlling others; imagine that it lies in discovering, respecting and responding to people's real needs.

How can we identify the processes that trap us in relations of domination, and how can we challenge such processes in a way which builds (rather than undermines) common cause between all concerned?

References and resources

Blaser, Mario (2004) 'Life projects: indigenous people's agency and development', in Blaser, Mario; Feit, Harvey and McRae, Glenn (eds.) *In the Way of Development: Indigenous peoples, life projects and globalisation.* London: Zed Books.

Climate Safety (2008) www.climatesafety.org (a report that provides a summary of the latest science and describes ways to avert climate change).

Forest Peoples Programme. www.forestpeoples.org (an organisation supporting forest people's rights).

Griffiths, Tom (2007) *Seeing 'RED'?: 'Avoided deforestation' and the rights of indigenous peoples and local communities.* Moreton-in-Marsh: Forest Peoples Programme.

Holyrood 350. www.holyrood350.org (describes four action points for the Scottish Parliament for averting climate change).

Kenrick, Justin (2005) 'Equalising processes, processes of discrimination and the forest people of Central Africa', in Widlock, Thomas and Tadesse, Wolde (eds.) *Property and equality, Vol. 2: Encapsulation, commercialization, discrimination.* Oxford: Berghahn. www.gla.ac.uk/media/media_106649_en.pdf.

Kirkby, John; O'Keefe, Phil and Timberlake, Lloyd (eds.) (1995) *The Earthscan Reader in Sustainable Development.* London: Earthscan.

Lohmann, Larry (2005) *What next? Activism, Expertise, Commons.* Dag Hammarskjold Foundation. www.thecornerhouse.org.uk/item.shtml?x=369050.

Shiva, Vandana (2005) *Earth Democracy: Justice, sustainability and peace.* London: Zed Books.

The Corner House. www.thecornerhouse.org.uk (an organisation that supports democratic and community movements for environmental and social justice).

Transition Towns. www.transitiontowns.org.

Chapter 7

Effortless Action

*The ability to fulfil human needs effortlessly
through working with nature*

Ling Feng

University of Sheffield

Effortless Action? This term, derived from Taoist philosophy, sounds passive and incompatible with our modern society, where effort seems decisive to success. I want to suggest that it can be very relevant to sustainability, and to explore some ways in which it might be applied by educators. Contemporary thought unconsciously conceives of 'effort' in a self-centred and modernist way that contributes to the unsustainability of our social and ecological system.

The notion of Effortless Action (*Wu Wei*) is one of the major themes of Taoism – an ecologically-oriented Chinese traditional philosophy that originated around 2,500 years ago with the classic work *Tao Te Ching* by Lao-Tsu (see Maurer 1982 for a full translation). Although Taoism originated in early China, over time practices in various cultural contexts have proved its wide applicability. It is philosophical yet practical,

Effortless Action.

seeking to inspire and instruct practitioners in how to obtain an optimal state of harmonic integration between both material and spiritual realms of existence with lessons derived from nature (Kirkland 2002).

As one of the most distinctive characteristics of Taoist thought, Effortless Action is "a form of intelligence – that is, of knowing the principles, structures, and trends of human and natural affairs so well" that achievements can be made through the least amount of effort (Watts 1975: 76). It is important to recognise that in Taoism, which urges 'selflessness' as opposed to 'self-centredness', 'effort' in Effortless Action refers to the total effort of all beings involved in and related to an action, instead of just effort of the self. Properly understood, then, Effortless Action is participative and inclusive rather than passive and anthropocentrically instrumental.

A recent advertisement for Volkswagen vehicles can help illustrate the difference between total effort and self effort. The advertisement shows how easy it is to drive and park the Volkswagen 4x4, followed by the slogan: "Tiguan, simply effortless". It makes perfect sense – easy to use, hence, simply effortless. But, is it really effortless? It may be for the driver, but it is certainly not effortless when viewed through the perspective of total effort: the engineers' effort in designing the car, materials and energy used in producing the car, the fuel imported from the warzone for running the car, the car parks and roads that need building, and the effort required to deal with the health consequences of pollution, accidents and the sedentary lifestyle of the driver. In addition, the fuels burned to build and run the car release carbon dioxide to the atmosphere, which requires current and future generations to make great effort to deal with the consequences of climate change. On the other hand, re-organising life so that most journeys can be conducted on foot, by bicycle or wheelchair, requires physical movement but, in comparison, is Effortless Action, since it flows with the natural order of things, which is for humans to expend bodily energy in moving from one place to another.

Learners could engage in practical active learning exercises to mind-map the total effort that goes into the production of daily products and services. This requires little more than a basic understanding of social and natural systems, and might be the easy bit. The more challenging bit is whether learners are able to think or are willing to think beyond the world of the self, to think of the self as a part of the social and ecological environment and build a holistic worldview in order to discover effortless alternatives for themselves.

Because our social system gets more and more complex, mutable and uncertain, it is increasingly difficult to trace every single effort involved, and it is easy to be misled by Greenwash and the supposed benefits of new technologies. For example, the generation of energy from nuclear fusion is one of the major ongoing projects that people count on to save humanity by providing clean and unlimited energy: no need to worry about peak oil and global warming once we get hold of the technology. However, the extension of human power through the use of fossil-fuel energy has led to immense damage to ecosystems, and has massively accelerated the depletion of literally 'vital' resources like fresh water. Even more unlimited energy is not a 'solution' in itself, since it could be used to exponentially increase efforts to deplete vital resources and further accelerate the damage to ecosystems.

Effortless Action reminds us of our place in the world, and also points out the way to be truly effortless – through working with the flow of nature. As Ames (1986) describes, Effortless Action is a model for creative participation in the cosmos in a manner that coheres with nature rather than resists it. This does not have to be an esoteric or mystical notion; it can be one which is intensely practical. An example is flood control. Typically, flood control is dealt with using 'hard engineering' – the building of concrete barriers and the hardening of channels. This approach is the path of effort since it depends on complex machinery, large amounts of energy, and highly skilled labour. It is a path which generates multiple further problems along the line, as the National Trust (2008) points out:

> Hard engineering works tend to increase the speed at which water moves through rivers, thereby increasing flood risk further downstream. Canalised rivers and drained floodplains are also bad for wildlife, and increased or more rapid run-off from land has a negative impact on water quality. Furthermore, the effects of climate change are already causing an increase in flooding, particularly as a result of extreme rainfall. Unless a new, more strategic approach to flood risk is adopted, flood risk management will require more and more expensive (and carbon-intensive) hard defences.

Instead, The National Trust is promoting a 'soft engineering approach' based on 'making space for water'. This path of Effortless Action involves:

> wetland creation, woodland planting and soft engineering of the river course to return it to a more natural state, which have all helped to make space for water, with benefits for biodiversity and water quality, as well as reducing the risk of flooding. (The National Trust 2008).

Solutions which restore and enhance the natural flood resilience of ecosystems end up providing multiple solutions rather than multiple further problems, and therefore save vast amounts of effort. There is also the case of 'missing-the-point' conservation projects such as 'Save China's Tiger', which has chosen to conserve the endangered south China tigers by transporting them from China to southern Africa for breeding and re-wilding (an action of great effort), instead of focusing on looking after their natural habitat in China. Lao Tsu uses a water metaphor to explain the benefits of the 'softer path':

Nothing beneath heaven
is softer and weaker than water.
Nothing is better
To attack the hard and strong
And nothing can take its place.
The weak overcome the strong;
The soft overcome the hard.
There is no one beneath heaven
Who doesn't know this,
Yet no one who practises it[2]

Tao following nature.

In general, Effortless Action means wisely and intelligently making use of what is already available in nature (the so-called 'ecosystems services') to fulfil human needs rather than taking the hard path of conquering nature through immense fossil-fuel subsidies, excessive use of technology, or inappropriate civil, chemical, genetic, nuclear or planetary engineering.

The significance of Effortless Action goes beyond ecologically sensitive design, however, to address one of the root causes of unsustainability – self-centredness and the overwhelming preoccupation with competition that results from it. We are facing a situation where huge amounts of effort are being expended in self-centred ways in order to compete and achieve goals such as having a high salary, a high status at work, a large car, or a prestigious address. These goals are not pursued because they are worthwhile for their own sake, but because people want to appear to be better than others.

This mindset is largely rooted in a form of individualistic self-centredness. Individualism has been seen as one of the achievements of Western modernisation, a form of human development through self-realisation. However, the rich and the powerful have used individualism for serving the goal of consumerism through education systems, advertising, and the media. As Hartley (1997: 62) observes, "New forms of individual identity are rooted in conspicuous consumption." Our identity is now less about who we are and more about what we have, with the priority to have more things, different things, and better things than others. In the meantime, while more consumers keen on getting better things and different things are being generated, "the drugged, the deranged and the depressed" (Hartley 1997: 63) are also mounting up, because not everyone can have more things than everyone else.

As Olive et al. (2003:237, 170) claim, the "major cultural error" of Modern culture is the "hyper-individualistic self", since "we lose our continuing commitment and capacity to participate in and negotiate culture within a fuller range" of possibilities for relationships with nature, and are left with "a much more limited quality of 'self' or 'being'" than we realise (Hilson-Katzenbach 2006). On the other hand, Lao Tsu describes a more holistic way of being-in-the-world, a way of achieving self-realisation without self-centredness or competition:

> True goodness is like water.
> Water benefits the ten thousand things,
> but does not compete with them.
> It stays in humble places,
> Therefore comes close to Tao.
> . . .
> If you do not compete,
> You will not be faulted.
> . . .
> [The sage] does not compete with anyone,
> and no one beneath heaven can compete with him.

. . .
Don't exalt the worthy:
People then will not compete

Taoism, then, represents a gentler way, a softer way, a way that flows with nature, that blurs the rigid boundaries between self and other, thereby tackling the obsession with competition at its source. How can 'I' compete, if 'I' exists only in interconnection and interdependence with other people and natural systems? (see *Being-in-the-World*, p.185). By avoiding the competition altogether and moving beyond the concept of winners and losers, beyond the idea of better people and worse people, we cannot lose, and therefore become invincible, and, importantly, more sustainable, because we are not building our sense of superiority on the repression of other people or the destruction of the environment.

Looking around us, movements such as Permaculture and Transition Towns (see www.permaculture.org.uk and www.transitiontowns.org) show us hope and alternatives. Why compete against each other and build success upon other's failures, when we can work together to create stronger and more resilient communities? Why expand competition culture through globalisation, unnecessarily multiply wants, and satisfy them through immense international efforts, when so many human needs can be fulfilled through the local community and ecosystems. Movements like the above have no place for competition culture, instead, they bring back a sense of community and trust and provide ways of acting effortlessly, flowing with nature to fill both basic and deeper human needs. There is, of course, a lot of physical work, design work, and teamwork that occurs when communities come together to fulfil their needs through practical local projects. This is not 'effort', though, because it is the kind of work that humans, as social animals, are naturally adapted for, work that resonates with who and what we are, as opposed to the effort of sitting isolated in front of computers, steering wheels, screens, and production lines, playing out a meaningless role in an unsustainable society.

Not only is our modern civilisation built upon competition, the changes that are occurring are accelerating competition between individuals, between communities/societies, between humans and the rest of nature. Environmental degradation, resource depletion, economic crises and the continuing growth of population and consumption make being critical about the entire competition culture at personal, social, national and international levels, a significant part of Education for Sustainability.

Unfortunately, competition culture is extremely evident in formal education as well, mainly through evaluation based on exams and league tables. As Sterling (2001:21) suggests: "We are educated by and large to compete and consume, rather than to care and conserve." This means that, in terms of sustainability, "education is both part of the problem and the solution" (Sterling 1996:18). If learners are to gain skills in 'effortless action', they will need to overcome the competitive atmosphere of educational institutions. They will need opportunities to work co-operatively with other learners, members of the local community, and local natural systems, in real projects of value for the future, rather than putting in effort just to get better marks than their peers. This is 'active learning', and if it is done in a way which flows with nature it becomes 'effortless active learning'. But how can this be taught? Lao Tsu has some useful advice here about effortless teaching:

> Therefore the sage
> achieves without striving
> teaches without talking

Teaching without talking.

Notes

1. Calligraphic stone stamps by Jiehua Gong.

2. All translations of the work of Lao Tsu are from Maurer (1982), with some small adjustments by the author.

References and resources

Ames, Roger (1986) 'Taoism and the nature of nature'. *Environmental Ethics*, 8:8, 317-50.

Hartley, David (1997) *Re-schooling Society*. London: Falmer.

Hilson-Katzenbach, Mimi (2006) 'Wu wei all the way'. *International Journal of Leadership in Education*, 9:3, 269-77.

Kirkland, Russell (2002) 'Self-fulfilment through selflessness: the moral teachings of the Daodejing', in Barnhart, Michael (ed.) *Varieties of Ethical Reflection: New directions for ethics in a global context*. Maryland: Lexington Books.

Maurer, Herrymon (1982) *Tao, The Way of the Ways*. Cambridge: Cambridge University Press (includes one of the best English translations of the *Tao Te Ching* together with an insightful commentary).

Olive, Donald; Canniff, Julie and Korhonen, Jouni (2003) *The Primal, the Modern, and the Vital Centre: A theory of balanced culture in a living place*. Vermont: The Foundation for Educational Renewal.

Sterling, Stephen (1996) 'Education in change', in Huckle, John and Sterling, Stephen (eds.) *Education for Sustainability*. London: Earthscan.

Sterling, Stephen (2001) *Sustainable Education: Re-visioning learning and change*. Dartington: Green Books.

The National Trust (2008) *Nature's capital: Investing in the nation's natural assets*. www.nationaltrust.org.uk/main/w-natures_capital.pdf.

Watts, Alan (1975) *Tao: The watercourse way*. New York: Penguin.

Chapter 8

Permaculture Design

Designing our lives with nature as the model

Patrick Whitefield

Author of The Earth Care Manual: A permaculture handbook
for Britain and other temperate climates

The essence of permaculture is that it takes natural ecosystems as the model for our own farms, gardens, buildings and settlements. In most parts of the world where agriculture is possible, the natural ecosystem is woodland or forest. The annual production of biomass in a woodland is greater than in a typical agricultural system, such as a wheat field, because more niches are filled. In plain terms, the woodland is three-dimensional where the wheat field is two-dimensional. To produce this biomass it needs none of the energy and other inputs which agriculture needs. Present-day agriculture is so energy-intensive that on average, by the time food reaches our plates, ten calories of fossil fuel have been expended for every one contained in the food. Nor does the natural ecosystem produce any of the negative ecological impacts of agriculture, such as enhanced soil erosion. The catch is that only a very small proportion of the natural ecosystem's annual production is edible for humans. So the aim of permaculture is to produce systems which have the high yield, low level of inputs, and benign ecological impact of natural ecosystems but which also have a high proportion of edible or otherwise useful yield. In short, the aim is to create edible ecosystems. Permaculture approaches this end in two different ways.

In its early days permaculture focused on imitating natural ecosystems in a fairly direct way. Its key characteristics included, amongst others: a high level of plant and animal diversity, growing perennial food crops rather than annuals, and not disturbing the soil by digging or ploughing. These are typical characteristics of natural ecosystems which can be observed and reproduced empirically in food-growing systems. An example of this approach is the forest garden, which mimics the structure of a natural woodland but replaces native plants with edible equivalents: fruit and nut trees, fruit bushes and perennial vegetables (Whitefield and Cassel 1996). I call this approach original permaculture.

But before long permaculturists began to look beyond the visible characteristics of ecosystems and ask what the basic principle is which enables them to be so high-yielding and self-reliant. The answer lies in diversity, but not so much in the diversity of the component species themselves as in the diversity of beneficial relationships between them. One example of this kind of relationship is that between the flowering plants and the pollinating insects, in which one gets its food need met and the other its reproductive needs. An ecosystem consists of a whole network of relationships of this kind, both between living organisms and between them and the non-living components of the ecosystem such as soil, water and climate.

An example of how beneficial relationships can be created in a human system can be seen in a productive conservatory. The conservatory collects solar energy and passes some of it on to the house in the form of space-heating. Energy is also stored in the wall of the house and re-radiated at night, keeping the conservatory frost-free and warmer than a free-standing greenhouse. Thus each helps to warm the other. The conservatory is relatively narrow from front to back and goes all the way along the most southerly-facing wall of the house. This ensures the maximum gain of heat and minimum loss. The conservatory is also used for raising vegetable plants in the spring, and the ease of visiting what is in effect another room of your house, compared with going to an outside greenhouse in inclement weather, means that the seedlings get more attention. This means they get off to a better start in life, which is a very important factor in the final performance of the crop.

A house with conservatory attached does not look like an ecosystem, but it shares its most important characteristic: a network of beneficial relationships. This kind of permaculture is not dependent on direct imitations of nature; it depends on placing things in relation to each other so that beneficial relationships can be formed between them. In short, it is a matter of functional design. I call this approach design permaculture. It can be practised with or without the characteristics of original permaculture, though in practice most permaculture contains elements of both.

A central method used in permaculture design is what we call the key planning tools. These comprise the concepts of: zone, sector, network and elevation. By *zone*, we mean the amount of human attention which a piece of land receives. Crops and activities which need the most attention are placed where they will receive it with the least effort. For example, when confronted with the choice between a very small back garden or an allotment which is half an hour away by bicycle, wise gardeners may forgo the allotment and grow their fruit and vegetables in the garden. The constant presence of the gardener means that production can be many times more intensive and the garden may out-yield an allotment several times its size. In addition, more frequent harvesting means that a greater proportion of what is grown actually gets eaten. Although simple, this is a wonderfully powerful design tool, not only for households but for farms and whole settlements.

Perennial Vegetables form part of the edible plantings at Ragmans Lane Farm,
a permaculture course venue in Gloucestershire.

While the concept of zone deals with the human energy centred on the site, *sector* is about off-site factors which affect it. These include wind, light and shade, water, views, neighbours, and pollution. Many of these are climatic factors and the concept of microclimate – the characteristic climate of a small area – is important in permaculture design. Whilst creating a totally new microclimate, such as a conservatory, can be worthwhile, it is not the first priority. The first step is to observe the site carefully through all the seasons and then match the planting to the various microclimates the site contains. For example, a tough fruiting tree such as a damson will yield as well in a windy or shady spot as it will in a south-facing suntrap. Not so a peach. Matching the plants to the microclimates available means that a wider range of plants can be grown, including more demanding ones, and the overall yield of the system will be higher than if they were placed at random.

Network is similar to zone but it comes to bear when there is more than one centre of human activity. This means it is more often relevant on larger sites such as farms and whole settlements than in domestic gardens. It is concerned with access and links between different nodes of activity. An example in settlement design is to ensure that all frequently used services, from shops to allotments, are within easy walking distance of people's homes.

Elevation is concerned with altitude, both relative and absolute, and degree of slope. It is particularly relevant when dealing with water, both in domestic and broad-scale situations. For example, the conventional approach to siting a pond for farmland irrigation is to place it on flat ground at the bottom of the slope and use fuel to pump the water to wherever it is needed. The permaculture approach is to find a spot which combines three characteristics: low enough in the landscape to be able to collect water; high enough so that it is above the area to be irrigated; and on a relatively flat piece of land for economy of construction – you need a taller dam to make a pond of given size on a steep slope than on a more gradual one. A pond in such a position may have to be a little smaller or may be a little more difficult to construct than one sited on the flat land at the bottom. But throughout the fuel-hungry ages which stretch before us it will irrigate the land entirely by gravity.

When they are used together as a set, the synergistic effect of these planning tools is powerful. They are far from being the only design method used by permaculturists but they are perhaps the most effective. A frequent theme which runs through them is the reduction of energy expenditure, both human and fossil fuel. In the examples I have chosen here: excessive travelling is cut out and more food is produced per unit of energy invested; tender fruit can be grown without the need for glasshouses or imports; journeys can be made by foot instead of powered transport; and water is available where it is needed without any pumping. In the past, human needs were met largely by muscle power, which meant unremitting drudgery for the majority of the population. In the present our needs are met by throwing unlimited quantities of under-priced fossil fuel at any problem. People often assume that these are the only two options but permaculture seeks to provide a third, one which is based on design.

Most of the elements of permaculture design, from conservatories to irrigation ponds, are not unique to it. Even the less familiar elements which are associated with original permaculture, such as the forest garden, have their equivalents in other parts of the world or in other times. The contribution which permaculture brings to the practice of sustainability is less to do with the elements it contains than the connections between them. The network of beneficial relationships which characterises a permaculture system is an alternative to the excessive use of energy which is characteristic of present-day systems. Although I am focusing here on energy use, permaculture is about much more than energy, just as the challenges which face us in the twenty-first century are not confined to climate change and peak oil. But these are certainly the biggest and most urgent of those challenges and permaculture has an important role to play in confronting them.

Whatever design methods are used, they are used within a clearly defined design sequence. The stages of the sequence are: making a map of the existing situation; conducting a site survey; asking the people who inhabit or use the site what they want from it and what work and skills they can provide; evaluation of the information gathered; formulating design proposals and drawing these on a map; and finally re-evaluation. A great emphasis is placed on the early stages, those of observing and listening. The temptation to rush into making design decisions early on is always there but a good, workable design is unlikely to result if the receptive part of the process is rushed. Listening rather than speaking, valuing the passive above the active, is the antithesis of our contemporary culture. We find it very hard to do. Yet it is a cultural change we need to make if we are to learn to live with nature rather than in spite of her.

Ideally the designers should be the inhabitants themselves. The time they are able to give to the design, compared with a consultant designer who will complete the job in a few days, is important. It allows for observation during all the seasons so that microclimates can reveal themselves. It allows time for all the people involved to have their say and be well listened to. It also allows initial ideas to be mulled over in the light of experience. There is a place for permaculture consultants, but most people who want to practise permaculture prefer to learn how to do it themselves and only bring in professional help to check that their design is on the right track.

At present, permaculture tends to be taught outside formal education in short courses in a two-week block, a series of weekends or evening classes. These courses provide a good model for how permaculture design could be introduced in formal education in dedicated modules, although permaculture principles could also be woven in right across the curriculum. Active learning is essential for gaining permaculture skills. The core of the standard permaculture course consists of a series of design exercises, usually one for each of the stages in the design sequence listed above. This is carried out on an actual piece of land but with a fictitious inhabitant. The land gives the exercises the element of reality and the tutor who plays the part of the 'client' can choose a scenario which will give the best learning experience. Having learnt how to do permaculture design in this practical way, the students can go home and do it on their own place.

That place need not be the idyllic smallholding or large garden which may spring to mind as the sort of place you need in order to practise permaculture. One of the strengths of permaculture is that it can be used to make the most of unpromising situations. Balconies, shady back yards, odd scraps of unused land, even flat roofs have their potential, and the permaculture design process can seek out these potentials and maximise them. It is also well adapted to community situations, where many voices need to be heard, and often the human aspect is more of a challenge than the physical. In the twenty-first century, the long, vulnerable, energy-intensive supply lines which presently keep us fed are unlikely to perform as smoothly as we have become used to. It is likely that we will need to cultivate every scrap of land available to us, especially in cities, and to learn how to work together as we do it. Permaculture design skills therefore have an important role to play if we are to survive and thrive in the difficult times ahead.

References and resources

Goldring, Andrew (ed.) (2000) *Permaculture Teachers' Guide*. Hampshire: Permanent Publications.

Holmgren, David (2002) *Permaculture: Principles and Pathways Beyond Sustainability*. Holmgren Design Services.

Jacke, Dave and Toensmeier, Eric (2005) *Edible Forest Gardens* (2 vols). Vermont, USA: Chelsea Green (includes an excellent account of the science that supports original permaculture).

Mollison, Bill and Slay, Reny Mia (1991) *Introduction to Permaculture*. Tasmania: Tagari

Permaculture Magazine. www.permaculture.co.uk (an excellent source of inspiration and practical ideas).

The Community Solution UK Permaculture (2006) *The Power of Community: How Cuba survived peak oil* (DVD). www.permaculture.org.uk.

Whitefield, Patrick (1993) *Permaculture in a Nutshell*. Hampshire: Permanent Publications

Whitefield, Patrick (2004) *The Earth Care Manual: A permaculture handbook for Britain and other temperate climates*. Hampshire: Permanent Publications.

Whitefield, Patrick and Cassel, Tricia (1996) *How to Make a Forest Garden*. Hampshire: Permanent Publications.

Chapter 9

Community Gardening

*Skills for building community and working
within environmental limits*

Alma Clavin

Leeds School of Architecture, Landscape and Design
Leeds Metropolitan University

The challenges of a changing climate and a peaking oil supply are an opportunity for educators to rethink the kind of community and world we would like to live in. As oil peaks, intensive farming becomes less economical, since it depends on oil and natural gas for pesticides, fertilisers and farm machinery. At the same time, climate change, ecosystem degradation, the demand for biofuels, an increasing population and increasing demand for milk and meat in developing countries, is putting further pressure on food supplies. For many communities, particularly those hardest hit by economic turbulence and extreme weather events, high food prices will present a challenge for survival, and even in rich countries it will become increasingly difficult for many to afford a varied and healthy diet. The ability to work with communities and design and implement gardens that can provide organic produce from minimal resources is therefore an important sustainability literacy skill, for both sustainability in the sense of surviving in the face of the challenging conditions of the twenty-first century, and the efficient use of resources so as not to contribute to making those conditions even worse. Developing skills in designing and implementing community gardens requires active engagement in real projects. This chapter describes how the form of active learning involved in community gardening helps learners gain skills not only in garden design but also a wide range of other sustainability literacy skills that are useful in other contexts.

Community gardens are urban plots of land which provide opportunities for learners and educators to work together with the local community to design spaces according to goals, such as creating an attractive space, demonstrating permaculture principles, building resilient communities, providing food, health, and environmental education. Community gardens can be sited on derelict urban brownfield sites, on allotments, or on the grounds of educational institutions themselves. Within community gardens, learning is a social process: learners, educators and members of the local community all learn from each other and from interaction with the built and natural environment (see *A Learning Society*, p.215). Working with nature and a local community in establishing and maintaining a community garden can enable learners to gain sustainability literacy skills in ways which would not be possible in a regulated classroom environment. This is a form of "experiential learning" (Orr, 1992), providing a direct participatory learning experience through active engagement.

The activities involved in designing, implementing and maintaining a community garden contribute to both environmental sustainability and the health and well-being of the learners. A well-being approach encourages the learner to think positively about sustainability since they have something to gain directly for themselves, while at the same time they can learn how environmental impacts are related to everyday choices and values. The approach demonstrates that the health of the environment and the well-being of the learner are interlinked – our natural environment generates the conditions for organic life, of which human life is one form, existing only in interdependence with other forms of life.

The sites are ecologically designed, contained spaces. Energy and waste inputs and outputs are minimised by natural and designed-in cyclical processes: organic food growing, natural seasonal growth, composting, rainwater harvesting, the use of solar energy, and the reusing and recycling of waste materials generated on site. In this way, activities within the sites enable the learner to become aware of environmental limits and ways of living within those limits. The sites also facilitate connection with the knowledge and skills for sustainable living that are embedded in local communities.

Table 1 overleaf summarises just some of the sustainability literacy skills that can be gained directly through the activities involved in designing, implementing and maintaining a community garden.

Because sites tend to be compact in size, learners can readily see the negative consequences of wasted resources, and the positive impacts of recycling and reusing the site's resources. Ecological design principles can be employed within the site in order to integrate natural processes with learning activities. Examples of this include using coppice willow in building structures, composting with organic waste from the site, using harvested rainwater to water crops during the summer months, eating food produced on the site and using a compost toilet. Such activities demonstrate how individual choices made within the site can enable or undermine conditions for other choices to be made in the future.

Table 1 – skills and activities in community garden projects

Skills	Activities
Community building	• Designing, planning and implementing a project collectively brings people from different ages and walks of life together. • Social events such as cooking with food grown in the garden, eating and working together help to develop social skills for bonding with others.
Ecological design and observation	• Participating in maintaining a non-rigid design and natural evolution of site. • Learning about the natural history of the site. • Working within the existing natural features of site: soil testing, aspect, shading, seasons, microclimates etc. • Seeing the consequences of one's actions within the site. • Caring for plants; growing food organically; recycling; reusing; encouraging wildlife.
Appropriate technology	• Designing, building and using rainwater harvesting systems, compost toilets, cold frames, wormeries etc.
Holistic health	• Working physically outdoors, being able to choose activities to match body limits. Eating organic, locally grown vegetables and fruit, becoming aware of interrelationships between a healthy body and healthy environment.
Communication skills and stakeholder engagement	• Talking with others within and about the local natural environment, solving problems together, consulting people when making decisions, overcoming disagreements and working with people who have different agendas.

Since each learner is actively involved in the evolving design process, they can develop the important quality of *mindfulness*, becoming aware of how their actions affect and are constrained by the natural processes around them across the changing seasons (see *Permaculture Design*, p.64). This can lead to the emergence of what E. O. Wilson (1984) calls 'biophilia', as learners begin to love the site and the unfolding structures, plants and wildlife within it. Since learners have a stake in the success of site activities such as growing food, participating in community events, building structures such as teaching rooms, digging ponds and making compost bins from natural and recycled materials, the activities are purposeful and meaningful.

The sites are embedded in place and community, and solutions to design problems are worked out within the site. Learning is through experiencing the

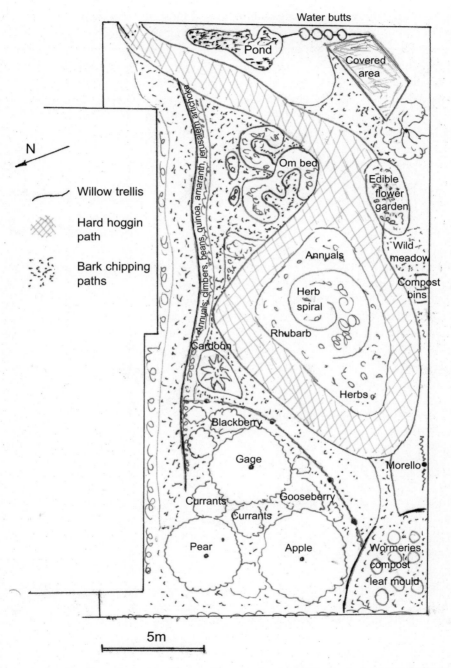

Water butts

Pond

Covered area

N

Willow trellis

Hard hoggin path

Bark chipping paths

Annuals, climbers, beans, quinoa, amaranth, Jerusalem artichoke

Om bed

Edible flower garden

Wild meadow

Annuals

Compost bins

Herb spiral

Rhubarb

Cardoon

Herbs

Blackberry

Gage

Morello

Currants

Gooseberry

Currants

Pear

Apple

Wormeries, compost leaf mould

5m

Design for the Edible Garden at the University of Gloucestershire produced by Mike Bush in consultation with the community (www.ecoling.net/garden.html).

success or failure of food crops, different composting techniques, methods of mulching and natural pest control. Diverse groups work together, learn from each other, eat food produced on site together, and gain observation skills through learning about the natural history, soil type, aspect and shading within the space. The informal and sometimes contested nature of reclaiming a public space for group activity gives those involved a sense of ownership, empowerment and community. The design evolves as the site evolves with the seasons, the food grown, with changing types and numbers of people and groups involved. In this way participants learn to deal with uncertainty, design for the future where appropriate and 'let what happens happen' where appropriate.

Because of the informal structure of community gardens, the learner has a choice in what activities/tasks to participate in. If they are not interested in being involved in a high level of physical activity such as digging or building on a particular day, they are free to choose a less strenuous activity such as weeding or harvesting. In this way, they can test and realise their own bodily limits, gaining intuitive knowledge of themselves as embodied beings acting within an environment. Since taking on tasks is voluntary and there are no deadlines, learners can focus on achieving tasks slowly, using simple technology such as hand tools to allow mindful attention to the task at hand. Such choices and experiences are in contrast to a usually high-tech and regulated urban educational setting. Activities such as planting and harvesting in natural surroundings while chatting with others absorbed in the same activities, provide sensory stimulation and can lead to a highly enjoyable learning experience.

By thinking holistically, learners realise their role as active *agents* of change both within the site and in their daily lives. Agency is the ability to exercise choice and live according to deeply held values and is enabled or constrained by physical health, social structure and environmental limits. Through being an active participant within a community garden, learners can become free from the artificial and often rigid constraints of disciplinary-based education and instead, exercise their agency within the very different constraints of community and environment.

In everyday activities, the concept of sustainability may be perceived as restricting choices. People may be 'locked-in' to unsustainable behaviours; for example, recycling opportunities may be limited, local organic food too expensive, or greywater systems impractical, given constraints on building alteration. There may, therefore, be many instances where actions which contribute to sustainability are desirable but cannot proceed because there are no enabling structures. Community gardens provide learners with such enabling structures by allowing access to skills, knowledge and support to grow food organically and be creative in the reuse of waste materials. They provide a space for active sociable participation in a natural environment which can fulfil human needs for belonging, community, physical exercise, healthy food and entertainment in ways which do not demand high consumption of resources. Because taking part provides so many enjoyable experiences, community garden projects can bridge the gap between valuing a sustainable life and having the enabling skills to act on such values.

The environment provides the resources we require for human life, and the activities and experiences within the site help learners understand the natural processes that make life possible for all life-forms. Goodin (1992) describes how these larger ecological cycles and processes provide a continuity and context in which humans understand their own individual plans and projects, and hence shape their own well-being. However, in a built-up urban environment, learners may not be aware of such cycles of activity. Community gardens enable such a realisation by creating a self-contained, ecologically designed space, within which the learner plays an integral part. In this way, they are transformative spaces in which the learner realises both human and environmental limits, and the intrinsic value of the natural environment.

Summary

The ability to design and create community gardens is a skill of considerable importance for surviving and thriving in the twenty-first century. It is not a skill that can be learned merely in the classroom, but one which requires learners to become actively engaged with educators and the local community in creating working community gardens for themselves. The sustainability literacy skills involved in participation in community garden projects reach far beyond gardening, and include a wide range of skills, from community-building to ecological design, which may be transferred to other spheres of life.

Within a community garden project there is a positive focus on both the health of the environment and the well-being of the learner. Education for sustainability within the sites is based on the premise that simply accumulating knowledge about problems such as climate change, pollution or threats of a peaking oil supply, is ineffective and may be disempowering. Including community gardens in learning programmes provides a resource hub for learning about the processes of nature and gaining a range of sustainability literacy skills. It is a transformative environment which enables a holistic way of thinking and of making choices about resources in everyday environments. Gaining skills in community gardening can help learners shift from thinking about sustainability literacy as being about self-restraint, to conceptualising it as a route to personal well-being, community resilience and the health of the systems that support life.

References and resources

Federation of City Farms and Community Gardens. www.farmgarden.org.uk.

Goodin, Robert (1992) *Green Political Theory*. Cambridge, UK: Polity Press.

Orr, David (1992) *Ecological Literacy: Education and the transition to a postmodern world*. Albany: State University of New York Press.

The Edible Garden Project. www.ecoling.net/garden.html (detailed information about a community garden project involving university staff, students and the local community).

Van der Ryn, Sim and Cowan, Stuart (1995) *Ecological Design*. Washington: Island Press.

Whitefield, Patrick (2004) *The Earth Care Manual: A permaculture handbook for Britain and other temperate climates*. Hampshire: Permanent Publications.

Wilson, Edward O. (1984) *Biophilia*. Cambridge, MA: Harvard University Press.

Chapter 10

Ecological Intelligence

Viewing the world relationally

Stephen Sterling

Schumacher Reader in Education for Sustainability,
Centre for Sustainable Futures, University of Plymouth

The shape of the global future rests with the reflexivity of human consciousness –
the capacity to think critically about why we think what we do – and then to think
and act differently. (Paul Raskin 2006)

If we want the chance of a sustainable future, we need to think relationally. That's
it, full stop. No need to write any more . . . or there wouldn't be, if it was that
obvious. It's because we *don't* think in a relational way that we need to explore
why we don't, how we can, and what it means. The world is increasingly
complex, interdependent and unsustainable, yet conversely, the way we perceive,
think, and educate tends to be fragmentary and limited, and we tend to live 'like
there's no tomorrow'. Addressing this mismatch requires developing competencies in systems thinking, critical thinking and creative thinking, but it requires
something more fundamental and challenging besides: no less than our
becoming "conscious agents of cultural evolution" (Gardner 2001: 206) towards
a more ecological culture and participative worldview, consistent with and able
to address the highly interconnected and endangered world we have created (see
Finding Meaning Without Consuming, p.178).

Worldviews are "epistemological structures for interpreting reality that
ground their picture of 'reality' in their own construction" (Milbrath 1994:117).
The contemporary challenge is to transcend our self-referential constructions,
recognising that the increasingly pressing sustainability problems we face are
rooted in the dominant underlying beliefs and worldview of the Western mind,
which, according to Clark (1989: 472) has grown "maladaptive" (see also *Beauty
as a Way of Knowing*, p.191). Rather, we need to move towards an ecological or
'participative' consciousness – or what Raskin et al. (2002:91) call, a "strong

ecological sensibility"– supporting a culturally shared ecological intelligence that is now well overdue (despite welcome and growing signs of its emergence).

This chapter provides some outlines of the meaning of ecological thinking and consciousness – as a response to the limits of the modernist worldview – and touches on the implications this has for education and learning. There is a need for "relearning on a grand scale", which should be "a core part of learning across society, necessitating a metamorphosis of many of our current education and learning constructs" (Williams 2004:4).

First, let's look at terms. Why ecological? One meaning of the term is reflected in the science of ecology. But at a broader level, the notion of an ecological worldview and sensibility arises from the identification of *ecology* as an ontological metaphor, to contrast with the underlying Newtonian metaphor of mechanism which informs modernist thought (see *Being-in-the-World*, p.185). There has long been tension between the dominant *mechanistic* and the alternative *organicist* ways of viewing the world. As Capra (1996:17) states:

> The basic tension is one between the parts and the whole. The emphasis on the parts has been called mechanistic, reductionist or atomistic; the emphasis on the whole holistic, organismic, or ecological.

Since the 1960s, Sachs (1999: 63) suggests that "The scientific term [ecology] has turned into a worldview. And as worldview, it carries the promise of reuniting what has been fragmented, of healing what has been torn apart – in short of caring for the whole." Notice that Sachs invokes caring here. So ecological thinking – reflected in ecophilosophy – is essentially relational or connective thinking, but it's also more than that: it is ethical, valuative, and expresses our humanity. In my doctoral thesis (Sterling 2003) I made a distinction between systems thinking and ecological thought, because while ecological thinking is systemic (relational), systems thinking is not necessarily ecological. Systems thinking can be used as a methodology for anti-ecological, as well as ecological, ends. Yet at the same time, systemic thinking can help sow the seeds of an ecological worldview; it can help facilitate the critical reflexivity – or deep questioning of assumptions – that Raskin (quoted at the start of the chapter) advocates (see *Systems Thinking*, p.84). This is important because, as the eminent anthropologist Bateson (1972:461) said years ago, we are "governed by epistemologies that we know to be wrong". That is, while we may be aware of the limits of reductionist and objectivist approaches and instrumental rationality, at both a deep and practical level they still tend to inform our perception and thinking – and much educational policy and practice (Sterling 2001). Through experience of the latter, educators and learners tend to be:

- good at *analysing* things – but less good at thinking 'out of the box', and at synthesising things

- good at *categorising* and *labelling* things (this is a 'health issue', an 'economic issue', a 'social issue' or an 'environmental issue', for example) – but less good at seeing the interrelated nature of the reality that often lies beneath the convenient label
- good at *seeing detail* and dealing with parts – but less good at appreciating overall patterns in events, in organisations, or other phenomena
- good at *focusing in* on one factor or one goal (e.g., maximising a particular achievement, increasing productivity, or maximising profits) – but less good at recognising and balancing multiple factors and goals (Sterling 2005).

This is a kind of lopsided competence, which is largely blind to relationships in both descriptive and normative terms (i.e., what is, and what should be). Getting beyond this depends on self-reflexivity, whereby dominant assumptions are brought to light for examination. I suggest such assumptions can be outlined as follows:

1. 'To every problem, there's a solution' *(belief in the power of problem-solving approaches)*
2. 'We can understand something by breaking it down into its component parts' *(believing a complex whole can be understood by looking at the detail)*
3. 'The whole (of something) is no more than the sum of its parts' *(there are no emergent properties)*
4. 'Most processes are linear and characterised by cause and effect' *(events and phenomena have a identifiable beginning and finishing point)*
5. 'Most issues and events are fundamentally discrete or may be regarded as such, and may be dealt with adequately in a segregated way' *(most issues are essentially unrelated)*
6. 'It is ethically acceptable to draw your circle of attention or concern quite tightly, as in "that's not my concern"' *(our system of concern is restricted – we do not need to look beyond our immediate concerns as an individual, a householder, a consumer, a businessman etc.)*
7. 'Objectivity is both possible and necessary to understand issues' *(it is important to exclude our feelings and values in our analysis and judgement)*
8. 'We can define or value something by distinguishing it from what it is not, or from its opposite' *(a belief that economics is separate from ecology, people are separate from nature, facts are separate from values, etc. – putting boundaries around that which we value)*
9. 'We can understand things best through a rational response. Any other approach is irrational' *(we need to downplay our intuition and non-rational knowing)*

10. 'If we know what the state of something is now, we can usually predict future outcomes' *(a belief in certainty, prediction, and the possibility of control)*

These ten assumptions can be re-stated as basic habits of thought or tendencies which characterise or exemplify the paradigm of modernist thinking as follows (in the same order as above):

1. problem-solving
2. analysis
3. reductionism
4. cause-effect
5. atomism
6. narrow boundaries
7. objectivism
8. dualism
9. rationalism
10. determinism

This kind of approach to issues has been phenomenally successful in the past, but arguably is now maladaptive to contemporary conditions of increasing complexity, uncertainty and volatility in intermeshed economic, social and ecological systems. Whilst they still have validity and applicability to simple and contained problems, they are unsuited to the 'messy' and 'wicked' problems that often characterise sustainability issues (see *Coping with Complexity*, p.165). Try applying these approaches for example, to issues of climate change or loss of biodiversity, or poverty, and their inadequacy becomes apparent. As Klein (2004:4) states:

> Arising from environments characterised by turbulence and uncertainty, complex problems are typically value-laden, open-ended, multidimensional, ambiguous, and unstable. Labeled 'wicked' and 'messy', they resist being tamed, bounded or managed by classical problem-solving approaches.

Such conditions require a different set of approaches and skills, which can be presented as follows. Each of the points is a corresponding rejoinder to the list of 'thinking assumptions' above (Sterling 2005):

1. Some solutions just produce more problems. Instead, we need to develop 'solutions that generate further solutions' (these are sometimes called 'positive synergies').
2. We often need to look at the whole, and at the larger context.
3. Complex systems show *emergent properties*; i.e., additional qualities that emerge from the interaction of the parts e.g., health in a human body.
4. We need to attempt to look at all the influences at the 'start', all the knock-

on effects at the 'finish' and any *feedback loops*. This complexity is characteristic of most human and environmental systems.

5. Most issues/events are related to other issues/events and can be better understood in the light of this interrelated reality.

6. Complexity means that we need to expand our view of the world and be more aware of the boundaries of concern we set ourselves.

7. So-called opposites are in relationship. We tend to devalue one side against the other (ecology against economics, nature against people, values against facts etc.), and instead, need to see them in relationship rather than in opposition.

8. The decision to try to be objective is a value judgement. Total objectivity is impossible. Better to recognise how our subjective self is involved in perception and interpretation of the world.

9. Intellect needs to be balanced with intuition, and rationality with non-rational ways of knowing; spiritual and aesthetic knowing (balancing our left brain with our right brain).

10. In human and most natural systems (that is, those systems which are not mechanical) it is impossible to predict outcomes. We need to be more flexible, accept uncertainty, and not try to control everything but participate in and learn from change.

The two sets of thinking approaches and assumptions can be summarised and compared as follows:

Two ways of thinking . . .	
• Problem Solving	• Appreciation / reframing
• Analysis	• Synthesis
• Reductionism	• Holism
• Closed cause-effect	• Multiple influences through time and space
• Atomistic/segregative	• Integrative
• Narrow boundaries	• Extension of boundaries
• Objectivism	• Critical subjectivity
• Dualism	• Pluralism / duality
• Rationalism	• Rational / non-rational ways of knowing
• Determinism	• Uncertainty, tolerance of ambiguity

It is not a matter of abandoning the left-hand side, even if this were possible. It is a matter of 'stepping out' of this paradigm, and recognising it – so that we master it, rather than it mastering us. In this way, we can employ these approaches but only when they are appropriate to the situation. Beyond this, developing an ecological sensibility, an understanding of interconnectivity, and an ability to design and act integratively requires attention to the more systemic set of approaches represented by the right-hand side of the diagram. In terms of educational practices, it means curriculum designers and teachers developing learning situations where the potential for transformative learning experiences is made manifest. Such situations will reflect implicitly in their design, and/or explicitly in their pedagogic approaches, such questions as the following:

- *holistic:* how does this relate to that?, what is the larger context here?
- *critical:* why are things this way, in whose interests?
- *appreciative:* what's good, and what already works well here?
- *inclusive:* who/what is being heard, listened to and engaged?
- *systemic:* what are or might be the consequences of this?
- *creative:* what innovation might be required?; and
- *ethical:* how should this relate to that?, what is wise action?, how can we work towards the inclusive well-being of the whole system?

Such learning will, ideally, be reflexive, experiential, inquiring, experimental, participative, iterative, real-world and action-oriented, invoking 'learning as change' in the active pursuit of sustainability and in designing and developing sustainable systems – rather than merely 'learning about change' or 'learning for change' which may be seen as rather more passive steps on the way to a deeper learning response (see *Institutional Transformation*, p.209).

The Future Leaders Survey (2008), which surveyed some 25,000 young people, makes it clear that they are 'intensely aware of the big challenges facing the planet', but also notes that they are also the last generation with a chance to put things on a more sustainable course. The only way to maximise this chance, is through the rapid flowering of ecological intelligence, a *collective connective consciousness* and *competence* that all of us, educators, learners and graduates alike, share in.

References and resources

Bateson, Gregory (1972) *Steps to an Ecology of Mind*. San Francisco: Chandler.

Capra, Fritjof (1996) *The Web of Life*. London: HarperCollins.

Clark, Mary (1989) *Ariadne's Thread – The search for new ways of thinking*. Basingstoke: Macmillan.

Farley, Joshua; Erickson, Jon and Daly, Herman (2005) *Ecological Economics: A workbook for problem-based learning*. Washington: Island Press.

Future Leaders Survey (2008) *The Future Leaders Survey 07/08*. Forum for the Future/UCAS. www.forumforthefuture.org/future-leaders-survey-07-08.

Gardner, Gary (2001) 'Accelerating the shift to sustainability', in Brown, Lester et al. *State of the World: Worldwatch Institute report on progress towards a sustainable society*. London: Earthscan.

Klein, Julie (2004) 'Interdisciplinarity and complexity: an evolving relationship'. *Emergence: Complexity and Organization*, 6:1-2, 2-10.

Meadows, Donella and Wright, Diana (ed.) (2009) *Thinking in Systems: A primer*. London: Earthscan.

Milbrath, Lester (1994) 'Stumbling blocks to a sustainable society', in McKenzie-Mohr, Doug and Marien, Michael (eds.) *Futures* (special issue: *Visions of Sustainability*) 26:2.

Raskin, Paul (2006) *World Lines – Pathways, Pivots and the Global Future*. Boston: Tellus Institute.

Raskin, Paul; Banuri, Tariq; Gallopín, Gilberto; Gutman, Pablo; Hammond, Al; Kates, Robert and Swart, Rob (2002) *Great Transition: the Promise and Lure of the Times Ahead*. Stockholm Environment Institute/Tellus Institute.

Sachs, Wolfgang (1999) *Planet Dialectics*. London: Zed Books.

Sterling, Stephen (2001) *Sustainable Education – Re-visioning Learning and Change* (Schumacher Briefing no.6). Dartington: Green Books.

Sterling, Stephen (2003) 'Whole systems thinking as a basis for paradigm change in education: explorations in the context of sustainability' (PhD thesis). Centre for Research in Education and the Environment, University of Bath. www.bath.ac.uk/cree/sterling.htm.

Sterling, Stephen (2005) 'Linking thinking, education and learning: an introduction', in Sterling, Stephen; Irvine, Deryck; Maiteny, Paul and Salter, John *Linking thinking – new perspectives on thinking and learning for sustainability*. WWF-Scotland. www.wwf.org.uk/scotland (contains many ideas and practical activities that can be used in educational settings).

Williams, Morgan (2004) Preface, in Potter, Nick et al. *See change – learning and education for sustainability*. Wellington, New Zealand: Parliamentary Commissioner for the Environment.

Chapter 11

Systems Thinking

The ability to recognise and analyse the
interconnections within and between systems

Glenn Strachan

International Research Institute in Sustainability,
University of Gloucestershire

The formal education experience of most learners could be summarised as moving from a multidisciplinary approach in their early years, grounded in their limited experience of the world, through to an increasingly reductionist experience in which they become more specialised and less prepared for the interconnected complexity of the world in which they have to live and work. This is a gross generalisation, but it does partly explain some of the unsustainable activities that have had such a detrimental impact on the natural systems of the Earth. In particular it helps to account for the large catalogue of examples of well-intentioned solutions to problems having unforeseen consequences and resulting in greater problems than the one being tackled.

Increasing numbers of analysts writing about the crises facing the world are identifying the interconnected nature of the crises and the need for interconnected and interdisciplinary solutions. For example Jeffrey Sachs in his latest book *Common Wealth* comments that "The problems just refuse to arrive in the neat categories of academic departments" (Sachs 2008:14). The established structures of the formal education system are resistant to change, and nowhere in the formal system is there a co-ordinated attempt to bring together the array of knowledge, skills and attitudes which learners gather through their educational career so that they can use them to make better sense of our complex world. Developing the ability to think systemically gives learners of all ages the potential to maximise the application of their diverse learning experiences and contribute to how we can better understand our complex interconnected world.

Ray Ison provides the following concise definition of the term *system* which leads us into the area of interconnectedness: "A system is a perceived whole whose elements are 'interconnected'" (Ison in Reason and Bradbury 2008:140). Systems thinking has developed a substantial body of knowledge, drawn from a number of areas of study including cybernetics, ecology and complexity theory. References to resources which provide some of the theoretical underpinnings of systems thinking are offered at the end of this chapter. The purpose of this chapter is to focus on one aspect of systems thinking, which is the ability to recognise interconnections and understand the relevance and the importance of the relationships represented by these interconnections. This is essential for understanding the nature of the sustainability crises we face and therefore essential in finding solutions.

The use of pesticides on crops is one example of how a solution to one problem has created further and greater problems. While trying to combat a pest or disease to improve food production, pesticides in many cases have disrupted ecosystems, some of which indirectly support the crop being grown, and have had adverse health effects on people from pesticide residues on food crops. Place the use of pesticides into the context of the 'Green Revolution' of the 1970s where they were part of a package with artificial fertilisers, financial credit, irrigation and increased mechanisation, and the interrelated social, environmental and economic consequences become complex.

According to Ison (2008), most people have some degree of systemic awareness; the question is, how can educators develop and increase that awareness? In the same way that we need to understand unsustainability in order to fully grasp sustainability, so by highlighting an obvious lack of systems thinking in an example it is possible to demonstrate to learners the nature of systems thinking in a practical way. One way of approaching this is to look for examples in everyday life that illustrate a lack of systems thinking through an inherent contradiction that may not be obvious to many people. Advertisements can be a rich source of these examples: for instance, in a recent Sunday newspaper an advert for a large 4x4 SUV pictured the vehicle driving down a flooded street and promoted the vehicle as a solution to living in adverse weather conditions. When the connections have been made in one's mind that the adverse weather conditions may have been the result of climate change and that CO_2 emissions from vehicles contribute to climate change, then suddenly the incongruity of the image leaps out. Once these types of connections have been demonstrated to learners, some of them (but, as Ison rightly says, not all) will start noticing similar examples, developing a perspective that highlights connections and will be thinking more systemically. As Fritjof Capra puts it, "Systems theory entails a new way of seeing the world and a new way of thinking known as systems thinking or systemic thinking. It means thinking in terms of relationships, connectedness and context" (Capra 1999:2).

This approach enables learners to discover an understanding of systems thinking for themselves, and this can be reinforced if they are given the oppor-

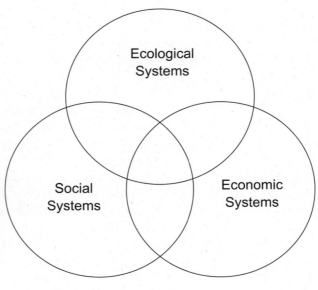

Figure 1.

tunity to apply that understanding to a context with which they are familiar. In so doing they can become more at ease with the interconnected nature of the world and less overwhelmed with its complexity. A simple exercise for learners to apply systemic thinking and discover how everything is linked involves them selecting an object with which they are very familiar and investigating it by asking a series of questions. (Questions can be simple, e.g. What is it made of? Where has it come from? Who made it?; or more searching, e.g. What needs does it fulfil? Is it necessary? What will happen to it in the future? Could it be redesigned to have a smaller environmental footprint?). Learners record their answers to the questions on a large sheet of paper and then start identifying connections between their answers, producing a web-like diagram. This activity can extend almost indefinitely depending on the enthusiasm of the learners and it will lead them across economic, social and ecological systems.

Developing an understanding of the relationship between elements within a system is a building block in learning to appreciate the relationships that connect systems to each other. The concept of 'nested systems', where there is a hierarchy of interconnected systems, is an aspect of systems thinking that has particular relevance for conceptualising sustainability from a systems perspective. Educators can explore this with learners, and gain an insight into the perspectives held by learners, by presenting the two most common diagrammatic representations of sustainability and asking the learners to describe the 'messages' that the

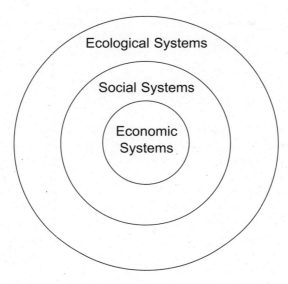

Figure 2.

diagrams convey to them, particularly about the relationships between the three sets of systems.

Having used this activity with a range of learners I have found that there are a number of common areas that usually emerge for discussion. The response from learners with regard to Figure 1 usually generates discussion around the idea that the relationship between the systems in the three circles is one of 'balance' or possibly 'trade-off'. There is often the suggestion that the relative size of the circles could be changed and that a much larger economic systems circle would be more representative of the three sets of systems when it comes to decision-making in the world of today. Learners recognise that there is a strong connectivity between the systems represented by the three circles, but are much less clear about the relationships associated with these connections.

The response to Figure 2 often generates a dichotomy in terms of responses from learners, illustrating the different perspectives they hold. Some see the ecological systems as representing a known fixed boundary inside which all the human social systems must exist, and economic systems existing within the boundaries of social systems since they are one of those systems. Others see economic systems as being at the centre of everything and therefore being the most important.

Systems thinking has much to contribute to sustainability literacy: it can provide a perspective that enables learners to engage with the complexity of sustainability and the complexity of the world around them. Recognising the interconnections within systems and between systems, and exploring the relationships which these interconnections represent, is a learning pathway to a systems thinking perspective.

References and resources

Capra, Fritjof (1994) *From the parts to the whole: systems thinking in ecology and education.* Berkeley: Center for Ecoliteracy. www.hainescentre.com/pdfs/parts_to_whole.pdf.

Capra, Fritjof (1999) *Ecoliteracy: the challenge for education in the next century.* Schumacher Lecture. www.ecoliteracy.org/publications.

Ison, Ray (2008) 'Systems thinking and practice in action research', in Reason, Peter and Bradbury, Hilary (eds.) *The Handbook of Action Research: Participative inquiry and practice.* Sage: London.

Laszlo, Ervin (1972) *The Systems View of the World.* Blackwell: Oxford.

Maiteny, Paul (forthcoming). 'Completing the Holistic Perspective: Emotions and Psyche in Education for Sustainability and the Emergence of an Ecosystemic Conscience'. *UNESCO Encyclopedia of Life Support Systems* (theme 6.46: Education for Sustainable Development. Article 6.61.4.2). www.eolss.net.

Sachs, Jeffrey (2008) *Common Wealth: Economics for a crowded planet.* London: Allen Lane.

Bowers, Chet. *Writings on education, eco-justice, and revitalizing the commons.* www.cabowers.net (a large collection of articles and online books by Chet Bowers).

Centre for Ecoliteracy. www.ecoliteracy.org (includes a range of relevant writings by Fritjof Capra).

Systemic Development Institute. http://systemicdevelopment.org (an international network of professionals committed to fostering systemic thinking and practice for ethical action in a turbulent world).

Chapter 12

Gaia Awareness

Awareness of the animate qualities of the Earth

Stephan Harding

Co-ordinator of the MSc in Holistic Science at Schumacher College

As the ecological and social crises bite deeper and deeper into the fabric of our lives, there is an urgent need for an education that addresses the question of how we can develop lifestyles that are truly sustainable in the ecological sense of the word. A key idea that people will need to understand is the notion that our planet seems to have regulated its own surface conditions within the narrow limits that life can tolerate over a vast span of time thanks to tightly coupled feedbacks between life and rocks, atmosphere and water. This is the key insight of Jim Lovelock's paradigm-shifting Gaia Theory. Students need a basic understanding of how to think in terms of feedback loops and of the surprising emergent properties that often appear when many such loops are linked together. They will also need to see how these concepts can help us to understand the possible consequences of our heedless lust for material growth that is now seriously disturbing the Earth, and they will need to use these ideas to think through possible solutions.

Wherever we look in the biological world we find astonishingly complex feedbacks, whether it is within the physiology of individual organisms, in the ecological interactions within ecosystems, or indeed amongst the interactions between rocks, atmosphere, oceans and living beings that constitute Gaia. Such complex systems can behave in unpredictable ways. Their precise behaviour will depend not only on which relationships are present, but also on their relative strengths. Systems with non-linear relationships will invariably exhibit a range of behaviours, from predictable to chaotic, although even a system with linear relationships can behave in unexpected ways. Simply put, in a linear relationship, a component's response varies in direct proportion to a change it experiences, and in a non-linear system it does not. A good example of non-linearity is the stockmarket, where a slight change in consumer confidence can ripple through the system very quickly to bring about rapid and unexpected change. It is also possible for tipping points to exist in which a small disturbance triggers a sudden and unexpected change. Take a pencil and line it up parallel to the edge of a table, not too far from the edge. Now give the pencil a slight push towards the edge and nothing dramatic happens – the pencil has moved a little, and just as you expected, it is still on the table. Now give it another small push, and another. Again you observe a predictable response. Eventually, of course, another slight push equal to one of the previous ones takes the pencil through a rapid tipping point as it falls over the edge and into a new 'stable state' on the floor. Non-linear systems are riddled with tipping points, but often a system is so complex that it is impossible to know exactly when these will be encountered.

Learners will need to discover that the Earth is replete with self-regulating negative feedbacks that tend towards constancy as well as self-amplifying positive feedbacks that can propel the Earth either towards cooling or warming. Without such an understanding, they might believe that half-measures are enough, that every little carbon dioxide saving makes a difference, that weak targets are better than no targets. They are not. Arctic sea ice is a clear example. If a little of it melts, dark ocean is exposed to the sun, which warms the region and thus more ice melts. This warms the region further, melting even more ice, and so on. The result is runaway warming. Our carbon emissions are edging closer and closer to triggering a series of additional self-amplifying feedbacks, with potentially catastrophic consequences for the entire planet. Once we push the Earth beyond critical thresholds, these additional self-amplifying feedbacks will warm the earth by various means: burning the Amazon, melting the icecaps, and releasing methane from permafrost, are but a few. As a result, it seems increasingly likely that the Earth will, by the end of this century, end up at least 4°C hotter than now, with dire consequences for our civilisation and millions of our fellow species.

To remedy the situation, if indeed this is still possible, we will need to stop emitting greenhouse gases and remove carbon dioxide directly from the atmosphere. If implemented immediately, these measures would allow the polar sea ice to recover, they would prevent the Amazon from burning, and would ensure that marine algae continue to cool the Earth by absorbing carbon dioxide and by producing planet-cooling clouds. We have found physical ways of vastly reducing our emissions of carbon dioxide (if not political ones), but as yet there is no failsafe way of extracting it directly from the atmosphere.

It is essential that learners understand the nuts and bolts of Gaian feedbacks if they are to understand the dangers of climate change as well as possible solutions. I have taught Gaia theory for almost twenty years, and have found that students (apart from those with good scientific backgrounds) are not enlightened by the dry language of conventional scientific discourse normally used to describe these feedbacks. In my experience, storytelling works best. Like those few daring teachers of chemistry who have found that the difficult concepts of their subject come alive when they speak of chemical reactions *as if* they involved interactions between sentient, feeling *persons*, I have developed story-based explorations of Gaian feedbacks that often awaken within students a deep sense of embeddedness in the astonishing self-regulating processes of our breathing planet (see Harding 2006).

Scientific knowledge about the Earth as a complex system is gradually permeating educational initiatives around the world. But by focusing only on thinking (albeit in a more enlightened mode known as 'systems thinking') our scientific understanding ignores the equally vital contributions that our sensory experience, our ethical sensibilities and our intuitive capacities can make to a more holistic understanding of the Earth and of our place within it. The problem, more succinctly put, is that our current educational paradigm emphasises quantities at the expense of qualities, and prioritises facts over values. The result is that we promulgate a rather dry soulless approach to the world that is inherently dualistic and which leads us to believe that our Earth is nothing more than a vast machine which we can control as we wish by using the detached, 'God's eye' view of rational scientific analysis. Thus, as a society, we feel strangely disconnected from the Earth – it seems as if we were aliens from some other planet placed here to prod and poke this world with our scientific instruments whilst feeling no sense of meaning, belonging or closeness to her ancient crumpled surface or to her rich, teeming biodiversity. With this worldview firmly in place in our minds, we engage in sustainable actions only out of fear, or if we are compelled to, by law. It is essential therefore that learners both understand modern science's predilection for quantities and gain an awareness of Gaia that embraces both quantities and qualities.

The denigration of qualities was deliberately built in to mainstream science at its inception some 400 years ago during the 16th and 17th centuries. The great pioneering scientific geniuses of that period such as Galileo, Bacon and Descartes convincingly argued that only quantities have validity, that nature has no intrinsic value, that the whole cosmos is in essence a vast machine, and that we have the right to use rational analysis to ruthlessly control and exploit the Earth and all her other-than-human creatures for our own ends. Is it any surprise, then, that this worldview has delivered us into the maw of a planetary crisis of such massive proportions that scientists talk about us being the cause of the sixth mass extinction and of the threat posed to civilisation by the looming spectre of anthropogenic climate change? Is it any surprise that a culture that sees the world as no more than a dead object will eventually seriously perturb the web of life on which it depends? Modern science is perhaps the greatest cultural achievement of the Western world, but it needs to be seriously reformed and expanded if it is to contribute to solving the urgent problems of the twenty-first century. It is time for science to heal its self-imposed split between quantities and qualities, and between facts and values, if it is to become part of a tenable solution.

It was C. G. Jung who pointed out that we gain reliable knowledge by means of the four modalities of thinking, feeling, sensing and intuition. Perhaps the reunification we are seeking will take place when we educate our students to consciously cultivate their ability to think in tandem with their other three ways of knowing, for it is with these that we become sensitive to the qualitative aspects of our experience.

Our efforts to educate for a genuinely sustainable relationship with the Earth must therefore attempt to reunite quantities with qualities by developing the four ways of knowing in our students, an approach that we are pioneering on our MSc in Holistic Science at Schumacher College. When working with our students to give them the deepest possible sense of connection with Gaia, we use Gaia theory to teach them how to think holistically about the Earth in the way we have outlined above. We look at the consistencies or otherwise between Gaia theory and natural selection, we build mathematical models of the carbon cycle coupled to an active biota, and we look at how the Earth could respond to climate change as a fully integrated complex system consisting of life coupled to its abiotic 'environment'.

Then we go further. We use this rational knowledge to fuel our intuitive sense of connection to the whole community of nature by engaging in rigorous meditative explorations and by recreating Gaia's long and complex evolutionary trajectory in our imaginations (see *Finding Meaning Without Consuming*, p.178). We deliberately connect with the qualities of rocks, atmosphere, oceans, clouds, individual organisms and entire ecosystems by spending quiet time savouring their essences much as we would that of a poem or a piece of music. As we deepen our perceptual abilities, we find a remarkable degree of commonality in what we discover by means of this more phenomenological approach to nature. In addition, we work with exercises that help to shift our everyday perceptional frameworks. We lie on our backs outdoors, feeling how our planet's gravity dangles us upside down over the vastness of space, and we gain a palpable sensation of her great curving spherical body as it arches away beyond us in all directions. The deep experiences of connection and communion that arise out of this radical holistic approach lead us to conclude that the mechanistic metaphor that has so seriously misguided our culture during these past four centuries must now be replaced by the more ancient understanding of the Earth as a great psyche in which we are deeply immersed and with which we are in constant communication. This intuition enriches our sensory experiences, so that we no longer see the world around us as a set of isolated mechanical objects, but as a unified field of experiencing subjects.

Now, with our ethical sensibilities alive and awake, Gaia enters into our awareness and we see why it is wrong to seriously harm the great turning world within which we have our being and which gave us birth. Our rational minds become the servants of this deeper sensibility by helping us to articulate our deep experiences of belonging to Gaia and to tease out to what extent our lifestyles are consistent with them. External compulsion or a sense of duty are no longer necessary to make us act correctly. The integration of our reasoning, feeling, sensing and intuition fill us with an inspiring sense of the mysterious personhood of the Earth. This unleashes tremendously powerful feelings of energy and dedication that lead us spontaneously into right action, wherever our own particular paths might lead us.

References and resources

Abram, David (1997) *The Spell of the Sensuous*. London: Vintage Books.

Berry, Thomas (1999) *The Great Work*. Kent: Bell Tower.

Capra, Fritjof (1997) *The Web of Life: A new synthesis of mind and matter*. London: HarperCollins.

Goodwin, Brian (2007) *Nature's Due: Healing our fragmented culture*. Edinburgh: Floris Books.

Harding, Stephan (2006) *Animate Earth: Science, Intuition and Gaia* (2nd edn). Dartington: Green Books.

Leopold, Aldo (1968/1949) *A Sand County Almanac*. Berkeley: Oxford University Press.

Lovelock, James (2009) *The Vanishing Face of Gaia*. Harmondsworth: Penguin.

Margulis, Lynn and Sagan, Dorion (1997) *Microcosmos*. University of California Press.

Swimme, Brian (1996) *The Hidden Heart of the Cosmos*. New York: Orbis Books.

Chapter 13

Futures Thinking

The ability to envision scenarios of a more desirable future

Sue Wayman

University College Plymouth, St Mark and St John

> The future can't be predicted, but it can be envisioned and brought lovingly into being. Systems can't be controlled, but they can be designed and redesigned. We can't surge forward with certainty into a world of no surprises, but we can expect surprises and learn from them and even profit from them. We can't impose our will upon a system. We can listen to what the system tells us, and discover how its properties and our values can work together to bring forth something much better than could ever be produced by our will alone. (Meadows 2001)

This chapter provides a brief conceptual introduction to Futures Thinking, and offers an insight into the practical implications and applications of this approach for engaging learners in the critical understanding, personal reflection, dialogue and collaborative action required to put futures thinking into practice. Sustainability literacy involves both social and environmental aspects, taking account of the economic, social and environmental power our actions exert through space and time, the historically, socially and culturally diverse ways in which we construct ourselves in relation to natural systems, and how we might learn to live in greater harmony within these systems.

It has been noted that the future is generally a missing dimension in education (Hicks 2002), to the detriment of individual aspiration and empowerment as well as positive social and environmental change. As Hicks and Holden (1995:24) note:

> The images we hold of the future motivate and influence what we choose to do in the present. . . . Having faith in our abilities may persuade us to reach for greater heights in the future. If life today is not to our satisfaction, for ourselves or others, we may strive to create a better and fairer world in the future.

Educators, while often feeling constrained in their own practice, are politically envisaged as "best placed to change society, by changing the habits and instilling the ideas of future citizens" (Tripp 1992:22). Educators and learners need to gain space for intuitive and emotional expression, creativity and imagination, vision and action to shape the future on behalf of the rights of current and future generations (Meadows et al. 1992; Dator 2002).

In some ways, this stance alludes to a 'Futures Movement' (Dator 2002), with an explicit purpose of contributing to social and ecological sustainability rather than engaging in more technical 'Futures Research' which is often aligned with prediction of social actions in markets. It involves Futures Thinking, drawing on the works of, for example, Jungk, Ziegler, Boulding, Pike and Selby, Slaughter, Dator, and Inayatollah, who have developed the field over the past 40 years. It engages learners in 'Futures Studies' that deconstruct and reconstruct images of the future, helping them to gain skills in working towards scenarios they see as possible and preferable. For Hicks, the crucial pedagogical question educators should ask themselves is how they can engage learners in a process that is both liberating and empowering. He suggests using case studies that embody the visions and actions of sustainability, and processes of 'envisioning' that learners can act on themselves. The idea here is not to be prescriptive but to facilitate learners' choices by directing them to wider philosophical and practical resources.

Futures Thinking for Sustainability is not, however, an easy task for learners to undertake, particularly when, for example, current global environmental predictions paint such a gloomy picture. Couching sustainability in terms of global systems and survival, abstract theories, and persistent structural inequality can overwhelm learners, leading to denial (Tilbury and Wortman 2004) or psychic numbing which disables learners cognitively, affectively and actively. However, we cannot ignore the issues nor indeed afford a 'wait and see' approach. Rather than avoiding this potential disempowerment of learners, it is useful to present a little humility and holism in the learning process, at some point, by offering scenarios that might usefully capture feared and favoured alternatives. Dator (2002) provides the scenarios of "continuation, collapse, disciplinary society, transformational society – high technology or high spiritual". These provide a way of facilitating learners' abilities to name and frame their own ideas and concerns, and their positionality and potential for change within such debates. Robertson (1983) uses similar categories – "business as usual, disaster, authoritarianism, hyper-expansionist and humane ecological". Hicks (1995) offers scenarios entitled "more of the same, technological fix, edge of disaster and sustainable development". Learners can use scenarios such as these as starting points, filling in examples of each and debating their desirability before generating and naming their own sets of scenarios.

While change is often discussed as the natural state of affairs for the twenty-first century, stability of certain ideas and practices is also the norm, and we need therefore to be critical and look beneath the surface of current orthodoxies, how we internalise and act on them, and which we believe are worth sustaining (see *Values Reflection and the Earth Charter*, p.99). This lies at the heart of critical thinking, which seeks to identify and challenge assumptions, recognise the importance of the social, political and historical contexts of events, interpretations and behaviour, and to imagine and explore alternatives (Brookfield 1987). The marriage of critical thinking with interpreting images of the future can be a powerful tool for informed purposive action.

Pike and Selby (1999:241) offer an exercise called 'Futurescapes' which provides a way of prompting learners to engage with Futures Thinking for Sustainability. This exercise provides ten scenarios covering a range of topics, for which learners need to decide the probability/improbability, possibility/impossibility and desired/undesired nature of the scenario within their lifetime.

Some example scenarios adapted from 'Futurescapes' (Pike and Selby 1999:241) are given below. In the original, each scenario was followed by the following options for learners to circle: *During my lifetime: possible, probable, improbable, impossible, desired, undesired.*

- Around half the world's energy will be created through solar, wind and water power, with desert solar panels and offshore wind farms connected to a new international grid.

- There will be a major breakthrough in genetic engineering so that we will have farm animals, looking quite different from those we now know, which will produce a higher yield of meat for less food intake in a shorter space of time.

- In a worldwide attempt to end famine in Africa, all surplus food grown on other continents will be shipped to various African ports and then taken by UN trucks to the towns and villages where the food is needed.

- For sustainability, health and to avoid cruelty to animals, diets around the world will be increasingly based on fresh fruit and vegetables, with only small quantities of high quality, sustainably farmed meat consumed.

- The cost of a new car will be four times higher than today because laws will require manufacturers to pay for the environmental damage caused by making cars.

Envisioning desirable as well as undesirable scenarios is important because, as Hicks (2005) points out, we need to know what we are fighting for rather than just what we are fighting against, and the judgement of scenarios can stimulate learners to articulate their individual, social and environmental concerns and ideals. Timelines (Pike and Selby 1999; Hicks 2002) can facilitate this. The object is to get learners – usually working in pairs to begin with – to draw a timeline (say 2009 to 2050) on one side of which they note the local/global events, trends and issues that they *expect* to unfold, while on the other side they note the future that they *hope* for. Once completed, they are prompted to focus further on their hopes and ideals through an envisioning process. They have to imagine and articulate what proof they would accept that their preferred futures have come into being – what evidence of individual and social change they could see. The images and metaphors they use to represent their ideals can become a useful source for discussion, and a valuable resource for future sessions.

However, while this exercise may stimulate thinking and dialogue, it does not necessarily prompt action for sustainability. Holden (cited in Pike and Selby 1988) suggests the need to incorporate questions about what actions would be required for these ideals to realised. She cites her work with younger learners where she asked them to compile ten questions they might ask about the future, and ten things they could give up to make the future better. Of course, associating sustainability with the need for altruism could be problematic, particularly when working with learners from disadvantaged groups. Hicks and Holden (1995) note that those with little sense of control over their lives, or those who are in fear of the future, tend to adopt an understandable 'live for today' mentality, and therefore security of self-identity and self-esteem in education and empowerment for sustainable living should be the measures by which we evaluate our work. Learners could therefore be asked to imagine ten personally life-enhancing ways to fulfil their higher needs in the future without relying on debt and consumerism (see *Emotional Well-being*, p.171). This could help empower learners to align their goals for a brighter personal future with efforts to create a generally more sustainable future.

While exercises such as Futurescapes are quite general in nature, more localised envisioning could help generate concrete and immediate action. One way of facilitating this is to begin with groups of learners describing a utopian vision of a more sustainable school, university, or local community, and giving a fixed date in the future for when this vision becomes a reality, say 2020. They can then use the technique of 'backcasting' to describe the policies and programmes that led up to this desirable future along a timeline stretching back to the present. For example, "In 2015, the university reached the target of growing 80% of the food consumed in the canteens in community-based permaculture gardens." In this way, visions are grounded in the local personal and shared experience of the group, and learners gain skills in planning for the future and articulating concrete courses of action.

At heart, Futures Thinking for Sustainability needs, as Pike and Selby (1999) maintain, to be "person centred and planet conscious", promoting learning that is affirmative of self and others, participatory, co-operative and experiential. Only by imagining the future is it possible for learners to extend the realms of possibility for what that future holds. The history of the future is not yet written and, as Inayatullah (2002:110) notes, there are no limits to the growth of our imaginations in all their diversity.

References and resources

Brookfield, Stephen (1987) *Developing Critical Thinkers*. Milton Keynes: Open University Press.

Dator, James (ed.) (2002) *Advancing Futures: Futures studies in higher education*. Westport: Praeger Publishers.

Hicks, David (2002) *Lessons for the Future: The missing dimension in education*. Oxford: Trafford Publishing.

Hicks, David and Holden, Cathie (1995) *Visions of the Future: Why we need to learn for tomorrow*. Stoke-on-Trent: Trentham Books.

Inayatullah, Sohail (2002) 'Pedagogy, culture and futures studies', in Dator, James (ed.) *Advancing Futures: Futures studies in higher education*. Westport: Praeger Publishers.

Levitas, Ruth (1993) 'The future of thinking about the future', in Bird, John et al. *Mapping the Futures: Local cultures, global change*. London: Routledge.

Meadows, Donella (2001) 'Dancing with Systems', *Whole Earth*, Winter 2001. www.wholeearth.com/issue/2106/article/2/dancing.with.systems.

Meadows, Donella; Meadows, Dennis and Randers, Jørgen (1992) *Beyond the Limits: Global collapse or a sustainable future*. London: Earthscan.

Orr, David (1992) *Ecological Literacy: Education and the transition to a postmodern world*. Albany: State University of New York Press.

Pike, Graham and Selby, David (1988) *Global Teacher, Global Learner*. London: Hodder and Stoughton.

Pike, Graham and Selby, David (1999) *In the Global Classroom*. Toronto: Pippin.

Robertson, James (1983) *The Sane Alternative: a Choice of Futures*.

Tilbury, Daniella and Wortman, David (2004) 'Engaging people in sustainability'. IUCN. www.unece.org/env/esd/information/Publications%20IUCN/engaging%20people.pdf.

Tripp, David (1992) 'Critical theory and educational research'. *Issues in Educational Research*, 2:1, 98-112.

Chapter 14

Values Reflection
and the Earth Charter

The ability to critique the values of an
unsustainable society and consider alternatives

Jeffrey Newman

Director, Earth Charter UK

Education for Sustainable Development is based on values of justice, equity, tolerance, sufficiency and responsibility. It promotes gender equality, social cohesion
and poverty reduction and emphasises care, integrity and honesty, as articulated in
the Earth Charter. (UNESCO Bonn Declaration 2009)

Educators are now teaching learners whose prospects seem to be darkening year
on year. Presently jobs are scarce, the economic outlook is poor and the
timescale for recovery uncertain. In the background looms the shadow of an
environmental crisis that threatens to degrade or even destroy the life-
supporting and life-enhancing systems of the Earth. This calls for a response at
a deep level of values, a rethinking and reorganisation of what is valuable, important, and worth sustaining in an uncertain future. Educators are, however, faced
with a double-edged sword. If values were explicitly incorporated in the
curriculum, they could be accused of imposing ideologies on learners. But if all
mention of values is expunged from education, then this leaves little choice but
for learners to draw their values from the unsustainable society around them, or
from the values latent in the 'hidden curriculum' of their educational institution.

Values reflection is one way out of this dilemma. Rather than having values
imposed on them, learners reflect on the dominant values of society and their
institution in the context of the changes that are occurring in the world around
them, and ask themselves whether these values are now outdated, or even
dangerous. They may reflect on a wide range of things that tend to be valued in

unsustainable societies, such as economic growth, profit at all costs, personal success defined in terms of salary, conspicuous consumption, directionless technological progress, convenience defined in terms of avoiding physical tasks, human superiority over other species, cold rationality, mastery over nature and so on.

If learners do find fault with the dominant values of the society around them, then they will also need to consider additional and alternative values, ones which might help contribute to a more sustainable future. This is where the Earth Charter (2000) is useful, not as a doctrine to be forced on learners, but as one among many places to seek possible alternative values. The alternatives, of course, will need to be subjected to just as deep and critical a process of reflection as the dominant values.

It is easy for learners to find nothing but despair as they discover the situation that the world finds itself in, but the Earth Charter provides a framework that offers hope – a way responding to a time of exceptional challenge and opportunity. The Charter's opening words spell this out succinctly: "We live at a critical moment in Earth's history, a time when humanity must choose its future", and "The future at once holds great peril and great promise" (p.1).[2]

The Earth Charter is a declaration of fundamental principles for a just, sustainable and peaceful global society which has been formally endorsed by thousands of organisations including UNESCO and the IUCN (International Union for Conservation of Nature). The preamble states that "We urgently need a shared vision of basic values to provide an ethical foundation for the emerging world community" (p.1), and the remainder of the Charter attempts to create such a vision through sixteen principles under four main headings: *Respect and Care for the Community of Life; Ecological Integrity; Social and Economic Justice;* and *Democracy, Non-violence and Peace.* Given the intensity of the arguments and disagreements which took place during the drafting process – considered the widest ever undertaken, involving more than 5,000 individuals and hundreds of organisations – the existence of the Charter is itself a symbol of hope and provides opportunities to explore its own Principle 14: "Integrate into formal education and life-long learning the knowledge, values, and skills needed for a sustainable way of life."

The Charter recognises that a deep change in values is imperative: the preamble states that "Fundamental changes are needed in our values, institutions and ways of living" (p.1), with the conclusion calling for "a change of mind and heart" (p.4). This can encourage learners to move beyond isolated economic, political and technological responses, to consideration of the more fundamental ethical, psychological and spiritual responses needed to cope with emerging ecological crises. The importance of this is well expressed by Theodore Roszak (2001):

The great changes our runaway industrial civilisation must make if we are to keep the planet healthy will not come about by the force of reason alone. . . . Rather, they will come by way of psychological transformation. . . . What the Earth requires will have to make itself felt within us as if it were our own most private desire.

One area where the Charter calls for a deep change in values relates to consumerism. It describes production and consumption, which were once valued as the foundation of human development and economic well-being, as instead being a root cause of unsustainability when taken to excess: "The dominant patterns of production and consumption are causing environmental devastation, the depletion of resources, and a massive extinction of species" (p.1). Rather than consumerist values of 'having more', the charter extols the value of 'being more': "We must realise that when basic needs have been met, human development is primarily about being more, not having more" (p.1).

Studying the Charter enables learners to imagine alternatives to the anthropocentric values that lie at the heart of many unsustainable cultures – values which may be unhelpful as we face the future. It encourages learners to question the place of humanity in relation to Earth and life itself and introduces them to ecocentric values. Principle 1a reads: "Recognise that all beings are interdependent and every form of life has value regardless of its worth to human beings." Reading through the Charter, students come across expressions such as "the Earth community" (p1); "the greater community of life" (p1); "a unique community of life" (p1); "a magnificent diversity of cultures and lifeforms" (p1); "reverence for life" (p4); "respect for nature" (p1) and the "joyful celebration of life" (p.4). The expressions encode a worldview quite different from lonely human beings surrounded by a sea of 'natural resources' worth something only for their utility value. Learners will discover that recognition of the intrinsic value of life in its many forms is basic to many indigenous cultures and this then may help them form a necessary "new sense of global interdependence and universal responsibility" (p.4).

Values such as intellectualism, competitiveness, rationalism, technical instrumentalism, reductionism, and scientism may well be hidden within the presuppositions of the curricula of learners' institutions, their textbooks, formal lectures and assessment strategies (see *A Learning Society*, p.215). The Earth Charter provides a set of alternative values that learners may never come across in the day-to-day business of formal education. These include valuing: co-operation (p.4); humility (p.1); the spiritual potential of humanity (p.2); compassion (p.2); love (p.2); human dignity (p.3); the Earth's beauty (p.1); reverence for the mystery of being (p.1); traditional knowledge and spiritual wisdom (p.3); loving nurture of family members (p.3); human solidarity (p.4); peace (p.4); and the sacred (p.1). Exploration of these alternative values is essential for the future since technical instrumentalism, scientism and rationalism are capable of as much harm as good, particularly when combined with a neoliberal world economy bent on profit. They therefore need to be complemented by deeper ethical values such as compassion. The Charter also provides opportunities for reflection on values in relation to crucial issues such as biological diversity (Principle 5), the precautionary principle (Principle 6), population (Principle 7), democracy (Principle 3), poverty (Principle 9), international finance (Principle 10) and gender equality (Principle 11).

The Charter not only provides potential alternative values, it also models a process where a diverse range of people come together to reflect on, negotiate and carefully express values. The process demonstrates how even the choice of a capital letter or definite article can be significant, for example in the two-year debate over the term 'Earth' as opposed to 'earth' or 'the earth'. Capitalisation for planets is common practice in the scientific community and was widely supported by representatives of indigenous peoples, but opposed by some religious conservatives who were concerned about pantheism or deifying the planet. The decision was eventually made to use the capital since "when one speaks or writes of 'the earth' . . . [t]here is a tendency to imagine [it] as merely a thing that is taken for granted and to view it as nothing more than a collection of resources that exists solely for the purpose of human use and exploitation" (Rockefeller in Corcoran 2008).

Studying the history and evolution of the Charter and its drafting can help learners become clearer how, as the Charter states, "Life often involves tensions between important values" (p.4). For example, leaders of the Inuit Circumpolar Conference objected to the use of the term 'compassion' in the original draft of Principle 15, which covers attitudes to animals in hunting and fishing communities. An Inuit leader challenged: "Mr Rockefeller, have you ever killed a whale?" (Rockefeller in Corcoran 2008). Eventually it was agreed that the word 'compassion' be moved from Principle 15 which now reads: "Treat all living beings with respect and consideration" to Principle 2: "Care for the community of life with understanding, compassion and love." This was acceptable to the Inuit and it particularly pleased the Buddhists, Hindus and Jains that the concept of compassion now had a prominent place early in the Charter. Learning about this history of joint values reflection and negotiation could help introduce the skills of conflict resolution, mediation, collaborative working and networking which will play a significant role in developing a sustainable, just and peaceful world. Learners need to learn how to express and explore differences in creative and flexible ways so that they can help "deepen and expand the global dialogue that generated the Earth Charter . . . for we have much to learn from the ongoing collaborative search for truth and wisdom" (p.4).

The Charter demonstrates that there is growing international awareness of the Earth's sickness, and that paths for healing are taking shape. The Charter is not only a text; it is also a movement, and this global perspective enables us to note the contrast between those of us for whom *sustainability* is the issue and the increasing number of us for whom the issue is *survivability* (Manteaw 2009). It is also practical, that is *action*-orientated – every Principle and sub-principle is introduced with an imperative verb which strongly encourages readers to follow the principle in their lives. The Charter shows that there need not be an end to dreams of a better world or to the belief that life can be well lived. Learners can feel there is a global movement acting for their well-being that they can become part of if they wish. If they do decide to work within such a framework, they will become more keenly aware of what needs to be done and sufficiently resilient in spirit to do it.

Some texts are so powerful that they can transform our way of thinking, enabling us to see the world in a new way. The Charter may be such a transformational text. Striking claims have been made for it, comparing it with Magna Carta and the American Declaration of Independence which "stirred human imagination and changed the quality of life of peoples all over the globe" (Hassan in Corcoran 2005). One leading Hindu has even suggested that, "Like the Gita, the Bible, the Quran, or whatever holy book you may follow, the Earth Charter, too, requires serious consideration, re-reading, re-interpreting and meditation" (Chowdhry in Corcoran 2005).

The Earth Charter, however, has not yet been officially recognised by the UN. Presumably our globalised world is not yet ready for the values which it expresses, particularly those which might interfere with economic growth. There was a proposal by the Netherlands that it be presented at the Johannesburg Summit, but when it was clear that there was insufficient support it was decided not to go ahead. Nevertheless, the Charter has been endorsed by thousands of organisations including educational institutions at all levels, in many different parts of the world. If it can be widely used as a resource in education for stimulating learners to reflect on values that are marginalised by their institution and the unsustainable society in which they live, then, perhaps, the final, hopeful words of the Charter will be realised: "Let ours be a time remembered for the awakening of a new reverence for life, the firm resolve to achieve sustainability, the quickening of the struggle for justice and peace, and the joyful celebration of life" (p.4).

Notes

Many thanks to John Pickering of Warwick University and the editor for help and advice. Unless otherwise stated, all references are to the Earth Charter (2000).

References and resources

Corcoran, Peter and Wohlpart, A. James (2008) *A Voice for the Earth*. University of Georgia Press.

Corcoran, Peter (ed.) (2005) *The Earth Charter in Action*. Amsterdam: Kit Publisher www.earthcharterinaction.org (includes over 60 authors, many of them world figures such as Wangari Maathai, Ruud Lubbers, Hazel Henderson, Jane Goodall and Leonardo Boff, from more than 30 countries – literally from 'A' [Algeria] to 'Z' [Zimbabwe] – this is an outstanding source of material for comparative work on the Charter).

Earth Charter (2000) 'The Earth Charter'. www.earthcharterinaction.org/content/pages/Read-the-Charter.html.

Earth Charter International (2007) *Good practices using the Earth Charter*. www.earthcharterinaction.org/resources/files/Good Practices 2 Earth Charter Stories in Education Full Document.pdf.

Earth Charter International (2009) 'A Guide for Using the Earth Charter in Education'. www.earthcharterinaction.org/content/attachments/12/EC_Education_Guide_2 APRIL_2009.pdf.

Manteaw, Bob (2009) 'People, places and cultures: education and the cultural politics of sustainable development'. *International Journal of Development Education and Global Learning*, 1:2.

Roszak, Theodore (2001) *The Voice of the Earth* (2nd edn). Grand Rapids: Phanes Press.

Snyder, Gary (2003) *The Practice of the Wild*. San Francisco: Counterpoint.

UNESCO Bonn Declaration (2009) *UNESCO World Conference on Education for Sustainable Development*. www.esd-world-conference-2009.org.

Chapter 15

Social Conscience

*The ability to reflect on deeply-held opinions
about social justice and sustainability*

Myshele Goldberg

University of Strathclyde and the Centre for Human Ecology

What is social conscience, and why is it relevant?

Conscience can be described as internalised values: a person's intuitive 'moral compass'. While rational, philosophical, or religious arguments are often used as justifications, conscience itself is primarily emotional: we associate feelings of pleasure and pride with right action, and feelings of guilt and shame with wrong action. These emotions help to motivate choices and behaviour, playing an important role in the maintenance and transformation of social norms. In many ways, the norms of society are the sum of our collective values and priorities – as society shapes us, we shape society.

In addition to a sense of right and wrong for personal action, individuals possess a sense of right and wrong for collective action – what might be called *social conscience*. Individual conscience compels us to act morally in our daily lives, avoiding or helping to relieve the immediate suffering of others, whereas social conscience compels us to insist on moral action from the wider institutions of society and to seek the transformation of social structures that cause suffering. While individual conscience is reflected in norms of personal interaction, social conscience is reflected in the ways we organise ourselves more broadly.

Across the political spectrum, most people experience a gap between the kind of world they see and the kind they want. On a personal level, social conscience is what bridges that gap. If we can understand our own social conscience, we can make more conscious choices to help shape society according to our values. If we can understand the social conscience of others, we can find common values and goals among seemingly diverse groups and build movements for change. Under-standing social conscience, whether our own or others', helps to identify assumptions, values, and visions, making it an important element of sustainability literacy and a useful tool for effective social and ecological transformation.

A model for understanding social conscience

Social conscience is shaped by a person's moral framework, but its interconnected elements – *consciousness, structure, and agency* – can be examined independently of particular values or political views.

Consciousness

The words conscience and consciousness are often used interchangeably, but they are not the same. Consciousness, as used in expressions such as 'raising consciousness', describes a person's knowledge and awareness, and in this case, their knowledge and awareness of the gap between their ideal world and the real world. Information and experience can be seen as neutral, while consciousness implies a process of value judgement, classifying situations broadly into right, wrong, or neutral. Consciousness also calls upon a person's assumptions and worldview to explain situations, identifying them as fair or unjust, individual or systemic, safe or dangerous, etc. Consciousness can (but does not always) link "personal troubles" with "public issues", to use the phrases of American sociologist C. Wright Mills (1959).

To give an example, homelessness is an issue of both social and environmental sustainability – while homeless people contribute least to pollution and environmental destruction, they are the first to suffer from them. Homelessness may or may not be on the moral 'radar' of someone who is not experiencing it first-hand; it may be considered a normal part of city life – a non-issue, morally speaking. If considered an issue, a person becoming homeless might be seen as the result of unlucky coincidence, personal failure, punishment for sins, or particular social forces. These four examples are not mutually exclusive, but each fits into a particular kind of worldview, dominated respectively by random chance, individual choice, divine will, or complex social systems; and each would elicit a particular kind of response – charity, tough love, evangelism, or social change. Each person's worldview influences the way they treat new information or experiences, but information itself only sometimes has an impact on worldview. Raising consciousness of an issue, while important, is only one element of motivating action to transform it.

Structure

What sets social conscience apart from individual conscience is its structural or systemic focus. In the first three explanations about homelessness above

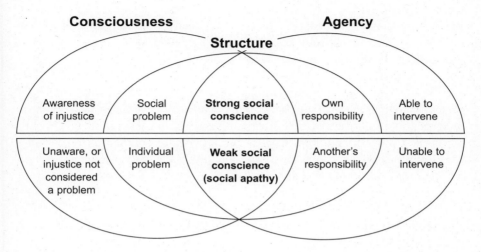

Figure 1.

(unlucky coincidence, personal failure, or punishment for sins), someone may feel compassion and a desire to help a person who has become homeless, on an individual level, from a personal sense of conscience. In the fourth explanation (social forces), they might question the structural reasons for homelessness and want to pursue solutions at a social or political level. Social conscience therefore moves beyond personal, individual interactions, to a wider desire to contribute to a more ethical society.

Conversely, a lack of understanding of social structure contributes to the opposite of social conscience, what might be called social apathy – the feeling that, despite sympathy or compassion, "it has nothing to do with me", or that "it's not my problem". When an unfortunate situation is the result of mysterious or misunderstood social forces, it is easy to misplace blame, for example, by blaming marginalised groups such as immigrants, ethnic minorities, or women for acting in a way which leads to their marginalisation. It is also easy to assume a bureaucratic solution is underway, or should be, without making efforts to ensure that it is. Even when government and civil society are seen as incompetent or inefficient, it is a common assumption that they alone have the responsibility for solving social problems.

Agency
The third element of social conscience is agency, which is a sense of personal power, as well as personal responsibility. While consciousness identifies situations

where the reality falls short of the ideal, a person's sense of agency allocates responsibility for action – is it possible to intervene personally, or should someone else be intervening? Individuals cannot care deeply and act effectively on every social and ecological problem they come across, but they can identify problems they feel are both important and that they have the agency to act on. Both consciousness and agency are based on an understanding of social structure, and ultimately, on values. Therefore, a crucial skill is the ability to identify areas where we feel a sense of agency, and find ways of effectively intervening in those areas that align with our deepest concerns, our knowledge of social structure, and our personal values.

All three elements – consciousness, structure, and agency – must be in place for a strong sense of social conscience (see Figure 1). Different combinations of these elements will shape different forms of social conscience. Although the term 'social conscience' is most often associated with the left end of the political spectrum, it is just as applicable to the right when seen as the expression of particular values. As an analytical framework, then, this model can be used to understand and relate different types of social conscience regardless of the political values they express.

Reflection on values and social conscience

Because social conscience is entwined with emotionally-charged assumptions and worldviews that may seem self-evident to those who hold them, it is not necessarily an easy topic to discuss. But the model above can be used to identify values, find emergent patterns of social conscience and understand how different worldviews work. Taking a step back can help learners avoid judging other people's social conscience, even if it may seem incompatible with their own, and realise that each person believes their way of looking at the world is 'correct'.

The questions below are intended to encourage learners to talk about their personal values and motivations, but can easily be adapted for less formal spaces outside the classroom. They could be used for self-reflection, or conversations in pairs, with one person 'interviewing' the other. Participants could be instructed to listen carefully for assumptions and ask for clarification, paying attention to the language being used. Each set of questions builds on the previous one, and it may be helpful for the 'interviewer' to weave themes from one response into the next set of questions, asking for points of clarity or drawing out patterns. Clearly, the categories of questions are not set in stone – one answer may cover several or all of the categories – and there are no right or wrong answers.

Background – developing rapport and setting the context

- What was it that led you to this course? Why were you initially interested in it?
- What do you enjoy about the course?

- When the course ends, what do you think will 'stick' with you?

Consciousness – values / 'other'

- In terms of social and ecological sustainability, what do you consider most precious about the world as you see it today?
- How close are the world as you see it and the world as you'd like it to be? Which elements are close together, and which are far apart?
- Which of these do you feel most passionately about? Why?
- If you had to describe these issues as moral issues, how would you frame them?

Structure – worldview / society

- Thinking about these issues, how are you connected to them?
- Does your daily life have a direct effect on these issues? Indirect effect?
- What are the root causes of these issues?

Agency – action / self

- Whose responsibility is it to take care of the issues that concern you?
- Do you have the power to be part of the solution on any level?
- If so, how are you using that power? If not, what blocks it?
- Who or what do you serve?

Constellations of social conscience: using this model as a tool for understanding

It will become clear in the course of conversation that each person has a unique 'constellation' of social conscience – their own particular blend of consciousness, structure and agency. Many people are passionate about similar issues, but understanding *why* they are passionate, *how* they are passionate, and about *what*, exactly, will help us work more effectively with them. In a world on the brink of collapse, none of us can transform everything, but each of us can transform something. If we reflect on our values and where we feel called to serve, we can focus our efforts and better understand the efforts of others, rather than getting caught up in what we 'should' be doing or criticising those working in different ways from us.

Thinking about social conscience is also a way to understand the motivations of people whose politics are very different from our own. Most people act in ways they believe to be morally correct, but if we do not understand their moral code, then their actions may seem irrational, misinformed, or evil. Lakoff (2002) presents a model describing fundamental differences in the ways conservatives and liberals view morality. Both groups have a strong social conscience, but in very different constellations – to the point where some phenomena that one group considers a problem, the other considers a solution (for example, social welfare programmes). But this makes perfect sense when we consider the two groups' different understandings of social structure, different ideas about personal responsibility and agency, and different values about what is precious in life.

In pairs or groups, learners may wish to discuss the origins of their own constellations of social conscience – for example, family or religious upbringing, social conditioning, life events, significant books or films, role models, etc. To what extent do learners feel they 'own' their social conscience? To what extent has it been passively accepted from outside sources? Where has it been shaped by life experience? Having discussed these questions from a personal perspective, there will be rich material to consider more broadly the effects of life history and moral worldview on the way other people approach social and environmental issues. More importantly, the experience of exploring these questions can help learners gain skills in reflecting on their own values and motivations – skills which are crucial for sustainability literacy.

Social conscience and social movements

The remarkable diversity in modern social movements is not just a diversity of issues, approaches, or demographics – it is also a diversity of values. On one level, we are all working toward the same goals of sustainability and social justice, and seeing people with so many different concerns working together is a great cause for hope. But are we really clear about the goals that we and others are working towards? If learners can develop awareness of social conscience within themselves and others, they will have a better understanding of what they are working for, who they are working with, and why it matters, ultimately creating space for more effective co-operation.

References and resources

Lakoff, George (2002) *Moral Politics: How liberals and conservatives think*. Chicago: University of Chicago Press.

Mills, C. Wright (1959) *The Sociological Imagination*. Oxford: Oxford University Press.

Neafsey, John (2006) *A Sacred Voice is Calling: Personal vocation and social conscience*. Maryknoll: Orbis Books.

Chapter 16

New Media Literacy

Communication skills for sustainability

John Blewitt

Director of Lifelong Learning, Aston University

Given that a great deal of our understanding of the environment – its habitats and peoples – is derived from new and traditional media, it is imperative that any notion of sustainability literacy is connected with ongoing work on media literacy. Many individuals and virtually every organisation have websites, and the growth of user-generated content, social networking, online games, online distance learning and 3-D virtual worlds suggests that our relationship with the physical world, including what passes for the natural environment, is increasingly mediated. Actual heritage sites, urban reconstructions and lost cities can be re-imagined virtually. It is possible to walk with dinosaurs or fly through the emergent ecocities of Dongtan or Masdar. Numerous sustainability scenarios are envisaged and communicated by governments, corporations, think tanks and NGOs, offering a powerful visual and aural persuasiveness. In this context, sustainability literacy, however defined, requires a sensitivity to virtual realism, to media ecology, and to those ongoing processes through which we shape and are shaped by increasingly ubiquitous technologies.

Umberto Eco (1979) wrote that if we stop worrying about the media feeding us pap and propaganda, which we gleefully and thoughtlessly are supposed to consume, and "turn on our critical freedom", then we will perceive the media, traditional and new, as essential tools and instruments for learning and development. Media literacy and sustainability literacy are both practices rooted in critical reflection and action. Both emerge and evolve by way of the environments in which they operate, and today those environments are a combination of the real and hyper-real, the virtual and the virtuous, the critical and the seductive, the imagined and the engineered. Indeed it is sometimes difficult, if not impossible, to maintain clear binary distinctions, for the media does not so much extend our experience of the social world beyond our own, rather narrow, temporal and spatial confines, but rather constitutes a significant and seamless development of it. Communities and neighbourhoods are giving way to networks, e-tribes and simulations. There is a depth that comes with the potential of new technologies and the unrealised creativities and skills of the individuals, groups and organisations using them. Consequently, our diverse media ecology has a key influence on what we are and what we might or can do (Altheide 1995; Boler 2008).

The new media ecology is self-evidently multi-modal. Words are no longer the dominant force. Text is no longer squiggles on a page but remains as signs and symbols nonetheless. Literature is not dead, and nor are television, cinema or radio, but they are no longer the same. New possibilities have opened up for generating the image of the human form in 3-D realism, and for animators to trace over live action movement with spectacular effects. The technologies are not only visual but haptic, aural and potentially immersive. *Second Life* is, for some, a genuinely alternative world with images functioning interactively as an interface between the user and computer or other devices.

This brings new cultural and educative possibilities. Just as the algorithms of the Google search engine seem to predetermine the salience or very existence of knowledge, so Manovich (2008: 15) argues that "our contemporary society can be characterised as a *software society* and our culture can be justifiably called a *software culture* – because today software plays a central role in shaping both the material elements and many of the immaterial structures which together make up 'culture'."

The digital image we see in our morning paper or on its increasingly important internet space may not have an iconic relationship to its actual referent – it may not actually depict what was. It is something potentially ungrounded, making it not simply an issue of media ethics, of image manipulation, but one which involves the nature of knowledge and the critical freedom to apprehend where the burden of visual truth lies (Newton 2001). This means that it is necessary to establish a new civil contract between the image, the text, the sound and the senses, determined by the political and pragmatic project of living and learning in our uncertain and risky world. It means literally visualising new possibilities which must communicate, and fashion, a more ecologically sensitive and sustainable global environment. In *How Images Think*, Ron Burnett (2005: 77) writes:

> Humans are as much within images as they are creators of images. They coexist with what is pictured and build hypotheses about the future and past through visualizations. It is in this sense that images are an expression of various levels of intelligence – images are visualizations of thinking, feeling, seeing and knowing.

The new technology re-mediates existing modes of communication, pedagogy, personal relationships and our participation in the various environments we inhabit. It offers new opportunities to produce messages, even perhaps memes, that resonate effectively with everyday life experience by connecting people with issues, cultures, actions, systems and philosophies. Social networking, indymedia, wikis, digital archives and computer games have become major elements in formal and informal learning. They have lead to the creation of collective knowledge, transcultural communication, and the linking of local to global concerns. Many websites communicate sustainability messages via a menu of virals, blogs, tweets, news, art, science, environment, comedy, music, networks, film and TV.

The key to success is harnessing new media to capture imagination and interest and transform understanding, values and knowledge. There are many arenas where one can view or make short, sharp, engaging and powerful audio/visual communications. Most campaigning organisations publish and promote sophisticated ideas that sometimes spread virus-like round the planet. The low cost of disseminating messages with new media, in comparison with traditional print-based and broadcast media, offers new opportunities for self and group expression, giving voice to those who have for too long been silenced. It offers a chance for others to connect with those who have been isolated in their subjugation (Blewitt 2008). The digital film festival Pangea Day in 2008 was an attempt to make McLuhan's notion of a global village a reality. The video *We* is universally available on the internet and graphically re-articulates the passionate words of Arundhati Roy's *Come September* speech of 2006 on power and powerlessness, liberty and justice. There is never just a single story, she says, just ways of seeing and telling stories.

The natural world too is highly mediated (Elliot 2006). No sooner is a rare bird sighted than pictures of it appear on the internet. The Bristol-based media and animal conservation organisation *Wildscreen* offers a stunning archive of still and moving images, oral histories, and a kaleidoscope of learning resources that document, stimulate and motivate the activities of many people across the world to visualise a human ecology that is sensitive to the imperatives of sustainability.

Clearly, although certain media skills can be taught, the capability to communicate is best acquired and learnt through doing, participation and engagement. As Hartley et al. (2008:61) discuss, it is important to understand how digital literacy evolves in informal learning contexts before it becomes transformed, emasculated and instrumentalised by formal organisations such as universities, colleges and schools. In its fresh democratic, participatory, sustainable and socially creative state, digital media provides a space where:

> . . . learning by doing is the norm. . . . Digital literacy is generated by its uses, not by a body of knowledge or 'critical' values. It is a demand-led literacy. (Hartley et al. 2008:61)

The user-generated content on the photo-sharing website *Flikr* is testimony to the reality that with new media, the consumer is also the producer. In an era of ubiquitous computing, citizen journalism and pervasive media is becoming quite commonplace.

However, there are plenty of media critics and sceptics. The democratic and perhaps utopian projections of Nicholas Negroponte, Bill Gates and Sir Tim Berners-Lee have certainly not been fully realised, while some of their fears have. Private corporations have enclosed vast tracts of cyberspace. Government surveillance, often in the name of security, and personalised commercial marketing, often in the name of convenience, have segmented the public sphere into a series of fractured semi-privatised spaces where participation is disconnected from individual empowerment. As Andrejevic (2004: 197) writes:

> The advent of digital interactivity does not challenge the social relations associated with capitalist rationalisation, it reinforces them and expands the scale on which they operate.

Media hardware also uses considerable amounts of energy, natural resources and, unless intelligently recycled or reused, (toxic) waste. In 2007, the carbon footprint of the information and communications industry overshot that clocked up by global aviation. Complex, visually dynamic websites are serious emitters of CO_2, and just browsing a simple website produces 20mg of CO_2 every second, with software glitches adding to the pollution tally. So new media are part of the problem, but can also be part of the solution. The McKinsey report, *SMART 2020: Enabling the low carbon economy in the information age*, describes the potential of Information Technology for saving energy: "No other sector can supply technology capabilities so integral to energy efficiency across such a range of other sectors or industries" (GeSI 2008: 11). For example, in higher education, digital media are enabling the development of smart campuses, e-learning and blended learning environments and a more efficient utilisation of physical space. A study by the UK's Open University (Roy et al. 2005:4) concluded that online distance learning courses consumed nearly 90% less energy and produced 85% fewer CO_2 emissions than conventional campus-based university courses.

The critical understanding of sustainability communication and new media can best be achieved through an informed engagement with the emerging technological affordances evident in many areas – social marketing, viral messaging, community development, environmental campaigning, media learning and sustainability education. In a highly mediated society, it is important to be critically aware of how the current and emerging mediascape influences our perceptions of the real and the possible, and how this mediascape can itself be altered through active engagement with it. Of course, this participation must also be informed by a sincere commitment to sustainability principles and global democracy. We are all media practitioners now. We need to be sustainability practitioners, too. Otherwise, where will we be? In the overcrowded dystopia depicted so vividly in the film *Soylent Green*?

Activity: change the world with a viral video

'A viral video is a video clip that gains widespread popularity through the process of Internet sharing, typically through email or instant messaging, blogs, and other media sharing websites.' (http://en.wikipedia.org/wiki/Viral_video)

Produce a 59-second viral video using an unsophisticated digital moving image camera to communicate a key sustainability message to an identified target group.

The viral may be produced by an individual or a small group who will be responsible for the design, production and dissemination of the product, e.g. uploaded to the institution's intranet, YouTube, Green TV, Planet 2025 Network or similar platform. Assessment should encompass self-reflection and peer evaluation. Did it work?

References and resources

Altheide, David (1995) *An Ecology of Communication: Cultural forms of control.* New York: Aldine de Gruyter.

Andrejevic, Mark (2004) 'The webcam subculture and the digital enclosure', in Couldry, Nick and McCarthy, Anna (eds.) *Mediaspace: Place, scale and culture in a media age.* London: Routledge.

Blewitt, John (2008) 'Picturing the lives of others', in Blewitt, John (ed.) *Community, Empowerment and Sustainable Development.* Dartington: Green Books.

Boler, Megan (ed.) (2008) *Digital Media and Democracy: Tactics in hard times.* Cambridge, USA: M.I.T. Press.

Burnett, Rob (2005) *How Images Think.* Cambridge, USA: M.I.T. Press.

Eco, Umberto (1979) 'Can Television Teach?' *Screen Education*, 31, 15-24.

Elliot, Nils (2006) *Mediating Nature.* London, Routledge.

Global e-Sustainability Initiative (2008) SMART 2020: Enabling the low carbon economy in the information age. www.gesi.org/index.php?article_id=43.

Hartley, John; McWilliam, Kelly; Burgess, Jean and Banks, John (2008) 'The uses of multimedia: three digital literacy case studies'. *Media International Australia*, 128, 59-72.

Manovich, Lev (2008) 'Software takes command'.
http://softwarestudies.com/softbook/manovich_softbook_11_20_2008.pdf.

Newton, Julianne (2001) *The Burden of Visual Truth: The role of photojournalism in mediating reality*. London: Routledge.

Roy, Robin; Potter, Stephen; Yarrow, Karen and Smith, Mark (2005) Towards sustainable higher education: environmental impacts of campus-based and distance higher education systems. Open University Design Innovation Group www3.open.ac.uk/events/3/2005331_47403_o1.pdf.

Wissner-Gross, Alex (2009) 'How you can help reduce the footprint of the Web'. UK Times online, 11 January 2009.
www.timesonline.co.uk/tol/news/environment/article5488934.ece.

Web resources

Wildscreen (www.arkive.org), Pangea Day (www.pangeaday.org),
Green TV (www.green.tv), Current TV (www.current.com),
Planet 2025 (www.planet2025.net), Smart 2020 (www.smart2020.org),
Alex Wissner-Gross (www.CO2Stats.com), The Flip (www.theflip.com),
Soylent Green (www.imdb.com/title/tt0070723).

Chapter 17

Cultural Literacy

Understanding and respect for
the cultural aspects of sustainability

Kim Polistina

Award Leader – Outdoor Learning University of Glamorgan

Culture includes our whole system of beliefs, values, attitudes, customs, institutions and social relations. The global crisis facing humanity is a reflection of this system, and is therefore a cultural crisis (UNESCO 1997). Hawkes (2001) reasoned that culture is the fourth pillar of sustainability, the glue that holds the social, environmental and economic pillars steadfast. An important skill for dealing with cultural diversity is cultural competence, which Chrisman (2007:69) defines as "attitudes, practice skills, and system savvy for cross-cultural situations". The central thrust of most cultural competence work involves individuals' flexibility and capability to properly assess and treat all people respectfully and in a suitable manner appropriate to their culture. Cultural literacy includes cultural competence, but adds to it the ability to critically reflect on, and if necessary bring about change in, one's own culture. It also includes the ability to analyse the behaviours of dominant cultures in relation to other cultures: for instance, the impact of globalisation or cross-cultural partnerships on local cultures around the world. There may, for example, be exploitative elements of sustainable development partnerships implemented by Western multinational corporations in developing countries. Four key cultural literacy skills will be discussed in this chapter.

- Cross-cultural awareness
- Local cultural awareness
- Critical reflection and thinking
- Personal skills for coping with being a change agent

Cross-cultural awareness

Within the enormous cultural diversity that exists on Earth, there are cultures which manage to fulfil human needs from the local environment in ways which are sustainable, or at least, more sustainable than consumerism-based cultures. Cultural literacy therefore includes the ability to examine other cultures critically and gain ideas about sustainability from them. Learning about another culture can be as simple as using the internet, consulting academic literature or popular media. However, this can give a superficial understanding of another culture, a 'tourist gaze' where learning is inauthentic and artificial.

Rather than learning about other cultures, a deeper and more respectful learning for sustainability can be gained by 'paralleling' different cultural traditions, beliefs and social systems with the consumerist cultures of the West, and then utilising this learning as a tool for critical reflection on aspects of learners' own cultures as well as the paralleled cultures. The word 'parallel' is used to provide a more egalitarian view of cultural examination than the value-laden 'comparison' which insinuates that one may be more appropriate, successful, valuable than the other.

Time spent understanding and 'paralleling' different cultural traditions can be extremely valuable when carrying out international sustainable development projects, both to avoid damage to the local culture and to draw on aspects of the culture which are already sustainable. One example of such a project is the co-operation between Ugandan local communities, Welsh Water and WaterAid (see Welsh Water 2009). In this partnership, the Ugandan communities continued their cultural outdoor lifestyles but worked with the external agencies to enhance sustainable living practices and increase the quality of life for communities in relation to health, education, environmental protection and conservation (Watkins 2009). Sustainable technologies from both Western and Ugandan cultures were combined with the sustainable local traditional lifestyles and environmental practices of the Ugandan culture to implement sustainable development. This project can be utilised as an example of a beneficial use of cultural literacy for sustainability as it does not use sustainable development for the sole purpose of increasing trade and growth for Western countries, but rather uses it to maintain local cultural and social sustainability.

Not all projects which come under the label of 'sustainable development' are beneficial to local cultures, however, and it is important for learners to view partnerships for sustainability between the West and developing countries as intervention (which could potentially be negative) rather than development (which has intrinsically positive connotations in the West). One exercise that can help raise awareness of how sustainable development can be tainted by economic values of market expansion is to involve students in critical analysis of how sustainable development is represented by transnational corporations. For instance, a recent Kenco Coffee advertisement claims that the company assists local communities in sustainable development through their trade with them. This image of sustainable development is imperialist, with Western-style houses popping up out of rainforests, Western-style classrooms (desks and blackboards) in the middle of a culture with an exceptionally good natural environment for learning outside the classroom, and water gushing out of a Western-style irrigation system indicating that it is now possible to waste a valuable resource on a larger scale. The underlying message is that 'valuable', 'better' or 'progressive' development involves becoming more like the (unsustainable) societies of the West. Cultural literacy can help prepare learners to contribute to developing sustainable societies that reflect and maintain local cultural traditions rather than imposing dominant cultural values and social systems from the West.

Discussions of culture and sustainable development can lead on to topics such as race and sustainability, establishing a local sense of place and cultural identity, community versus individualistic cultural value systems, imperialist definitions of sustainability, neoliberalism and sustainable development, and the impact of globalisation on local cultures. There is a wide range of literature in cultural studies and cultural theory that provides well-defined, explicated and useful information on these areas. Furthermore, protocols that provide guidelines for culturally appropriate behaviours that assist with cultural sensitivity, awareness and respect when working with local cultures are often developed by the government of the host nation itself (e.g. Department of Aboriginal and Torres Strait Islander Policy and Development 1999). These guidelines are extremely useful in coming to an understanding of the complexity of cultural issues and the importance of cultural literacy for sustainability.

Local cultural awareness

Cultural awareness and respect is not just a cross-cultural skill. The ability to accept and respect knowledge within local cultures and communities is also necessary for developing cultural literacy. There may be knowledge and skills for living sustainably that are already embedded in the traditions of local cultures and passed on intergenerationally through non-formal education (Bowers 2003; Polistina 2001). Formal education tends to place little value on such practical knowledge and skills, preferring instead abstract, technical or generalisable skills suitable for further advancing industrialisation and economic expansion. Education for an ecologically sustainable future requires a shift towards valuing and revitalising local knowledge of how to build self-reliant communities, and protecting this knowledge from the forces of commercialisation and consumerism (Bowers 2003; Polistina 2007).

Outdoor learning is particularly suitable for drawing on the grassroots expertise in sustainability found in local communities. For instance, a series of outdoor learning short courses developed at the University of Glamorgan focuses on sustainability and global citizenship and recognises the extensive and long-term sustainable education already being undertaken in local communities in non-formal and informal learning contexts (Polistina 2003).

Examples of how formal education can incorporate local grassroots educators include local elders describing the traditional agricultural practices of the region, local mothers working directly with learners for health and sustainability in an outdoor walking group or organic garden; landowners explaining the installation of micro-hydro schemes, and representatives from sustainable communities demonstrating renewable energy and waste systems utilised on their property. Learners can also be inspired to make a shift from fast food, which is both unhealthy and unsustainable, to more sustainable foods such as local, seasonal organic fruits and vegetables through learning traditional cooking skills in local courses, volunteering in organic edible gardens, working in allotments, and participating in community-led health needs assessments.

In collaborative projects such as these, the primary formal educator takes a step back, enabling local people to become the educators. This learning experience creates a more social, informal and relaxed atmosphere than classroom education, and learners develop their understanding of, sensitivity towards, and respect for the sustainability knowledge and skills that can be found in local cultures. Having learners choose their own community-based project to complete the assessments makes the learning real and has immediate consequences for the learners' lives and the sustainability of their localities or regions. This direct experience of sustainability within local communities can act as a basis for an increased understanding of international development issues, particularly the need to conserve, rather than destroy, aspects of cultures around the world that are already sustainable.

Critical reflection and thinking

Contrary to a culture of specificity and difference is one of hyperculture and indifference. This hyperculture is detrimental to sustainability literacy as it silences the need for self-critique, self-reflection, or reflection on the trajectory that society is taking. Critical reflective thinking is a dialogue between learners and educators on aspects of cultural or social discourse; it considers the experiences of the group as a whole and provides a way of accounting for ourselves (Ghaye and Ghaye 2001). It demonstrates an awareness that actions and events are located in, and explicable by, reference to multiple perspectives as well as influenced by multiple historical and socio-political contexts (Hatton and Smith 2006).

One possible exercise to encourage critical reflective thinking consists of providing learners with a piece of discourse about sustainability from popular media, for example from magazines, websites, advertisements or newspapers. Learners write whether they agree, disagree, like, dislike, understand or are confused by the information being provided. Once learners have written down their comments, they take them home without discussing them. At home they are instructed to forget what they have written and reflect on the information from another person's perspective, e.g., a Buddhist, single mother, managing director of a multinational company, a teenager, or a father in a community in Tanzania. By the time they come back to the group there will be several different perspectives on the same piece of information. Seed et al. (2007) take this exercise one stage further in the 'Council of All Beings', an imaginative exercise where participants wear masks and take on the perspectives of both human and non-human beings affected by environmental issues, including animals, plants, or even whole ecosystems such as rivers. This process can be utilised for any level of education. In higher education the critical reflection and thinking process would naturally progress through levels until a comprehensive and critical examination of information is undertaken, with innovative and achievable actions for cultural and social change being provided by the learner.

Personal skills for coping with being a change agent

Whilst a cultural shift towards sustainability is being sought globally, learners in Western countries do not live in the kind of society that supports the types of widespread changes, diversity of cultural systems or challenges to the status quo that are required for this shift to occur. Learners need to 'survive' being change agents for this cultural shift as they will encounter a variety of mental, physical, psychological and emotional battles with those seeking to sustain the status quo. Cultural and social power-brokers may safeguard the prominence of their power positions by discrediting, ridiculing and devaluing groups they perceive to be a threat. Learners and educators therefore need to be empowered to cope with these unreceptive behaviours.

Knowledge itself is a form of power, and learners will need skills in seeking out reliable, up-to-date and accessible information, from the latest climate science to an understanding of neoliberal critiques of sustainability and global citizenship. This requires practical research skills gained through self-directed learning, and can be achieved through mentored projects that learners chose for themselves. Ultimately, the educator becomes a facilitator and enabler of change

rather than a disseminator of knowledge. Having gained knowledge for themselves and reflected deeply on their values within the context of the realities of
the twenty-first century, learners need skills in confident, persuasive public
speaking to express their vision of a better world and back it up with evidence.
They will also need skills in resisting bullying and harassment, which is, unfortunately, a common response to suggestions that change might be needed. This
requires a deep sensitivity to the cultural context and so is an important part of
cultural literacy.

Learners' self-confidence and self-esteem can be built through involvement
in supportive networks of people working towards common goals, both within
local communities and globally in the wider sustainability and global citizenship
movement. Being part of a group with shared values can provide learners with
valuable social support for their work as cultural change agents and a healthy
release for the stresses that they will experience.

Conclusion

This chapter has looked at cultural literacy as a fundamental skill required by
learners in their development of sustainability literacy. The role of educator itself
demands a high level of cultural literacy to ensure that education provides
chances for critical reflection on culture from multiple perspectives, rather than
being confined to limited imperialist views of other cultures. Reflection on our
own culture and other cultural systems can help reveal the complex social, environmental and economic relationships that need to be changed to make a
successful shift towards sustainability.

References and resources

Bowers, Chet (2003) *Mindful Conservatism: Re-thinking the ideological and educational
    basis of an ecologically sustainable future*. Lanham: Rowman & Littlefield.

Chrisman, Noel (2007) 'Extending cultural competence through systems change:
    academic, hospital, and community partnerships'. *Journal of Transcultural Nursing*,
    18:1, 68-76.

Department of Aboriginal and Torres Strait Islander Policy and Development (1999)
    Protocols for consultation and negotiation with Aboriginal people. Brisbane:
    Queensland Government Printing Service.

Ghaye, Tony and Ghaye, Kay (2001) *Teaching and Learning Through Critical Reflective
    Practice*. London: David Fulton.

Hatton, Neville and Smith, David (2006) *Reflection in teacher education: towards definition and implementation.* School of Teaching and Curriculum Studies, University of Sydney.

Hawkes, Jon (2001) *The Fourth Pillar of Sustainability: Culture's essential role in public planning.* Victoria: Common Ground Publishing.

Polistina, Kim (2001) 'The validation of alternative discourses in the lifelong learning systems of Australian appreciative outdoor recreationalists and Indigenous peoples', in McPherson, Gayle and Reid, Gavin (eds.), *Leisure and Social Inclusion: New challenges for policy and provision.* Eastbourne: Leisure Studies Association.

Polistina, Kim (2003) 'Towards environmentally sustainable lifestyles through outdoor leisure?', in Ibbetson, Adrian; Watson, Beccy and Ferguson, Maggie (eds.) *Sport, Leisure and Social Inclusion.* Eastbourne: Leisure Studies Association.

Polistina, Kim (2007) 'Outdoor leisure and the sustainability agenda: critical pedagogy on neoliberalism and the employment obsession in higher education'. *Tourism Recreation Research*, 32:2, 57-66.

Seed, John; Macy, Joanna and Fleming, Pat (2007) *Thinking Like a Mountain: Towards a council of all beings.* British Columbia: New Catalyst Books.

UNESCO (1997) *Educating for a sustainable future: a transdisciplinary vision for concerted action.* available from www.unesco.org/education.

Watkins, Mary (2009) 'Welsh Water, Water Aid – Ugandan water access project'. Presentation for the environmental and sustainability education network, Rhondda Cynon Taff County Borough Council. Trefforest: Wales.

Welsh Water (2009) 'Welsh Water – Uganda WaterAid Project'. www.dwrcymru.co.uk.

Chapter 18

Carbon Capability

*Understanding climate change
and reducing carbon emissions*

Lorraine Whitmarsh *School of Psychology, Cardiff University*

Saffron O'Neill *Tyndall Centre for Climate Change Research,
University of East Anglia*

Gill Seyfang *Centre for Social and Economic Research on the Global
Environment, University of East Anglia*

Irene Lorenzoni *Tyndall Centre for Climate Change Research,
University of East Anglia*

Introduction

The UK government's recent Climate Change Bill set an ambitious target of an 80% reduction in emissions by 2050. This level of response to climate change has profound implications for individual choices and behaviour, as well as for the social structures in which these operate. With over one third of many nations' carbon emissions coming from private travel and domestic energy use, individuals clearly have a key role to play in any potential shift towards low-carbon societies. An individual can take several roles in promoting a low-carbon society, such as by being a low-carbon citizen (e.g. voting for a 'green' policy), a low-carbon consumer (e.g. buying locally-sourced food) or a low-carbon employee (i.e. an employee with a commitment to a low-carbon future who acts as a change agent in the work-place). At the moment, however, public engagement with climate change in the UK is limited, and energy demand for both domestic uses and transport is rising. Although a large majority of the public recognises terms such as 'climate change', understanding and emotional buy-in are far smaller. One problem is that there is a general lack of knowledge about the urgency of the situation, the scale of social changes necessary to reduce carbon emissions by 80%, and about the emissions impacts of different actions – the UK public is not yet 'carbon capable'. In this chapter, we introduce the concept of 'carbon capability' before suggesting ways that education can help learners to become more carbon capable.

Why 'carbon capability'?

We define 'carbon capability' as follows (adapted from Seyfang et al. 2007):

> 'Carbon capability' captures the *contextual meanings* associated with carbon, whilst also referring to an individual's *ability* and *motivation* to reduce emissions within the broader institutional and social context.

Importantly, carbon capability is not defined simply as knowledge, skills and motivations (although these are important components); rather, if people are genuinely carbon capable they will understand the limits of individual action and the need for collective action and other governance solutions. Also, a genuinely carbon capable individual appreciates that there are barriers in current systems of provision which limit the ability of an individual to act, and that much consumption (and hence carbon emissions) is inconspicuous, habitual and routine, rather than the result of conscious decision-making (van Vliet et al. 2005). Many studies show people face considerable obstacles to low-carbon lifestyles. These range from insufficient knowledge about effective actions, through perceived social inaction and the 'free rider effect', to inadequate or unattractive alternatives to energy-intensive activities such as driving (Lorenzoni et al. 2007).

Carbon capability is similar to financial capability, and involves managing budgets, planning ahead, staying informed, and making choices (Seyfang et al. 2007). Indeed, there are similar driving forces and comparable consumer issues with both types of capability, necessitating a holistic approach to sustainable consumption in both financial and resource terms. Carbon and finance are inextricably linked since excessive material consumption in developed countries is widely acknowledged as a principal driver of economic growth and unsustainability.

Given the state's reliance upon economic growth as a measure of development, the response of governments has been to promote 'financial capability' as an important basic skill and to emphasise individuals' responsibility to successfully navigate financial markets for themselves using this skill. This implies a deregulated economy governed not by government, but rather by individual producers and consumers' self-restraint (Binkley 2006). The credit crunch, however, has shown the manifest failure of this approach. If government is relying on individuals to manage their behaviour in this way, then people need to be skilled, motivated and capable of doing so; but more than that, they need sufficient understanding of the limits of voluntary self-restraint in order to demand appropriate regulation.

Managing finance and managing carbon are also similar in the way that they have intangible aspects. Perhaps partly because of credit finance's innate intangibility compared with cash transactions, debt has become widespread. Similarly, the negative impacts of increasing carbon emissions are easily ignored because of their intangibility. One of the challenges therefore for promoting carbon capability is to increase the visibility of carbon and re-materialise energy use in day-to-day activities and choices. Carbon capability is about transforming understandings of carbon from an inevitable waste product of modern lifestyles, to a scarce and potent resource to be carefully managed.

Being carbon capable implies knowledge of:

- the causes and consequences of carbon emissions
- the role individuals – and particular activities – play in producing carbon emissions
- the scope for (and benefits of) adopting a low-carbon lifestyle
- what is possible through individual action
- carbon-reduction activities which require collective action and infrastructural change
- managing a carbon budget
- information sources – and the reliability (bias, agenda, uncertainty, etc.) of different information sources; and
- the broader structural limits to and opportunities for sustainable consumption.

In the light of these multiple dimensions, carbon capability can be seen as intimately linked with other aspects of sustainability, for example issues of well-being, community, food, transport, housing, social justice, climate adaptation, and governance.

Evidence of a shift towards promoting carbon capability includes the development of 'carbon calculators' and discussion about managing 'carbon footprints' (see *Materials Awareness*, p.137). Yet our research suggests these new concepts and tools are having little impact at the individual or household level (Whitmarsh et al., 2009). People talk about carbon in very abstract and impersonal terms, and others (e.g. industry) are blamed for causing climate change. Carbon emissions are rarely linked to personal actions and lifestyle choices: for example, few people are aware of the significant climate impact of eating meat. Also, very few people have used a carbon calculator or are taking significant steps to lead a low-carbon lifestyle. Importantly, it is rare for citizens to consider political action a valid response to tackling climate change (Whitmarsh et al., 2009).

Promoting carbon capability

Carbon capability is a capacity pertaining to individuals, but, as discussed earlier, there are many changes that are necessary at the higher level of economic and social structures in order to create an enabling environment so that people *can* reduce their carbon emissions if they wish. It is essential then that learners go beyond gaining skills in reducing their own carbon footprint, to skills and understanding which can help them influence social institutions and organisations. Examples of two directions that this influencing could take relate to 'materialising' and 'budgeting' carbon emissions:

Materialising carbon emissions involves using tools and techniques which make carbon emissions more tangible in daily activities. Tools such as smart electricity meters and carbon labelling of consumer products work to make carbon emissions associated with consumption and manufacture visible and accountable, encouraging awareness of carbon costs associated with particular actions and everyday choices. Materialising carbon emissions allows development of enabling contexts in which people are able to act on their knowledge about carbon and its impacts if motivated to do so.

Budgeting carbon emissions relates to the management of personal carbon quotas, and typically involves community engagement with like-minded people. Through goal-setting and support networks, participants are helped to achieve their goals. Members of the Royal Society of Art's CarbonDAQ, for example, report their personal carbon emissions within a 'personal budget' framework and trade carbon allowances in a virtual market. Similarly, Carbon Reduction Action Groups (CRAGs) are community-based voluntary groups ('craggers') who adopt a 'weight-watchers' approach to cutting carbon footprints: regular meetings provide support for reducing carbon emissions and include a 'weigh-in' to calculate actual emissions against personal carbon allowances (which are reduced each year). While the number of people engaged in such activities is small, particularly in the light of an 80% reduction target, national frameworks such as carbon rationing could make this form of activity inclusive of a far wider range of people.

Learners need to think beyond the simplest energy-conservation measures, however, since interventions are needed at a larger scale than the household level. They could consider small-scale interventions such as car-share clubs, sustainable energy projects, the linking of personal emission-reductions with community benefits (Prescott 2008), to larger institutional and corporate transformation, and right up to the level of national carbon rationing or global agreements for emissions trading.

Conclusions

This brief exploration of carbon capability suggests a need for learners to gain skills not only in reducing their own carbon emissions, but in influencing social and economic structures through skills in communication and public education. This needs to go beyond simply providing information, since information provision alone is not enough to encourage lifestyle change or promote public acceptance of policy (e.g. Lorenzoni et al. 2007). Also, it should be acknowledged that scientific knowledge will be interpreted in diverse ways by different individuals according to their prior beliefs, knowledge, emotions, and situational factors (e.g. Whitmarsh et al. 2005). This chapter has argued for the need for learners to explore the implications of carbon emissions and energy usage in everyday life, within the broader context of structural opportunities for, and barriers to, low-carbon lifestyles. There are far more aspects to carbon capability than could be covered in this short chapter, but a central component of carbon capability must be the ability to resist – and create alternatives to – the social structures that underpin consumerism.

Activity: cutting carbon

The purpose of this exercise is to demonstrate that individual action is only one part of the carbon-management picture, and there is a limit to what can be achieved by individuals acting independently. To achieve the necessary cuts in carbon emissions, collective action and action by business and government are essential to shift fundamental infrastructures of society.

(a) Investigate your carbon footprint using the following web sources:

www.carbontrust.co.uk/solutions/CarbonFootprinting/
wi.footprint.wwf.org.uk
actonCO2.direct.gov.uk/index.html

- who is providing these calculators?
- what do you think their aims are in providing the calculator?
- what are your scores for each of the footprint calculators?
- what assumptions are made in each of the footprint calculators?
- how useful do you think calculators like this are for contributing to a low carbon future?

(b) How could you, acting on your own, reduce your carbon footprint?

(c) How could the following people or organisations help to create an environment which would make it easier for you to reduce your footprint?

- your fellow household members
- your community
- businesses
- government
- other organisations?

References and resources

Binkley, Sam (2006) 'The perilous freedoms of consumption: toward a theory of the conduct of consumer conduct'. *Journal for Cultural Research*, 10, 343-362.

Lorenzoni, Irene; Nicholson-Cole, Sophie and Whitmarsh, Lorraine (2007) 'Barriers perceived to engaging with climate change among the UK public and their policy implications'. *Global Environmental Change*, 17, 445-59.

Prescott, Matt (2008) *A persuasive climate: personal trading and changing lifestyles.* London: Royal Society for the Encouragement of Arts, Manufactures and Commerce.

Seyfang, Gill; Lorenzoni, Irene and Nye, Michael (2007) *Personal carbon trading: notional concept or workable proposition? Exploring theoretical, ideological and practical underpinnings.* CSERGE Working Paper EDM 07-03. Centre for Social and Economic Research on the Global Environment (CSERGE), University of East Anglia, Norwich. www.uea.ac.uk/env/cserge/pub/wp/edm/edm_2007_03.pdf.

van Vliet, Bas; Chappells, Heather and Shove, Elizabeth (2005) *Infrastructures of Consumption.* London: Earthscan.

Whitmarsh, Lorraine; Kean, Sharon; Russell, Claire; Peacock, Matthew and Haste, Helen (2005) *Connecting Science: What we know and what we don't know about science in society.* British Science Association. www.britishscienceassociation.org.

Whitmarsh, Lorraine, Saffron O'Neill, Gill Seyfang and Irene Lorenzoni (2009) 'Carbon Capability: what does it mean, how prevalent is it, and how can we promote it?'. Tyndall Working Paper 132. Tyndall Centre for Climate Change Research, University of East Anglia. http://tyndall.ac.uk/publications/working_papers/twp132.pdf.

Chapter 19

Greening Business

The ability to drive environmental and sustainability improvements in the workplace

Zoe Robinson

School of Physical and Geographical Sciences, Keele University

Introduction

The business sector accounts for a significant proportion of the UK's environmental footprint, in addition to having a major influence on wider social and economic sustainability issues both nationally and internationally. Making improvements in the environmental and sustainability performance of businesses and organisations is therefore crucial for achieving a more sustainable society. In order for employees at all levels to be able to contribute to making these improvements, a sustainability-literate workforce is needed. This sustainability literacy must involve, alongside appropriate values and ethics, the practical knowledge, understanding and skills to drive positive environmental change within an organisation.

Sustainability issues are relevant to all organisations of all sizes and in all sectors. Increasingly, organisations themselves are demanding sustainability literacy skills for a wide range of roles and responsibilities. If learners can gain these skills they are therefore improving both their own employability as well as their ability to contribute to making their future workplace and society more sustainable. Yet despite this, and an ever-growing emphasis on employability within the education sector, there are currently few examples of sustainability literacy being addressed across the curriculum in mainstream education. This chapter describes how 'greening business' skills can be incorporated into the curriculum and gives some example exercises which can help learners gain those skills.

Integrating 'greening business' skills into the curriculum

In order to effectively contribute to driving environmental and sustainability improvements in their (future) workplaces, learners need to acquire knowledge, understanding, skills and experience in identifying opportunities for improvements and designing effective strategies for realising them. They also need skills in effectively and persuasively presenting the proposed changes, sometimes in difficult circumstances if the change goes against the ingrained culture of the organisation. Arguing persuasively requires an awareness of both the ethical and business case for improvements, and the benefits of, and barriers to, making those improvements. Helping students prepare to become effective change agents in their future working life involves introducing them to aspects such as the following within the curriculum:

- Environmental and sustainability legislative requirements (including national and international legislation), and the techniques that corporations frequently use to evade them (see Achbar et al. 2005)

- The benefits of environmental and sustainability improvements to an organisation (e.g. financial savings; attracting and maintaining a high-calibre, motivated workforce; customer/stakeholder expectations; accessing new markets; company image; creation of innovative new products/processes)

- The risks of not addressing sustainability issues (e.g. being closed out of future markets/tendering opportunities; attacks on company image; legal risks and liability; supply problems with raw materials and energy; damage to people and the environment)

- The potential barriers to making environmental and sustainability improvements within an organisation (e.g. perceived costs; ignorance; lack of interest and scepticism; practical limitations such as available time and space and existing building stock)

- Techniques for environmental auditing (covering resource efficiency/waste management, utilities management, transport and purchasing practices and policies)

- Underpinning knowledge and understanding of the science of climate change and other human impacts on the environment, life-cycle analysis, environmental footprinting etc.

It is essential that learners are introduced to 'real world' examples and case studies. This could involve, for example, engagement with local organisations and employers or their own institutions by conducting informal environmental audits for them, or researching the activities of larger organisations to expose environmentally damaging practices and to identify paths for improvements.

The following are important generic employability skills essential for achieving environmental and sustainability improvements within an organisation, and can be developed as part of an effective active-learning focused 'greening business' curriculum:

- research skills, including the investigation, interrogation and evaluation of the reliability of resources and evidence, for example determining assumptions used in claims of environmental benefits and improvements, and an awareness of bias and 'greenwash' (see *Technology Appraisal*, p.150)

- numerical skills and confidence in the handling and manipulation of numerical data, for example, the quantification of environmental and financial costs and savings across an organisation

- accurate observation, monitoring and recording skills for the auditing of observable environmental and sustainability practices within an organisation

- question setting and question posing to access information on environmental and sustainability practices that are not directly observable as part of an environmental audit

- action planning to produce a feasible and actionable strategy for organisational change

- negotiation skills to agree an achievable and worthwhile action plan and influence practices and behaviour of individuals within an organisation

- report writing and visual and oral presentation skills for the professional, confident and persuasive presentation of environmental audit findings and action plans for environmental and sustainability improvements

Wider benefits of 'greening business' skills

In addition to the direct benefits to learners from gaining sustainability literacy skills, the greening business curriculum has many wider institutional, societal and environmental benefits. Despite regular coverage of the unsustainability of society and reports of a newly environmentally conscious generation, a significant segment of society still remains disinterested and sceptical about their responsibility to work towards a more sustainable future. In particular, many learners claim to be bored with hearing about climate change and have become disengaged with environmental and sustainability issues, primarily because they can see that, on its own, the reduction of their personal environmental footprint will make little difference overall. A greening business approach has the potential to interest and engage learners both by making sustainability relevant to their future career prospects and by enabling them to have a much larger influence on the sustainability of society through potentially influencing the decisions of a large organisation. In this way, learners can become empowered to contribute towards a more sustainable society and help generate a positive culture of organisational change and optimism. That optimism might influence their own lives, leading them to become better 'environmental citizens' and consider environmental and sustainability issues in their day-to-day behaviour and decision-making.

An active-learning based greening business curriculum provides opportunities to integrate campus and curriculum developments, and can act as a mechanism for learners to influence environmental and sustainability developments within their institutions. As well as being able to apply their knowledge and skills to their own immediate environment, opportunities to work directly with local businesses can prove beneficial to the learners and businesses alike.

Society will be faced with many major environmental challenges and changes in the twenty-first century, including peak oil, climate change, population growth, declining water resources and ecosystem destruction in parts of the world. Businesses and organisations will need to be prepared to operate within a very changed society. They will need to contend with changing markets and growing insistence from government, customers and employees for more sustainable products and practices. During the twenty-first century, business will experience changes in the costs and supply of energy and water and have to contend with potentially unstable supply chains caused by environmental, societal and economic degradation in different parts of the world. Businesses and organisations that fail to adapt to these challenges will struggle in the future while those companies that have embraced a more sustainable organisational culture will thrive. Already examples are being seen of companies which are struggling because they have resisted adopting more environmentally sound and sustainable practices. By acquiring greening business skills for driving environmental and sustainability improvements in the workplace, learners will be well-placed to contribute to the success of businesses and organisations in the twenty-first century and to a thriving and sustainable society.

Active learning exercises

'Greening business' material can be integrated into the curricula of a wide range of disciplines, or can equally well stand alone as an autonomous module which is accessible and applicable to learners from any discipline. This is an area of learning which lends itself to active learning strategies, through analysis of case studies and the practice of acquired knowledge, understanding and practical skills. Some examples of learning activities are outlined below:

1. Environmental audits within the learners' institution (or partner organisation)

Training in a basic framework for environmental auditing provides learners with the practical skills to identify areas for environmental and sustainability improvements. There are many basic environmental-auditing frameworks publicly available which are suitable for introductory auditing activities (see *References and resources* on p.136), or learners can draw up their own auditing frameworks. Learners can apply their auditing training to an area of their institution's (or on placement in another organisation) activities or estate, identifying areas for improvement and formulating realistic, well-researched and justifiable proposals for implementation of the improvements.

- Development of a spreadsheet for recording directly observable environmental and sustainability practices

- Formulation of a list of questions to establish environmental and sustainability practices which are not directly observable

- Carrying out an audit of a particular aspect of an organisation's operations (this could be a specific building, a specific aspect such as purchasing or transport, or a particular area of an organisation's operations such as a manufacturing process)

- Talking with management and employees to understand the organisational culture and identify any barriers to change

- Development of recommendations for improvements and the formulation of realistic, well-researched strategies for implementation of the proposed changes

- Presentation of the audit findings and recommendations as a report, oral and/or poster presentation.

The need for a well-researched and professional presentation of the project findings can be emphasised through arranging for learners to present their findings to those responsible for implementation and policy-making of the environmental and sustainability practices of the organisation/institution that has been studied. This can be effectively carried out at a poster presentation session, for example.

Through these activities learners practise a wide range of employability skills, and gain experience in applying their new knowledge, understanding and skills to drive environmental and sustainability improvements within their own institutions or partner organisations.

2. Carbon footprinting an organisation's operations and prioritising strategies for change

The quantification of the different components of an organisation's carbon footprint can highlight priority areas for change and emphasise the carbon and financial savings that can be made through changes to the organisation's activities. The importance to an organisation's carbon footprint of making small changes can be emphasised when the savings resulting from changes are multiplied up to an organisational scale. There are several publicly accessible online resources reporting on aspects such as transport and utilities usage within an organisation's activities (see *Carbon Capability*, p.124 and *Materials Awareness*, p.137). These can be used in combination with standard tables of average CO_2 emissions per unit of activity to calculate the size of an organisation's carbon footprint, determine the most polluting activities and hence identify priority areas for action. This can be followed by discussion of appropriate and realistic strategies to reduce the organisation's carbon footprint. Example tables for these exercises are available at www.esci.keele.ac.uk/greeningbusiness.

3. Interrogating and evaluating environmental policies and corporate social responsibility reports

There is a vast array of online resources and environmental and sustainability literature available from corporations and organisations, including environmental policies, corporate social responsibility reports and life-cycle analysis reports. Exercises which involve interrogating and evaluating these resources provide learners with skills in evaluating the potential bias of resources and also provide examples of positive activities being carried out by organisations. Group debates centred on a selected resource can provide a useful vehicle for the evaluation and discussion of these resources. Learners, or groups of learners, can take on different roles, for example acting as representatives from the senior management of the company, an employee environmental action group, a major customer and a representative of a major environmental group such as Greenpeace or Friends of the Earth. Each debater scrutinises the resource in question and presents a critique of the report from the perspectives of the viewpoint that they are representing. Where the resource under scrutiny is a document from the learners' own institution, this provides a further vehicle for increasing awareness of environmental and sustainability developments and driving positive environmental and sustainability change within their own institution.

References and resources

Achbar, Mark; Abbott, Jennifer and Bakan, Joel (2005) *The Corporation*. Vancouver: Big Picture Media (a fascinating documentary about the growing prominence of large global businesses and the way that their decisions are impacting on the world).

Carbon Trust. www.carbontrust.co.uk (provides a wide range of resources aimed at helping businesses and organisations reduce their carbon footprint).

Friends of the Earth online office audit. www.green-office.org.uk/audit.php (an online tool designed to find out how to identify the environmental impacts of an office, find appropriate solutions and track progress).

Greening Business: an online educational resource. www.esci.keele.ac.uk/greeningbusiness (examples of teaching materials and learning activities for embedding 'greening business' curriculum developments).

Institute of Environmental Management and Assessment. www.iema.net (established to promote best-practice standards in environmental management, auditing and assessment, and promote sustainability through improved environmental practice and performance).

Chapter 20

Materials Awareness

*The ability to expose the hidden impact
of materials on sustainability*

Melinda Watson

University Centre Yeovil

Every day we individually engage in the creation and consumption of products
and materials in one way or another, whether it is the computer used to type this
on, or the reams of paper that learners use. Whilst consumption is necessary on
a personal, social and economic level, excessive over-consumption on an individual and macro-aggregate level is the primary cause of environmental problems. This chapter explores 'materials awareness' within the realm of everyday
experience as a way of empowering learners to become active citizens by lever-
aging their consumer power and effecting change.

Craft and designer-maker traditions and materials have evolved and changed
remarkably as the result of advances in technological industrialisation. In the
contemporary mass production context, a plethora of new products and materials is constantly being generated. The dominant paradigm of affluent developed nations blatantly promotes hedonistic consumerism and rampant materialism, and this ideology risks becoming entrenched across the world. The
constant modification and updating of products, where cost and convenience is
of primary concern, forms the basis of our capitalist economy and throwaway
culture. The whole system is premised on increasing levels of consumption.
Regardless of true needs, sophisticated marketing and advertising stimulate
unprecedented artificial wants, encouraging excessive consumption (see *Advertising Awareness*, p.37). A seemingly inexhaustible range of choices, representing
a vast array of powerful, symbolic, status-defining goods that establish self-
image and social-cultural relations, has blurred image with reality and altered
perceptions of well-being. Firmly ingrained, the addictive and habitual human
activity of consumption engages us daily with a multitude of products from
buildings to home furnishings, cars to electronics, clothing, food and garden

equipment. According to Leonard (2007), the proportion of products "that remain in use six months after purchase is a pitiful one per cent". Rapid product obsolescence, design for disposability and constructed needs have created a supremely wasteful system of production.

Overwhelmingly, consumption in rich countries is far greater than that in developing and poor nations. Paradoxically, nations demonstrating the highest levels of consumption exhibit the lowest levels of environmental degradation since problematic waste and pollution are externalised. Disparities are intensified by obsessive global economic growth and competition for profit, accelerating exploitative inequality and ecological injustice. To facilitate over-consumption, wealthy industrialised nations, transnational corporations and rich individuals strategically monopolise access to global natural resources, energy and trade. Maintaining and exacerbating their cross-national and socio-cultural power marginalises the poor both within nations and internationally. The exploding populations and phenomenal rates of growth of developing nations such as China and India, which aspire to match the material living standards of the West, indicate the growing scale of the problem. Resultant protectionism and security repercussions will only magnify current social unrest, fragmentation and exclusion. As Kofi Annan once said, "A path to prosperity that ravages the environment and leaves a majority of humankind behind in squalor will soon prove to be a dead-end road for everyone."

The Intergovernmental Panel on Climate Change (IPCC) confirms the science of anthropogenic climate change beyond reasonable doubt: our consumption habits, products, materials and associated production processes designed to feed this appetite are significantly out of step with the natural balance. Nature cannot keep up with either the unprecedented speed or scale of material exploitation, environmental degradation, and persistent toxic chemical contamination and pollution. These have an impact on all four of the Earth's ecological 'spheres' – air, organisms, water and soil. Choosing to purchase the latest mobile phone or a bottle of water is only the *visible* tip of a vast material iceberg. The moment an individual hands over money to purchase a product they are connecting to a web of global activity that is *invisible*. The crucial skill of *Materials Awareness* is the power to use knowledge and imagination to make that web visible, to understand the full implications of purchases and act on that understanding.

The problem essentially lies in the secret life of materials: the entire 'story' or life-cycle of materials and the consequences are hidden before, during and after consumer use. Therefore, the critical challenge for learners and educators at every level is to investigate and expose the *invisible* material trail. Capra's (1999) vision of an ecological framework and systems thinking are vital core concepts, entailing a "new way of seeing the world and a new way of thinking . . . in terms of relationships, connectedness, and context" which transcends disciplinary boundaries. Materials awareness can help learners develop this new way of thinking, since following the invisible material trail leads to discovery of connections of all kinds. Reconnecting consumers to the ecological networks of which they are part, and reviving more sustainable practices from the past, may help to move us towards a more sustainable future.

A common first exercise to link learners to their own daily actions and consumption habits is through carbon-footprint calculators, which give an indication of the scale of individual behaviour. However, this method has limitations: it fails to take into account the social and environmental impact of materials; the systematic erosion of the Earth's carrying capacity due to a wide variety of factors beyond climate change, and ignores the effects of *trans-boundary* toxic pollution of organisms that sustain the Earth's life support systems.

Synthetic plastic is a notorious example of a material with impacts across the web of life. The search to produce a cheap, durable, lightweight material that can be transported and stored efficiently has created a wide range of goods that we now depend on. It can be made into virtually anything, and is practically everywhere; we drink from it, eat from it, cook in it, sit on it, type on it, play with it, drive in it and pay with it. However the production, use and disposal of plastic causes widespread ecological damage: inadvertently, the very properties that make it particularly useful also make it a persistent pollutant (Moore 2002). Learners can explore the origins of plastic in petroleum, the impact of petroleum extraction on the environment, its role in international conflict, the pollution resulting from plastic such as the Great Pacific Garbage Patch which is now the size of Texas, and the impact of plastic pollution on marine and land wildlife. They can go further still, and investigate the highly toxic chemicals that are used during plastic production, the chemicals that can leach out when plastic is exposed to the sun, and examine the terrible health and environmental consequences when plastic is disposed of through landfill or incineration.

Plastic is just one example. There are countless other materials causing environmental damage and chemical contamination that learners can explore. For example, a toy duck:

> contains chemicals known . . . to cause cancer and birth defects or other reproductive harm. . . . What kind of culture would produce a product of this kind and then label it and sell it to children? (McDonough 2005)

Other examples, such as e-waste containing over 1,000 different substances, many of which are toxic, continue to create serious pollution on disposal in Asia, despite 'take-back schemes' and regulation. The likelihood is that learners will be completely unaware of the unfair occupational and environmental health threats that expose men, women and children to hazardous toxins in developing countries.

Beyond understanding the social and environmental problems associated with materials, learners also need awareness of solutions for avoiding or mitigating those problems. Dryzek (2005) identifies a range of different responses to environmental issues which can be usefully applied to materials awareness. He categorises responses according to two dimensions, *prosaic/imaginative* and *reformist/radical*. *Prosaic* responses involve action but without any commitment to political or social change. *Imaginative* responses, on the other hand, seek to rethink relationships between humans and the environment and build a different kind of society. Prosaic and imaginative responses can vary according to degree from *reformist*, involving slight adjustments to current systems, to *radical* which involves widespread, major change. Dryzek uses these two dimensions to categorise different environmental *discourses*.

The first discourse he describes is *environmental problem-solving*, characterised as *prosaic-reformist*. This discourse is gradually being adopted by industry, and seeks, among other things, to reduce the impact of environmentally damaging materials by using them more efficiently. Yet 'eco-efficiency' has yet to be fully implemented, and is not a long-term solution since increasing demand for products could outweigh efficiency gains. The second discourse is *survivalism*, characterised as *prosaic-radical,* and takes 'limits to growth' seriously, calling for major changes to allow the current system to continue into the future, but without challenging the consumerist basis of society. Of particular importance for this chapter is the *sustainability* discourse (*imaginative-reformist*), which widens the intellectual discourse to cultivate an attitude of inquiry. Learners are encouraged to consider alternatives to the systems of material flows and waste at a systemic level. Also of importance is the *green radicalism* discourse (*imaginative-radical*). This discourse seeks to re-vision wasteful, profligate 'human-centred' norms and promote instead an Earth-centred norm of reality and value, based on a deep approach that all life on Earth has intrinsic value (see Hannigan 2006 for more on environmental discourses).

Expanding perceptions and values can essentially move learners and educators beyond *reactive* and *adaptive* levels to *transformative* levels, to challenge and reframe present notions that are threatening the systems that support human life. This represents an entire paradigm shift. To contribute to creating this paradigm shift, learners will need to be motivated to think beyond their immediate cultural environment, which is preoccupied with self-centred over-consumption, materialism and competition. The challenge is to embody the basic principles of ecology, eliminate waste and cultivate sustainable communities to meet genuine human needs where competition is perceived in terms of the origin of the word *com-petare*: 'to strive together' (see *Effortless Action*, p.58).

Rather than endorsing cradle-to-grave products and materials that are dumped in landfills at the end of their 'life', McDonough and Braungart's (2002) *imagina-*

tive-reformist vision of a 'cradle to cradle' closed loop system offers an example of an innovative alternative based on ecological principles. Industry could be transformed by creating products whose materials are perpetually circulated in closed loop cycles. Maintaining materials in closed loop cycles maximises material value without damaging ecosystems, offering a new ethics of consumption. McDonough (2005) asks: "Why not set out, right from the start, to create products and industrial systems that have only positive, regenerative impacts on the world?" Cradle to cradle "envisions a world powered by the sun where growth is good, waste nutritious, and productive diversity enriches human and natural communities" (ibid.).

McDonough and Braungart (2002) distinguish two main cycles, modelled on the elegance and effectiveness of natural cycles and ecosystems. The biological cycle is composed of biodegradable materials called biological nutrients, and the technical cycle is composed of 100% 'pure' reusable materials called technical nutrients. For example, Climatex Lifecycle upholstery fabric is a blend of organic, pesticide-residue-free wool dyed and processed entirely with non-toxic chemicals. All materials and processes are chosen for human and ecological safety. As a result, the fabric's biological waste nutrients can be returned to the soil. In contrast, Shaw Industries, a commercial carpet company, provides a model for technical 'up-cycling'. The company guarantees that all nylon 6 carpet fibre and its polyolefin backing can be recovered and returned to nylon 6 carpet fibre and polyolefin backing. The underlying idea is pure raw material back into raw material. In conjunction with this, adopting principles such as design for longevity, disassembly and reuse can shift the strategic emphasis from efficiency to sufficiency and reduce material flows.

Once learners have gained an *imaginative-reformist* perspective it is possible for them to devise solutions for themselves which minimise the environmental impact of materials, or at least to exercise their consumer power in choosing products which have been ecologically designed. At a deeper level, however, gaining an awareness of how prevailing human exploitation of materials, material flows, and waste systematically causes ecological destruction can lead learners to reflect on the personal and social change necessary for reduction of consumption and 'de-materialisation'. By inviting engagement at the experiential level, the invisible impacts of habitual consumption of products and materials can be exposed, and alternatives explored.

Activity

The objective of this activity is for learners to evaluate visible and invisible materials and processes in order to understand how consumer habits affect the environment (see Thorpe 2008).

1. Identify an everyday consumer object/product that is immediately at hand. Describe the various materials and processes that contribute to its production and disposal.

2. After identifying the *visible* materials, consider other relevant aspects that may be *invisible*:

- *Scale:* how many of these objects are there in the world, and how fast do they 'turn over'?

- *Origin:* where have the components of the materials come from?

- *Content:* what chemicals and material types does the object contain?

- *Resources:* what raw materials are used, and what are the environmental and social consequences of their extraction?

- *Composition of materials*: are the materials used pure or hybrids? What consequences does this have for later recycling?

- *Size:* what is the relative size of components versus relative potential harm? (e.g. in mobile phones, some of the smallest quantities contain the biggest potential toxic harm)

- *Additives:* what hidden coatings, protective coverings or chemical treatments are added?

- *Packaging:* what impact does the packaging have on the environment?

- *Labels:* are they present, and if so, what do they really tell us?

- *Manufacture:* what are the processing methods and costs?

- *Energy:* how much energy is consumed at each stage of manufacture?

- *Distribution:* how is the object transported, and how many times?

- *Escape:* how do parts of the object, or the whole object, get back into the environment?

- *Social-cultural:* how do all of the above affect individual and community health and well-being?

References and resources

Capra, Fritjof (1999) *Ecoliteracy: The challenge for education in the next century.* Schumacher Lectures. www.ecoliteracy.org/publications.

Dryzek, John (2005) *The Politics of the Earth: Environmental discourses.* Oxford: Oxford University Press.

Hannigan, John (2006) *Environmental Sociology* (2nd edn). London: Routledge.

Leonard, Annie (2007) *Story of stuff.* www.storyofstuff.com (a 20-minute, fast-paced, fact-filled video by international sustainability expert Annie Leonard).

McDonough, William and Braungart, Michael (2002) *Cradle to Cradle: Remaking the way we make things.* New York: North Point Press.

McDonough, William (2005) 'The wisdom of designing cradle to cradle'. www.ted.com (offers a series of useful podcasts).

Moore, Charles (2002) 'The great pacific garbage patch'. www.greatgarbagepatch.com.

Thorpe, S. (2008) *Teaching Guide for the Designer's Atlas of Sustainability.* www.designers-atlas.net/teachguide.html.

Chapter 21

Appropriate Technology and Appropriate Design

The ability to design systems, technologies and equipment in an appropriate way

Mike Clifford

Faculty of Engineering, The University of Nottingham

Engineers and product designers have often been guilty of feeding on consumer wants rather than working to satisfy the basic needs of the global population. It is nothing short of scandalous that in the twenty-first century, one-third of the world's population – two billion people – do not have access to safe drinking water, whilst expensive projects such as the Large Hadron Collider (estimated final cost £5.5 billion) occupy the attention of engineers. Large projects with no obvious benefits are easy targets, but on the individual scale, a survey carried out by insurer Cornhill Direct found that the average UK teenager leaves the house with clothes, jewellery, watches and gadgets such as mobile phones worth £529.54 – a value roughly equivalent to the Gross National Income per capita of sub-Saharan Africa (estimated by the World Bank as £590 in 2006).

Up to the mid-twentieth century, engineering was usually a response to a physical need. For example, steam engines were developed by Newcomen, Watt, Trevithick and others, to pump water from mineshafts; Abraham Darby's efforts to refine iron production were motivated by the need for cheaper cooking pots; and the chlorination of water by John Snow was in response to the 1854 cholera epidemic.

Facing page: Examples of appropriate technology project work. From top, left to right: oxygen conservator produced from condoms; laryngoscope adapted to operate without batteries; mechanical solar tracker; solar still; bread oven, now in use in Soroti, Uganda; plans for candle-powered plastic bag sealer; bicycle-powered palm nut crusher; palm nuts; appropriate technology wheelchair; energy-efficient wood stove; cardboard composite furniture; clockwork syringe driver; mechanical battery recharger; and biomass briquetting in Ghana.

Maslow ranked human needs in a pyramid, with basic physiological needs such as the need to eat, to breathe and sleep at the bottom of the pyramid. The next layer includes the need for safety and security. Next comes the need to belong, to love and be loved, which are topped by esteem and other higher 'self-actualisation needs'. With basic needs having been largely met in over-developed countries, engineers have been aimlessly 'innovating' and relying on a massive advertising industry to convince consumers that the resultant products will satisfy their higher needs. Buy these trainers and you will be accepted. Use this deodorant and you will be attractive to the opposite sex. Subscribe to our mobile phone network and your talk will be unlimited (see *Advertising Awareness*, p.37). In the twenty-first century, consumerism – not necessity – is the mother of invention.

The influence that technology can have on culture is discussed by Postman, who classified cultures into three types: tool-using cultures, technocracies and techno-polies. Until the seventeenth century, all cultures fitted into the first type. Tools were invented to do two things – firstly to solve urgent basic physical problems such as grinding corn, ploughing land, transporting water and so on, and secondly to serve the symbolic world of art and religion. The integrity and dignity of the culture was not threatened by the use of such tools. However, in a technocracy, tools play a central role in the thought-world of the culture. The very instruments created to meet the needs of society threaten to transform and indeed overthrow it. In Huxley's *Brave New World*, the revolution is complete – technopoly eliminates alter-natives to itself by creating a culture that seeks its purpose and finds its satisfaction in technology. The means to an end has become an end in itself.

The Indian theologian M. M. Thomas (1993) expressed these concerns in an address to the Christian Medical College at Vellore:

> There is no doubt that the scientific and technological revolution of the modem period has been a tremendous expression of human creativity: it has eliminated dis-tances and created the global community materially. It has given us the knowledge necessary to produce goods and services in abundance. It has given us power for social, psychic and genetic engineering, to control disease and death as well as birth. But as we survey the world situation today, the general feeling is that along with many benefits, many of the promises of technology stand betrayed, and there is evi-dence of a lot of technology having become instruments of exploitation of peoples, destruction of cultures and dehumanisation of persons and pose a threat of destruc-tion not only to the whole humanity through nuclear war but also to the whole com-munity of life on the Earth through the destruction of its ecological basis.

As powerful marketing departments encourage consumers to switch their focus from one flashy technology to another, designers provide products to meet the latest fad, even though they know that the market for whatever it is they are producing will last perhaps a few years at the most. The rate at which technology becomes obsolete is increasing. For instance, it is estimated that mobile phones are replaced by users after eighteen months, whereas it takes approximately 1,000 years for a mobile phone to decompose naturally (see *Materials Awareness*, p.137).

Too often, engineers have ignored sustainability and designed equipment, processes and technologies without taking into account local factors such as culture, environment, gender, local availability of materials and local production methods. Market economics has pushed engineers into coming up with mass-produced 'one size fits all' solutions, which may be inappropriate for some. This is particularly evident when designing for remote communities both in economically well-off countries and, acutely, for those with fewer physical resources.

Cooking stoves make a good case study. Half the world cooks using wood as a fuel. With population pressures and climate change, it is becoming increasingly difficult in the twenty-first century for populations around the world to find sustainable sources of wood for cooking, leading to widespread deforestation. In addition, with some designs of woodburning stove there are issues of indoor pollution. The developed world's response to these problems has largely been to come up with new technologies which are designed and tested at considerable distance from the communities they intend to serve. Often research is carried out in academic institutions away from where stoves are used, and although the resulting stoves can be fuel-efficient, the neglect of social factors is a major barrier to successfully introducing improved stoves into the homes of those living in remote communities.

In Ethiopia and neighbouring Eritrea, the staple food *injera* (a spongy sour flatbread) is cooked on a large griddle on a *mogogo* stove. These inefficient, smoky stoves are made by individuals from a mixture of mud and clay, whilst the *mogogo* plates are supplied by the local ceramics industry. Two recently proposed 'improved' stoves are not suitable for cooking *injera*. The CleanCook alcohol stove, made in Sweden from aluminium, has two small burners which are insufficient to heat a *mogogo* plate. The change of fuel and stove also has adverse economic effects on local *mogogo* plate manufacturers and firewood sellers. A stove from Aprovecho with a more traditional appearance but made from concrete failed to take into account the even temperature distribution required, so although testing in the USA by boiling pots of water appeared to show improved efficiency, when it came to cooking *injera*, the results were inedible. Although these attempts have some merit, their use requires Ethiopians to change their eating habits, threatens local economies and could thus be regarded as intrusive and colonialist. There is also a design of *mogogo* plate promoted by the Eritrean government – the ETRC (Energy Research and Training Centre) *mogogo*, but the cost of £28 places it out of reach of many Eritreans.

Alternative approaches involving local stakeholders have tended to be successful on a small scale, but are much more labour-intensive. For example, on a recent trip with Engineers Without Borders UK to install wood stoves in a remote village in the Imbabura region of Ecuador, Nottingham University undergraduate Rob Quail found that although initially the villagers were rather shy, by involving them in the design and material selection process, they overcame scepticism. Returning to the village two weeks later, Rob found that the villagers had built two stoves from his design and had begun to experiment with modifying the stoves according to their own ideas.

It may be impractical to involve end-users at every stage of the process in the design of improved cooking stoves, but it is vital that users' requirements are assessed carefully before solutions are proposed. For instance, stove users in rural locations are more concerned about the cost of a stove than fuel efficiency, since firewood is often collected free, whereas urban dwellers may have to purchase fuel and consequently are concerned with both initial cost and fuel efficiency.

An alternative approach is to tackle the problems of poor fuel economy and harmful emissions by modifying stoves which are currently in use rather than starting with a blank sheet of paper. Indigenous stoves will have undergone a natural process of evolution, with good stoves being imitated and bad ones replaced. Indigenous technologies can inspire us to find solutions to engineering problems of the twenty-first century because they are addressed at solving real needs with limited resources. We must therefore exercise caution in defining the characteristics of good stoves. A project to replace smoky stoves in Nepal was successful in eliminating harmful indoor air pollution, but after six months, several dwellings collapsed due to termite damage; the previously used smoky stoves had been effective at killing pests whereas the new improved stoves did not fulfil this secondary (but essential) function.

Whilst the evolutionary approach to stove design is commendable for the way in which it builds up local communities, supports the local economy and fosters a sense of ownership, the process is frustratingly slow and costly in terms of the number of new stoves that have to be built and tested, many of which will not show any improvement on the previous generation. A novel approach is to make use of genetic algorithms and computer modelling. Traditional stoves are allowed to 'mate' with stoves with good fuel efficiency, such as the rocket stove. The offspring stoves are modelled using Computational Fluid Dynamics (CFD) and assessed in terms of fitness. Fitness can be defined to include factors such as fuel efficiency, temperature distribution, volume of material used to construct the stove (indicative of cost) and so on; although other cultural and environmental concerns, such as local availability of materials, may be harder to factor into the algorithms.

An excellent way to engender appropriate design is through project-based learning. Learners have tackled the following problems: designing a wheelchair suitable for use in Kenya; producing a small-scale cardboard briquetting machine for use on the Isle of Lewis (to avoid cardboard ending up in landfill);

designing medical equipment such as laryngoscopes and otoscopes which work without the need for replacement batteries in remote regions of Uganda; removing excess fluoride from drinking water using locally available materials in Ethiopia; designing a mechanical solar tracker for the Democratic Republic of Congo; and so on.

Working on projects designed with specific communities in mind encourages learners to develop communication skills, increases their awareness and understanding of the importance of cultural and social factors to engineers and promotes people-centred design. Involving users of technologies in the design and manufacturing process breaks down the barriers between learners and educators, and facilitates the discovery of solutions through mutual investigation and knowledge-sharing.

Understanding the principles of appropriate design and technology is important not just for engineers but for everyone, since everyone makes choices about what kind of technology to employ in particular circumstances. As fossil fuels become scarcer and their use increasingly constrained, appropriate design and use of technology will become increasingly important, not only in remote locations which lack physical resources, but everywhere. Skills in appropriate design and appropriate technology will be essential in order to confront real problems of survival rather than the artificial problems of satisfying fleeting whims created by marketeers.

References and resources

Appropriate Technology Research. www.nottingham.ac.uk/~eaxhtv/ATR (contains details of a growing number of student projects concerned with appropriate technology).

Clifford, Mike (2007) 'Engineering learning with appropriate technology'. *Education for Sustainable Development: Graduates as Global Citizens.* Second International Conference, September 2007, Bournemouth University.

Engineers Without Borders. www.ewb-uk.org (a student-led charity that focuses on removing barriers to development using engineering).

Practical Action. www.praticalaction.org (this charity, originally called the Intermediate Technology Development Group, addresses issues of poverty through simple and extremely effective technologies that give people the power to change their lives).

Robinson, Paul (1998) 'Microhydro in Papua New Guinea – the experiences of an electrical engineer'. *Power Engineering Journal*, 2:5, 273-80.

Schumacher, Ernst F. (1999/1973) *Small is Beautiful.* Dublin: Hartley & Marks.

Thomas, Madathilparampil M. (1993) 'The Church's mission and post-modern humanism'. The Indian Society for Promoting Christian Knowledge. www.religion-online.org/showchapter.asp?title=1448&C=1258.

Chapter 22

Technology Appraisal

The ability to evaluate technological innovations

Gavin Harper

The Centre for Business Relationships, Accountability, Sustainability and Society, Cardiff University

Consumers are being increasingly bombarded with so-called 'green-innovations' – devices that claim to have enhanced environmental performance, offer superior benefits over their competitors, or claim some kind of eco-advantage as the result of innovation. Indeed, in these fast-moving times of sustainable innovation, there is a plethora of devices, widgets and technologies all vying for the consumers' attention. Sustainable technologies, however, have not yet been codified into standards, and there is insufficient performance data to evaluate their 'real world' performance.

The ability to look at a new product, and, with some knowledge of the underpinning technologies, make a judgement on how well it is likely to work, how useful it is and whether it is an efficient solution that society should adopt, is likely to become an increasingly useful skill as the traditional orthodoxies of dominant technologies are challenged by new, more sustainable alternatives.

It is essential for all learners, not just those in technical disciplines, to gain skills in the appraisal of technologies, since everyone makes choices about which technologies to employ in one's personal and professional life, and must be able to see through the flashy marketing literature and unearth the true nature of claims made for devices. There is not space for a comprehensive discussion of the many aspects necessary for adequate technology appraisal, so this chapter describes a few examples as catalysts to engage learners in discussion, and for educators to create active learning exercises around. Through active exploration of the kinds of issues described in this chapter, learners can begin to develop a skill that is likely to become increasingly relevant as a smörgåsbord of competing technologies vie for their attention.

The role of materials in making a 'green' product

Often a product or technology will justify its superior environmental perform-ance based on the fact that it is made from materials that are in some way envi-ronmentally benign, recycled or re-purposed. In assessing the product's claim to green-ness, learners need to first consider the product itself and the worldview it embraces. The new Honda hybrid car for instance, has seeds embedded in the cover of its information booklet and the speedometer glows green when the driver is light on the throttle, but is nonetheless a large, heavy machine for trans-porting very few people at a time. By the time it rolls off the production line it has already used up a large amount of energy in the mining and manufacturing of its materials and parts, the transportation of those parts around the world and the final assembly. If learners have a clear idea of embodied energy, they can question innovations such as hybrid cars and compare them with smaller, lighter diesel cars or with alternative forms of transport such as trains.

An important question is: what are the product designers' motivations for choosing alternative materials? Are they subtly used to replace other materials where they can offer similar performance but with reduced impact, or are they brazenly displayed to add novelty to a product? Do they constitute the bulk of the product, or are they a thin veneer of eco-minded propaganda over an other-wise unsustainable product? Learners also need to question how the use of mate-rials affects the users' perception of the product – does the fact it is covered with an 'environmentally benign' material make it more acceptable to the user to throw it out and replace it than if it was made from a conventional material?

Bolt-on renewables

There is a current vogue in green product design for 'bolt-on renewables' as a solution to the energy crisis. By being able to generate (sometimes a tiny frac-tion) of the energy required to run the product from within itself, the product somehow lays claim to being 'greener' than the alternatives.

A useful example for learners to investigate is that of a 'conversion kit' marketed to drivers of hybrid cars. The kit allows the roof of the car to be coated in solar photovoltaic material, which will trickle-charge the batteries of the vehicle. To the bystander with no technical knowledge, this may create the deceiving impression of a solar-powered car, whilst at best the clean energy provided by the solar panels will be sufficient to run the lights or the radio of the car for a relatively short amount of time rather than producing enough energy to produce vehicle motion. Whilst some would still praise this as a noble attempt to 'green up' the vehicle, it is eco-façadism or 'greenwash' – a ploy to *appear* green without any real substance. If we enquire further, we could surmise that the vehicle's aerodynamic performance decreases as a result of the retro-fitted solar surface, the surface adds weight to the vehicle adding to the bulk the engine must carry around, and the solar material is unlikely to be perfectly oriented towards the sun for optimal efficiency, particularly when parked in the shade or in a garage. A far better use of the photovoltaic material would be to create a static array on the garage roof, with optimum orientation for solar collection which would also be able to collect solar energy for the duration the sun was in the sky rather than relying on fortuitous parking.

This mentality of bolting on renewables to add instant green credentials extends through all layers of society, with prominent politicians jockeying for enhanced green credentials by 'bolting on' micro wind turbines to their residences – save for the fact that turbulence in urban areas often means that the energy returned by small wind turbines in low wind regimes is disappointing, to the extent of not generating over its entire life-cycle the equivalent amount of energy used in the turbine's manufacture. A working knowledge of Energy Return On Investment (EROI) will help students calculate whether and how soon devices generate more energy than their embodied energy, i.e. the energy that went into making them in the first place.

A question of scale

The underlying message of the work of E. F. Schumacher is often misunderstood as being 'Small is beautiful' – a catchy title appended by his publisher to his work that was originally entitled *Economics as if people mattered.* However, the thrust of Schumacher's argument is, in fact, that 'there is an appropriate scale for any human endeavour', and the same can be said of technologies. For any technological endeavour, there is a scale at which it makes the best economic, social and environmental sense.

Small-scale solutions carry a certain allure to some environmentalists who believe that solutions should be decentralised as far as possible. It is possible to take this too far, however, and ignore basic economies of scale, physical reality and practicality. Solutions on a scale that is too small are futile, requiring undue duplication to produce questionable results.

There are often basic physical factors that underpin the performance of many engineered solutions. For example, with a solar array, as the area is doubled, so the power output of that array (all other things being equal) should double. Twice as many panels will cost twice as much – however, there are also 'fixed costs' that accompany such an installation: the cost of labour, and inverters and ancillary equipment. There is a scale at which the array becomes so small that the 'fixed' costs drown out the benefit of any valuable energy generated by the array – and as the scale of the endeavour increases, so the fixed costs appear smaller in comparison with the cost of purchasing panels.

Likewise, with wind power, the physical relationships between size of turbine, speed of wind and power output are not linear relationships. In fact the capture area of a turbine (the area its blades sweep) is πr^2, and the amount of energy in the wind is a cube relationship – double the speed and you multiply the amount of energy by eight. Increasing the diameter of a wind turbine from nine feet to ten results in a 23% increase in swept area. Suddenly, the economy of smaller wind machines begins to look dubious in contrast to the utility-scale counterparts, and investment in a community wind turbine looks a sounder investment than every homeowner bolting a turbine to the side of his or her house. Whilst some people might cherish notions of their own micro-generation keeping their lights on as their neighbours enter a blackout, for reasons of technology and economy the development unit that makes sense may require the co-operation and pooling of resources among members of communities.

Technology lock-in

There is an element of 'path dependency' in the selection of technologies. Decisions will need to be made in the evolution of new sustainable technologies, and standards will have to be selected and codified – either by national bodies, or informally selected by consumer decision-making and current public perception. These decisions and choices will doubtless result in increased energy and vigour being channelled into developing those initially selected solutions into versions with iterative improvements. However, there is ample evidence to suggest that neither the market nor official bodies are always right in their initial selection of standards.

The standards that 'win' are not always the standards that are technologically superior. In the Betamax vs. VHS formats war, VHS was the eventual winner even though Betamax offered higher horizontal resolutions, less video noise and less crosstalk between channels. A combination of factors, marketing availability and price led to the widespread adoption of VHS, which shaped video-player technology until the end of the 20th century when videotapes themselves were superseded.

We will inevitably see a degree of competition as sustainable technologies compete for market share, for subsidies and for recognition. Choosing the most suitable technologies involves an element of forecasting, looking not only at our present technology needs but also ensuring that if we pursue a particular path, there are no unhelpful dependencies or lock-ins.

A good example of how this will be played out in the next several decades is looking at the transition to alternative vehicles and fuels. Many technologies are vying for recognition as the answer to fuelling our transportation needs in a post-petroleum world. At the moment, no one solution emerges as a clear winner, partly because of the presently intractable nature of storing energy in the small weight and volume presently afforded by liquid hydrocarbons. Competing technologies – electric vehicles and hydrogen-fuelled vehicles, not to mention advanced biofuels – pertain to offer a solution at some point in the indeterminate future. Selection of any one of these technologies, however, will result in the creation of path dependencies. Adoption of new vehicle technologies is heavily reliant on the provision of infrastructure, which is costly to develop. It is also necessary to consider undesirable side-effects related to scale – for example, the impact on ecosystems of providing biofuels on a very large scale, or the contribution to climate change if electricity from coal-fired power stations is used to create hydrogen or power electric cars. In making decisions that will have a real impact on the future trajectory of green innovation, we need to ensure that learners are equipped to make sound, resilient technology choices today.

A question of necessity

All kinds of devices from aeroplanes to mobile phones are labelled 'green' or 'ecological' simply because they use slightly fewer resources in their manufacture or consume slightly less power than alternatives. However, learners need to compare these minor gains with the scale of energy reduction needed to cope with climate change and peak oil, and ask themselves whether small savings like these are of the right order of magnitude. They will need to consider the rebound effect, where efficiency savings result in more money available to spend in further energy consumption, such as reduced plane ticket prices due to fuel savings resulting in people flying more often. Cars are a good example of a technology which has become far more efficient over the years, while the overall energy use has increased significantly since there are simply more of them and people drive further in them.

Often, the only solution is not a slightly more efficient version of the same technology, but an entirely different technology. If the problem is restated from "What's the greenest kind of car I can buy?" to "How can I best fulfil my transport needs?", then walking, bicycles or trains might be the most appropriate technology for people in particular situations. In general, green advertisements attempt to convince people that by purchasing a slightly more efficient product they can continue to live their lives in exactly the same way as before but without the guilt. Learners need the ability to resist such messages and search for ways to change their lifestyle and business practices so that their needs can be fulfilled using significantly less energy. Without skills in doing so, they are unlikely to survive and thrive in a world where the use of energy is increasingly constrained by limitations on fossil-fuel extraction and environmental legislation.

Activity

Learners could engage in active learning exercises where they write down lists of the services they receive from energy-intensive technological devices. They could then search for available or possible ways of making the technology less environmentally damaging. A starting point may be considering advertisements for 'green' alternative products and estimating how much energy would be saved over the expected lifetime of the product, taking embodied energy into consideration. Going beyond that, however, they could think laterally about whether an entirely different form of technology could provide the same service if they changed their lifestyle in particular ways. For example, learners might write that they get the service of 'exercise' through using jogging machinery in a heated and lit indoor gym, but the same service could be supplied for free by running outdoors or even gardening with friends. They get 'entertainment' from the latest video games, MP3 players, chatting on the internet, and watching plasma televisions, but 'entertainment' could equally be provided through alternative, less energy-intensive ways that could, ultimately, be healthier and more fulfilling. Learners could calculate savings both in terms of energy and money, and think of ways of avoiding the rebound effect by channelling the money saved into something more meaningful than additional consumption.

References and resources

Arthur, W. Brian (1989) 'Competing technologies, increasing returns, and lock-in by historical events' *The Economic Journal*, 99, 116-131.

Kemp, René and Rotmans, Jan (2005) 'The management of the co-evolution of technical, environmental and social systems', in Weber, Matthias and Hemmelskamp, Jens (eds.) *Towards Environmental Innovation Systems*. New York: Springer.

Madu, Christian (1996) *Managing Green Technologies for Global Competitiveness*. Santa Barbara: Greenwood International.

Marinova, Dora; Annandale, David and Phillimore, John (2008) *The International Handbook of Environmental Technology Management*. Cheltenham: Edward Elgar.

Chapter 23

Complexity, Systems Thinking and Practice

Skills and techniques for managing complex systems

Dick Morris

Visiting Senior Lecturer, Faculty of Mathematics,
Computing and Technology, Open University

Stephen Martin

Visiting Professor and Advisor to the Pedagogic Research
and Scholarship Institute, University of Gloucestershire

I had a crisis of relevance and rejected the high ground of technical rationality for the swamp of real-life issues. (Shon, 1995)

Introduction

The journey towards sustainability is a 'wicked' problem involving complexity, uncertainty, multiple stakeholders and perspectives, competing values, lack of end points and ambiguous terminology (Martin et al., 2008). In a word, dealing with sustainability means dealing with a mess, and most people avoid messes because they feel ill-equipped to cope. The health, agricultural, financial and ecological problems we now face are qualitatively different from the problems for which existing scientific, economic, medical and political tools and educational programmes were designed. Without the right tools, learners faced with these wicked problems may fall back on the same old inappropriate toolbox with, at best, disappointing outcomes. Given the messy nature of the dilemmas and contradictions facing us, there can be no single recipe and no definitive set of tools. Yet some ways of thinking and of doing things do seem more useful than others in this context. These approaches are as much about 'problem-finding' and 'problem-exploring' as they are about problem-solving. Our contention is that learners cannot deal with the wicked problems of sustainability without learning to think and act *systemically*. There is a body of systems theory and practice, summarised and explained on the Systems Practice website (BBC Open University, 2008). This has been developed and tested through thousands of learners over the past 30 years specifically to accommodate such situations. The approach explicitly acknowledges the tensions between our current way of living and its impact on the planetary life support systems upon which we depend. Yet despite its relevance, repeated advocacy for including systems thinking and practice in education curricula seems largely to have been to no avail. This needs to change.

Systems thinking and practice

Although the concept of sustainability relates to the whole biosphere, at its core it is concerned with *sustainable human lifestyles*. To achieve such lifestyles, we all need to make decisions about a whole complex of interacting requirements, for food, housing, livelihood, health, transport etc., where decisions about one aspect can have unexpected, and perhaps undesired, effects on others and on our wider biophysical environment. Choosing to work from home can save transport fuel, but could use an even greater amount of extra fuel for home heating. To be effective, we need to learn to consider our whole lifestyle *system*, not just separate activities.

This word system has become so much a part of our twenty-first century vocabulary that we often take it for granted. We refer to 'the Transport system' (usually when it breaks down), 'the Social Security system' (ditto), a 'computer system' etc., without considering the full implications of the word. Really to *think and act* in terms of systems is often not easy, but is an essential part of our outlook if we are to develop our world in a sustainable manner. Learning to think in terms of systems, means moving away from our usual habits, so heavily influenced by the science-based model of post-Enlightenment European thought. Current thinking in science and its partner, technology, has produced enormous strides in our material well-being, but is not without problems. A key feature of classical science has been using carefully controlled experimental conditions, looking in detail at the effects of one factor at a time. The success of this has unintentionally engendered a widespread popular belief that we can isolate a single cause for any observed event. This is typified by headlines suggesting that children's behavioural problems arise from food additives, traffic accidents or congestion are the result of inadequate expenditure on the roads etc. All too often, political or societal responses to events are based on such *mono-causal* explanations. It's much easier for a politician or a manager to demonstrate that the supposed single cause is being tackled than to ask the much harder question as to whether this will really produce the desired result. The question of whether that result is indeed the best one in a wider context is even less likely to be asked.

A classic example arose from the series of rail crashes in England in the first years of this century. Tragically, several people were killed and the obvious 'cause' was problems with the rails. To avoid further loss of life, inspections and repairs to the tracks were instigated and draconian speed limits were imposed on trains. This certainly prevented further rail accidents, but also encouraged many people to abandon rail travel in favour of their cars. Given that the probability of an accident per kilometre travelled is a couple of orders of magnitude larger for car travel than rail travel, the decisions taken about the railways may actually have increased the subsequent number of travel-related deaths and injuries, rather than reduced them.

One response to the need to think beyond single cause-effect relations has been the movement, particularly in some aspects of medicine, towards so-called *holistic* approaches. These look beyond monocausality to embrace a whole range of factors affecting human health, such as diet, social relations, posture etc., and the complex interactions between them. This undoubtedly has its strengths, but can seem impossibly time-consuming and may even conceal or confuse simple solutions. Somewhere between the seductive simplicity of reductionist, monocausal explanation and the possibly unreal requirements of unbridled holism, we need to learn a pragmatic systemic approach that is both effective and efficient.

Dealing with complexity

Systems practitioners have found it helpful to differentiate between two categories of problems, namely *difficulties* and *messes*, although many problems do not fit these categories exactly and their characteristics overlap to varying degrees. Difficulties are problems which usually have a well-defined and clear boundary, involving few participants, short timescales and clear priorities, with limited wider implications. Examples might be an engineering problem involving routing a pipeline over a river or mountain range or a scientific problem concerning the impact of water stress on the yield of a crop.

Messes are typified by more human-oriented issues where values, beliefs, power structures and habit play a major part. There is no well-defined problem or solution, timescales may be long, and at best we can only seek to improve the

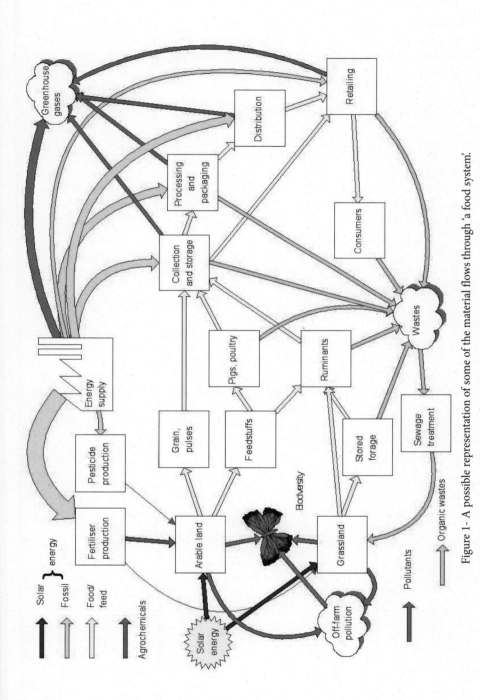

Figure 1- A possible representation of some of the material flows through 'a food system'.

situation as seen by the wide range of people involved. This is where a systemic approach can be more appropriate than traditional, scientific, technical or economic approaches.

Systems thinking and sustainability

Thinking about sustainability involves questions about what aspects of our existence we want to sustain, how much we are prepared to compromise with others' needs, and what unexpected results might arise from our actions. To develop a systemic approach to these questions will require some agreement about basic definitions and techniques for systems thinking. One key definition, based on work in the Open University's Technology Faculty, is that a system:

- is a collection of entities . . .

- that are seen by someone . . .

- as interacting together . . .

- to do something.

The various elements of this definition make clear that a system is not a single, indivisible entity, but has component parts (which may themselves be regarded as systems, and termed 'sub-systems') and that such components interact with one another to cause change. For example, questions about food supply are best understood in terms of a complex, interacting food system involving land, animals, machinery, people and organisations (Figure 1), not just unconnected crops, retail outlets, consumers etc. Models like Figure 1 are systems diagrams of the way that things currently are; in this case, a diagram of the current food production system as seen by one observer. They act as starting places for learners to consider how whole systems, or components of systems, can be redesigned along more sustainable lines. Figure 2, from Ho (2008), for example, is a systems diagram that attempts to provide a model for a more sustainable sub-system within Figure 1, a zero-emission farm.

Perhaps the most difficult aspect of the definition is the second one – that the collection of entities is *seen by someone as a system*. While the components included within a system often have concrete form, it is a human decision to group them together as a system. In that sense, systems are purely constructs and different individuals will see different systems in a particular situation. For example, a farm can be seen as a system to produce food, to produce a profit or to maintain a particular landscape. To a consumer a supermarket is a source of food, whereas to its operator and shareholders it is primarily a source of profit. Since we cannot simultaneously solve all the problems of global sustain-

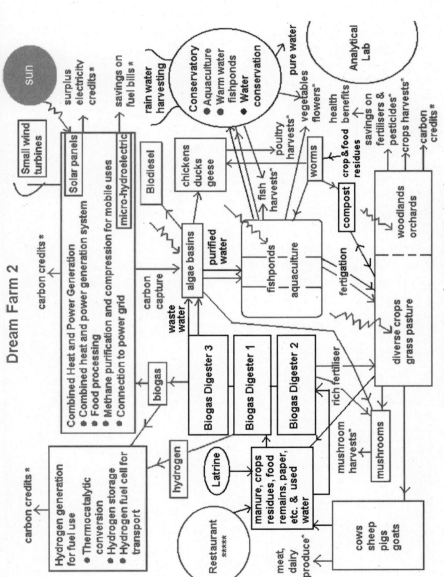

Figure 2: Dream Farm 2 by Mae-Wan Ho (2008)

ability, learning to choose an appropriate system for debate and decision-making is crucial. We need to establish a *boundary* around the system that we are debating, and different conceptions of the chosen *system of interest* will carry with them different criteria for the success or otherwise of that system. These criteria are chosen by the human participants – they are not a given of some pre-existing system. Choosing an inappropriate boundary and with it, inappropriate criteria, can be misleading. For example, choosing to put a narrow boundary around a system of using animals for food production can suggest that this is grossly inefficient, since it takes about 10kg of feed to produce 1kg of meat. However, if the system is redefined to include the available land, then a more appropriate measure may be the total amount of food produced from the total area. In this situation, some ruminant animals have an important role: to obtain useful human food from those areas that can only grow grass or other plant materials that cannot be used directly by humans. In our earlier example, a decision taken about the safety of *the railway system* may well have had completely the opposite affect to that intended when considered in relation to the wider *transport* system. Changing the boundary and the criteria can produce very different conclusions.

We are all stakeholders (with different emphases, timescales, and skills) in some sustainable, human-oriented system, but we are unlikely all to have the same vision of what it is, what we expect from it and how it functions. To share our visions, and to debate futures, we need to learn ways of explaining what we regard as the system of interest and its key features. We need to learn how to create some *model* of a relevant system which is necessarily simpler than the whole, complex situation itself, but still shows the important aspects. It might be possible to create this model in words, but it may be quicker and more powerful to use some sort of diagram. Words have to flow in a sequential manner to make sense, and one of the features of most systems is that the interactions between entities are often looped or recursive, where A may affect B which in turn affects C, but C can also affect A. In such a situation, a diagram can literally be 'worth a thousand words'. In the same way that a map highlights a selection of important features of the landscape, an appropriate diagram can make clear the key features of our interpretation of a system. Diagrams can provide the means for sharing different understandings of the world around us and of the potential outcomes of our actions within the multiple, complex systems of which we are a part.

Techniques for thinking systemically

Two simple diagrammatic forms that learners can find useful here are *Systems maps* and *Multiple-cause* (alternatively, *causal loop*) *diagrams*. Further detail and

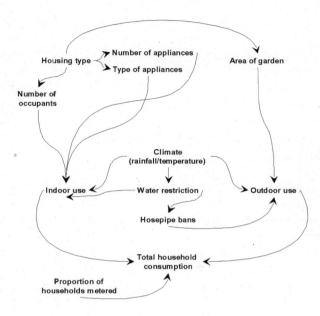

Figure 3 - A multiple-cause diagram of the factors affecting domestic water use

hints on learning to use these are provided on the Systems Practice website. A systems map uses closed shapes to represent the relatively unchanging components or sub-systems that the person drawing the map regards as important in the system that he or she sees in some situation. The spatial relationship between the shapes can be used to highlight some of the structural links between these aspects. So, the farms, food processors, the food distribution network and the supermarkets in Figure 1 are components of a food supply sub-system, and might be grouped together on a map of a larger economic system. Multiple-cause diagrams (Figure 3) highlight more dynamic aspects of a system, using arrows to indicate that one factor causes another to change, or causes some event to occur. Such diagrams can be developed into more formal, even computable, models of systemic behaviour. However, for many purposes, a diagram alone is more than adequate.

Systemic practice also involves learning a whole range of participatory diagrammatic, verbal and computational methods to draw out different perceptions of a situation, but this is only a start to the process. Learning to move towards sustainability requires us to think not only what *is* in a situation, but also to consider what *ought to be*. This is the role of critical systems thinking, and requires the learner consciously to face up to ethical issues. One widely used methodology requires consideration of the *customers* involved in a situation. Critical systems work explicitly recognises that this is too limited, and requires that we learn to take account of both *beneficiaries* and *victims* of any actions, rather than subsuming these into the economic class of customers. Systemic practice can also be characterised as a process of social learning, whereby those involved change both their common understanding of their situation, and their behaviours that arise from this understanding. Learning thus becomes embodied in action and vice versa. This will change the situation, so that under-standing and action need continually to develop together. Hence a final key characteristic of systemic practice is that it is iterative, never assuming that we have found the answer, because the questions associated with sustainability are always going to change. We must be properly prepared to recognise, and to be part of, these processes of systemic change.

References and resources

BBC Open University (2008) *Systems practice – managing complexity.* www.open2.net/systems/index.html.

Ho, Mae-Wan (2008) 'Food without fossil fuels *now*'. Institute of Science in Society Report. www.i-sis.org.uk/foodWithoutFossilFuels.php; also appearing in *Science in Society* 38, 8-13 (diagram reproduced with permission from Figure 3, members' version).

Linking Thinking. www.wwflearning.org.uk/data/files/linkingthinking-302.pdf (A flexible suite of learning and teaching resources designed to generate new perspectives, introduce systems ideas and develop relational thinking).

Martin, Stephen; Martin, Maureen; Jucker, Rolf and Roberts, Carolyn (2008) 'Education and sustainable development – learning to last?', in Larkley, Jasmine and Maynhard, Viola (eds.) *Innovation in Education*. VB: Nova Science Publishers.

Shon, Donald (1995) 'The new scholarship requires a new epistemology'. *Change*, 27:6, 26-34.

Chapter 24

Coping with Complexity

The ability to manage complex sustainability problems

Bland Tomkinson

University of Manchester

Wickedness, complexity and the role of education

In 1987, a commission led by Gro Brundtland identified a number of global issues which might fall within the broad area of sustainability, including:

- the burden of debt in the developing world, inequitable commercial regulations and a growing number of the world's population living at or below subsistence level

- overuse of non-renewable resources and growing competition for limited water supplies, threatening armed conflict over access to water and mineral reserves

- reduction of biodiversity and increasing desertification

- pollution of air, water and soil with detrimental influences on the global environment and climate change

- continuing growth of the world's population, coupled with additional economic pressures caused by increased life expectancy

- increasing nationalistic, political and religious extremism, terrorism, armed conflict, mass migration and social disruption, and

- the threats and consequences of climate change.

At first sight, some of these might appear to have little to do with formal education as it has been experienced until now, but politicians have a particularly short-term view of complex issues and time horizons dictated by the next election. Commercial organisations can be even more short-sighted, with a focus not far beyond the next balance-sheet. Resolution and amelioration of complex global problems in the longer term therefore fall to the professions and, through the education of professionals, to educational institutions.

The Brundtland list exemplifies some very complex issues that have not only technological aspects, but economic, political and social aspects as well. The nature of these issues is such that they mostly fall within Horst Rittel and Melvin Webber's definition of 'wicked' problems which:

- have no definitive formulation

- have no clear end, no 'stopping rule'

- have an answer that is 'good or bad' rather than 'right or wrong'

- have no immediate or ultimate test of their resolution

- have consequences to every solution – there is no possibility of learning by 'trial and error'

- do not have a well-described set of potential solutions

- are essentially unique

- can be a symptom of another problem, and

- have causes with no unique explanation.

Not all of these determinants have to be present for a problem to be *wicked*, but the complex global issues illustrated above demonstrate many of them. How, then, do educational institutions prepare learners to meet these challenges?

Tackling the insoluble

Traditionally we have tended to look at developing 'problem-solving' skills in our learners, but these become irrelevant in the face of the complexity of issues of sustainability and global social responsibility. There appears to have been an increasingly reductionist approach to teaching: subjects have become narrower and more specialised, and issues have been reduced and sanitised to make them solvable by learners. This creates the illusion of problem-solving, but fails to recognise that the approach makes exercises increasingly academic and divorced from reality. But how do we help learners approach real-world problems when they are necessarily complex?

A study into educating engineers for sustainable development (Tomkinson et al. 2008) brought out a consensus view that such issues have to be tackled in a systemic way, using learner-centred approaches such as case studies, role play and problem-based learning. Collaboration is central, involving small groups where the process of intellectual development is more important than a display of academic brilliance. A key feature identified by a number of leaders in the field is the need for interdisciplinary or inter-professional education. Complexity is best not tackled alone.

Finding a way forward

One approach is to develop problem-based interdisciplinary learning modules (Tomkinson 2009). The key to this approach is developing a range of complex scenarios for which there is no 'right' answer, and facilitating learners to work together on the problems in small, interdisciplinary groups. In terms of scenario design, the important things to consider are that scenarios are:

- topical
- contextual: the scenario is set in a situation that is realistic to the future professional interests of the learners
- interdisciplinary: this can include disciplines that are not represented amongst the learners
- integrated: learners become increasingly familiar with different disciplines and gain skills in applying relevant aspects of them to problems
- complex: the scenario involves aspects of 'wickedness'
- unresolved: the task is not one that has been 'solved' already, and
- cumulative: each scenario builds on the experience of previous ones.

The set of tasks needs time for learners to examine what the problem might be, what experience they can collectively bring to the task, to research specific aspects individually, and bring the knowledge learned back to share with the group. The table below gives some examples of scenarios, drawn from a third-year undergraduate pilot module. In this case the group was given two weeks to tackle each task, with set meetings at the beginning, middle and end of this period.

Key elements of the success of exercises such as this are:

- literature search: learners are adequately briefed on information retrieval and reliability of sources
- group work: learners are involved in setting their own ground rules and ways of working

Table 1: Examples of problem-based scenarios		
Title	**Task**	**Sustainability aspects**
Wheels	Recommend sustainable development initiatives for a large tyre-manufacturing company, aiming to achieve change within the company through involving different functions within the organisation. A consultant's letter provides a list of existing sustainability tools and projects that learners may decide to investigate and could choose to include in their plan.	Enabling change within an organisation; Sustainability definitions, tools and techniques; Corporate attitudes; Understanding stakeholders' perspectives.
Shelter	Develop a strategy for transitional accommodation (housing, schools, clinics, etc.) after a natural disaster. Analyse possible alternative approaches and propose a sound and sustainable strategy for their construction. Achieve a realistic and workable balance between international aid and local skills and manpower.	Enabling change across international and cultural boundaries; Impacts of natural disasters on communities; Stakeholder co-operation; Infrastructure and logistics; Cultural differences; Sustainable design.
Rules	As employees of a Regulatory Body, review the UK's implementation of recent EU directives concerning the electronics manufacturing industry, identifying strengths and weaknesses in minimising the negative life-cycle impacts. Predict impacts on small businesses and advise on preparation required for implementation.	Implementing change via regulation; Impact of environmental regulation; Impact on supply chain: Minimising life-cycle impacts.
Energy	For new-build housing, weigh up the social, financial and environmental impacts of incorporating micro-energy-generation technologies such as wind turbines, solar water heating, geothermal heat pumps and photovoltaic cells, through an initial cost-benefit analysis taking into account economic, social and environmental issues. Understand the implications of introducing new technology to the marketplace and how to overcome barriers to public acceptance of technical solutions.	Implementing change through new technology; Cost-benefit analysis; Barriers to new technology; Infrastructure support for new technologies.
Shops	Assess the sustainability of a major supermarket chain; evaluating the company against industry good practice in terms of the supply-chain sustainability, in response to serious criticism by shareholders. Recommend actions to urgently address the corporate social responsibility issues identified.	Implementing change through company policy driven by investor pressure; Corporate social responsibility; Supply-chain management; Assessing sustainability; Benchmarking.

- problem recognition: scenarios are written in such a way that groups need to identify for themselves what the 'problem' is – if necessary, redefining the problem in the process

- stakeholder analysis: learners understand who the various players are in the scenario and where their interests lie

- creative thinking: for some, the use of concept maps (see *Complexity, Systems Thinking and Practice*, p.156), mind maps (Buzan 2006) or 'rich pictures' (Checkland: 1999) may help to clarify the interactions of the various elements of the scenario

- communication skills: the task may call for a response expressed in a number of different ways appropriate to different intended audiences, and

- feedback: feedback is given promptly to allow for cumulative learning.

Exercises such as this, if well constructed, can contribute significantly to the development of the abilities and skills of lifelong learning and towards becoming skilled change agents.

Conclusions

Gro Brundtland's report has passed its twenty-first birthday, but the issues it raises are still very relevant today. It is in the nature of wicked problems that they never go away: they simply regroup and come back in a new form, just as complex as before. Indeed, some of the issues raised seem to have become even more complex and more entrenched. Learning to tackle these complex, wicked, problems is best done as a learner-centred, group-based activity. Use of problem-based scenarios and cross-disciplinary groups can heighten this process. In the academic setting, the assessment of the ability to deal with such issues has to be directly aligned to the learning process. Learning how to use some of the environmental and problem-solving tools could be done in a reductionist, mono-disciplinary way, but the real world is complex and messy, and a different approach is necessary in order to manage change and cope with complexity.

References and resources

Association of University Leaders for a Sustainable Future.
www.ulsf.org/programs_talloires_td.html.

Brundtland, Gro (1987) *Our Common Future: From one Earth to one world*. New York: United Nations.

Buzan, Tony and Buzan, Barry (2006) *The Mind Map Book*. London: BBC.

Checkland, Peter (1999) *Systems Thinking, Systems Practice* (2nd edn). Chichester: John Wiley.

Engel, Charles; Dangerfield, Peter; Dornan, Timothy; Maudsley, Gillian; Naqvi, Janette; Powis, David and Sefton, Ann (2006) *A whole system approach to problem-based learning in dental, medical and veterinary sciences*. Manchester: University of Manchester CEEBL. www.campus.manchester.ac.uk/ceebl/resources/guides (a useful introduction to problem-based learning).

Rittel, Horst and Webber, Melvin (1973) Dilemmas in a general theory of planning. *Policy Sciences*, 4, 155-69.

Tomkinson, Bland (2009) *Educating engineers for sustainable development: final report of a Royal Academy of Engineering sponsored pilot study*. www.eps.manchester.ac.uk/tlc/sd.

Tomkinson, Rosemary; Tomkinson, Bland; Engel, Charles and Lawson, Alvin (2008) *Education for sustainable development in engineering: report of a Delphi consultation*. Loughborough: Engineering Subject Centre. www.engsc.ac.uk/downloads/scholarart/delphi-consultation.pdf.

Chapter 25

Emotional Well-being

*The ability to research and reflect
on the roots of emotional well-being*

Morgan Phillips

Becoming Green (www.becominggreen.co.uk)

What do we want learners to become? Do we want them to be shallow, individualistic, infantilised, anxiety-ridden, status-obsessed, selfish consumers? Or do
we want them to have fulfilling and meaningful lives, characterised by
generosity, intelligence, community spirit and stable levels of self-esteem and
maturity? If our educational, political, societal and cultural systems continue to
foster learners who will become the former, sustainability may well remain, as
John Foster (2008) describes it, a "mirage". If sustainability is to become a reality,
we need learners to become the latter. Education has a very important role to
play in realising this.

This chapter will discuss the importance of understanding emotional well-
being. It will argue that learners need to critique their own understandings of the
'good life' and the foundations of happiness. The chapter is built on a core argument (explored in depth by James 2008) that our current ways of pursuing
happiness (through the accumulation of material wealth) benefit only an elite
few, whilst failing to bring long-term emotional well-being to the majority. Fail-
ings are not only evident in many individuals: society, the environment and the
economy are also chronically failing. Our misdirected pursuit of happiness
therefore seems to be a major barrier to sustainability. Unless we are more
literate in our understandings of emotional well-being, we will ultimately
continue on a path of unsustainable development as a society shaped by
consumerist values.

A consumer economy built around the idea that material wealth equals
happiness is, at the very least, a hindrance to sustainability and at worst a
complete sustainability show-stopper. At present we are over-consuming the
world's resources, causing huge ecological damage. We consume so much

because we want, or feel that we need, the things that natural resources are turned into. To put it bluntly, we want too many things, or just lots of varieties and the latest versions of the same things. But why? The answer to this question is not straightforward, and even if we do find it and understand it, behaviour change may still remain unappealing or insignificant. As many environmentally conscious people have found, behaviour change is far from simple, even when the prescribed change is entirely rational from an environmental or sustainability perspective.

The problem for environmentalists is that the environment is just one factor that we consider in our decision-making. While it is true that we can strengthen the influence of our environmental conscience, our behaviour is often simultaneously driven by other, competing, factors. In our materialistic consumer society it is often the case that the things we want to do are contradictory to our environmental beliefs. For the sake of the environment we know we should not fly to a nice hot country, we know we should not have an energy-intensive flat-screen TV, we know we should not leave our computers on all day and we know we should not shop in supermarkets. The list is long and probably endless. The broad reason why we do all of those things and more is because in some way we believe that they will make us happy, improve our emotional and physical well-being, or simply make our life easier. We **act** as if we believe that material wealth equals happiness, even if, on deeper reflection, we do not really believe it. We live in a consumerist society.

It is, however, possible that consumerism is built on sand. Works by Barber (2008), James (2008), McKibben (2008), Adam Curtis (2002) and the New Economics Foundation (NEF) are examples of a growing body of research by concerned economists, environmentalists, psychologists and sociologists who have recognised the shaky foundations of a consumer-led economy. Consumerism has caused the blurring of the needs/wants boundary; it is based on the (usually hollow) promise of a better life – a better life if only you had *this*, if only you lived *here*, if only you could afford *this holiday*, if only you could be *this attractive*. This supposed better life is repeatedly flaunted in the media, most conspicuously by celebrities. They have the cars, houses, lifestyles, clothes, parties and so on that we all (especially the young and/or immature) supposedly aspire to (see *Optimisation*, p.25). At the very least, we are actively encouraged to aspire to this better life when immersed in consumer culture. Over the last six or seven decades consumerism has been the chief stimulator of economic growth, but, as Layard (2005) argues, it appears to have struggled to improve people's subjective well-being, that is, how happy they *feel* that they are.

In the modern Western world we are too easily persuaded that emotional (and often physical) well-being will result from the purchase of gadgets, services, holidays, education, 'green' products and so on (see *Advertising Awareness*, p.37).

From where we are to where we need to be.
Illustration by David Fell using Wordle (www.wordle.net)

People, within and beyond environmentalism, are beginning to question consumer culture; they are beginning to opt out of it. They are realising that there are too many false promises and they have decided, or learned, to seek emotional well-being in more authentic ways. Happiness for them is not defined as a feeling. Happiness is a steady state of contentment; it is about having control over your own well-being, not relying on the approval of others or on external stimuli as sources of happiness.

It is not enough to chastise our current predicament, we need to move beyond it; we need solutions. The New Economics Foundation persistently and progressively promote the idea of a well-being-led economy. Through regular publications and public events they explore and advance ideas of how we could convert to an environmentally and emotionally less detrimental way of living. Theirs is an example worth following.

For most people, healthy emotional well-being comes second only to healthy physical well-being. Indeed, for many, it may be true that if they feel free from immediate threats to their physical well-being they will concentrate most avidly on their emotional well-being. Questions of what brings emotional well-being are, however, not simple to answer and have troubled many of history's greatest thinkers. Its inherent complexity means that it is extremely improbable that anyone will ever lay out a formula for emotional well-being that will be applicable to every different person in every different circumstance. However, the subject can be explored through a rich literature that stretches from contemporary examinations of well-being by, for example, Mark Vernon (2008), back to the musings of esteemed thinkers such as Aristotle and Plato. There is also empirical evidence of what brings about emotional well-being that has been gathered by ecopsychologists and other well-being scientists (see Pretty 2007). The New Economics Foundation (NEF 2009) distil a wide range of research into five evidence-based actions which can lead to emotional well-being, none of which requires a dependence on consumerism. They are:

- *Connect:* With the people around you. With family, friends, colleagues and neighbours. At home, work, school or in your local community . . .

- *Be active:* Go for a walk or run. Step outside. Cycle. Play a game. Garden. Dance . . .

- *Take notice:* Be curious. Catch sight of the beautiful. Remark on the unusual. Notice the changing seasons. Savour the moment, whether you are on a train, eating lunch or talking to friends . . .

- *Keep learning:* Try something new. Rediscover an old interest. Sign up for that course. Take on a different responsibility at work. Fix a bike. Learn to play an instrument or how to cook your favourite food . . .

- *Give:* Do something nice for a friend, or a stranger. Thank someone. Smile. Volunteer your time. Join a community group. Look out, as well as in.

The conclusions that can be drawn from the science of well-being are necessarily generalisations, but learners can gain more specific insight into what makes them personally happy through intuitive reflection. They can reflect, for example, on the times in their lives that they felt the strongest sense of well-being, and try to find out patterns and causes that led to those times (see *Finding Meaning without Consuming*, p.178).

An excellent starting point for learners to begin exploring emotional well-being is to consider the difference between happiness as feeling and happiness as authenticity. Arguably feeling good, being happy – and being seen to be so – is the main game in our society. We constantly aspire to have exotic holidays, celebrity lifestyles, fashionable clothes, food from trendy restaurants, fast cars, and everything else that advertisements associate with smiling faces. The ubiquitous use of sexual imagery in advertising and the heavy marketing of alcohol by big corporations pushes people into a meaningless search for temporary pleasures through binge drinking and casual sex. Consumer culture imbues us with these hedonistic values, makes us feel we are inadequate and/or missing out on things, then sells us what we are conditioned to crave. As a result we are tied to jobs we do not like, mortgages, wage-slavery and huge credit-card bills.

This is not to say that good feelings are a bad thing, there is no doubt that happiness or feeling good is desirable. However, if hedonistic values are the only ones we hold, we get locked onto a hedonic treadmill on which we are constantly searching for new sources of pleasure as the rewards from our last holiday or purchase wear off. The key thing here is that our happiness is determined by external forces and societal rewards. When this is the case we become puppets jerked around by social controls. The alternative is to, as far as possible, maintain control over our sources of happiness. This is happiness as authenticity.

People can be said to be behaving authentically when their observable behaviour is consistent with their internal values, innate talents and desires. Consistent authentic behaviour reinforces and develops the values and talents that underpin it. Aristotle argued that happiness, or well-being, is inseparable from well-doing (Hallam et al. 2006). The endurance of this idea in subsequent works by many other authors, suggests that it holds a strong degree of truth. When ethical values such as generosity, patience, tolerance, courage and kindness underpin behaviour, that behaviour is more likely to be beneficial to other living organisms as well as the non-organic world. As NEF (2009) show, most people experience a sense of well-being when they engage in well-doing. This is a result of their behaviour being consistent with their innate possession of ethical values: it is happiness as authenticity. Self*less*, ethical, values are in opposition to the self*ish* values associated with the accumulation of vast material wealth and hedonistic pleasure-seeking. Kasser

(2002) and James (2007, 2008) would argue that people who behave materialistically are also behaving authentically in that they are being consistent with their materialistic and hedonistic value systems. They would, however, also argue that these people are likely to suffer violent mood swings as they sway between hedonistic highs (happiness as a feeling) and hangover-like lows.

Happiness as *authenticity*, as opposed to happiness as *unstable mood swings*, derives from an ability to transfer one's selfless, ethical, values into one's observable behaviour. For many this involves a letting go, or resistance of, materialistic and hedonistic values. Given the social and cultural reinforcement of these selfish values, in what James (2008) calls our selfish-capitalist society, a switch to authentic behaviour underpinned by selfless, ethical, values is unlikely to happen instantaneously. A long-term approach is needed. Therefore questions of what we want our learners to be need to be at the centre of pedagogic and curriculum design in schools and universities.

It takes time to understand and accept the emotional and physical benefits of letting go of consumerist values. Fears of alienation from peer groups and the external influence of embedded family, work, community and social values make it a hugely difficult process when done in isolation. Social approval of new behaviours normalises and strengthens them, and can be built through representing materially simple lifestyles as not only socially acceptable but even desirable. Gladwell (2000) explains how social epidemics take off when 'early adopters' are joined by increasing numbers of people until a 'tipping point' is reached. A social epidemic can be anything from the mass consumption of a unique style of shoe to an influenza outbreak. When an idea, a fashion trend, or a disease reaches a tipping point it spreads exponentially and comprehensively through society. Kasser (2002) and James (2007) would argue that we are in the midst of an 'Affluenza' epidemic. Social epidemics, by their very nature, must be contagious. In the case of materially simpler, well-being-focused lifestyles, this lifestyle needs to be attractive if it is to become contagious. It can become attractive to those who develop a deep understanding of emotional well-being.

A solitary tutorial, lecture, seminar or workshop session is insufficient if learners are to explore emotional well-being in the depth required for them to become early adopters of well-being-focused, materially simple, lifestyles. Months, possibly years, of study, reflection and inquiry are needed during which the value of strong bonds within a community of learners are facilitated, capitalised on and nourished. Exceptional members of such a group may well emerge as the designers and deliverers of a well-being-led economy. The rest may become inspiring examples to those in their wider communities: the spreaders of a new social epidemic.

If avoiding social and ecological collapse is important, then all education should ultimately be education *for* sustainability as opposed to education *against* it. When consumer culture and its individualistic, infantilising, selfish-capitalist values are left largely unchallenged and indeed championed by educational establishments, it should not come as a surprise that learners become living examples of unsustainability. If consumer culture is left unquestioned, or is accepted as a 'fact of life' by educators, then learners are unlikely to develop sustainability literacy. They will be encouraged to be 'green', but not green to the extent that they might undermine the consumer economy. Rather than asking only the superficial question "How can we deal with the consequences of consumer culture?", it is time to ask the more fundamental question: "What lies beyond consumer culture?" Understandings of the true sources of emotional and physical well-being should be a central goal of education, and underpin and frame sustainability literacy. Sustainability literacy can then facilitate the materially simple dimension of a life lived to the full.

References and resources

Barber, Benjamin (2008) *Consumed*. London: Norton.

Curtis, Adam (2002) *Century of the self. Episode 1: Happiness machines*. BBC documentary.

Foster, John (2008) *The Sustainability Mirage*. London: Earthscan.

Gladwell, Malcolm (2000) *The Tipping Point: How little things can make a big difference*. London: Little, Brown and Company.

Hallam, William; Olsson, Craig; Bowes, Glenn and Toumbourou, John (2006) 'Being true to oneself: the role of authenticity in promoting youth mental health'. *Youth Studies Australia*, 25:1, 28-32.

James, Oliver (2007) *Affluenza*. London: Vermilion.

James, Oliver (2008) *The Selfish Capitalist: Origins of affluenza*. London: Vermilion.

Kasser, Tim (2002) *The High Price of Materialism*. Cambridge, USA: M.I.T. Press.

Layard, Richard (2005) *Happiness: Lessons from a new science*. London: Penguin.

McKibben, Bill (2008) *Deep Economy*. Oxford: One World Publications.

New Economics Foundation (2009) *Five ways to well-being: A report presented to the Foresight Project on communicating the evidence base for improving people's emotional well-being* www.neweconomics.org/gen/z_sys_publicationdetail.aspx?pid=265.

New Economics Foundation. www.neweconomics.org.

Pretty, Jules (2007) *The Earth Only Endures: On reconnecting with nature and our place in it*. London: Earthscan.

Vernon, Mark (2008) *Well-being: the art of living*. Stocksfield: Acumen.

Chapter 26

Finding Meaning without Consuming

The ability to experience meaning, purpose and satisfaction through non-material wealth

Paul Maiteny

Education for Sustainability Programme, London South Bank University
and ecological counsellor and psychotherapist in private practice

Since the 1960s, a wave of anxiety has welled up every fifteen to twenty years about looming ecological breakdown. Each time, anxiety intensifies with a growing sense that pressures on physical life-support systems are coming closer to tipping point. Yet, there is still resistance to accepting that the causes of apparently 'outer' problems are rooted in our 'inner' selves. Twenty years ago, systems thinker, Ervin Laszlo (1989:26), recognised this when observing that:

> We cast about for innovative ways to satisfy obsolete values. . . . We contemplate changing almost anything on this earth but ourselves. . . .

He insisted that:

> It is high time we engaged in an individual and collective soul-searching; in a much needed psychoanalysis of our inner limits. Even if the process is painful, its potential benefits should encourage us to carry it through. . . . By examining and identifying the arbitrary inner limits to our growth and development, we should learn to cast them off like the outgrown habits of our collective adolescence. (ibid.: 28)

We *know* that obesity, heart disease, chronic fatigue, depression, cancer and other health problems are often symptomatic of lifestyles and associated desires and priorities. The same is true of our ecological malaise. But beliefs and feelings have a far tighter hold over behaviour than mere knowledge of facts. We are so strongly attached to our ways of living, and our *convictions* that they are good for us, that we avoid acting on what we *know* – that we are the causes of our own disease. What we prefer to see as the 'problems' are actually ways of unconsciously avoiding these deeper causes within ourselves. These are the real problem, but this is just too excruciating to admit. Unless we do so, however, we will continue, ever more urgently and uselessly, to rearrange deckchairs on the ecological *Titanic* as it sinks deeper into the ocean. We have been doing this for decades already.

The 'inner' human causes of ecological breakdown are emotional and cultural. Emotions like desire, anxiety and fear are what *move* us. It's right there in the word – e-*motion*. But emotions are experiences which *we need to make meaningful sense of*. It's natural for humans to want to do so. And we do this using cultural-type thinking: through beliefs, models, purposes, priorities, prescription, decision-making and so on. What we attach to most ardently is generally what we are convinced can best satisfy or quell our difficult feelings and emotions.

After decades of avoidance, we're starting to own up to the fact that belief in ever more material consumption and possession as the way to satisfaction and happiness both causes ecological breakdown and is a phantom, as it does not ultimately satisfy (see *Advertising Awareness* p.37 and *Emotional Well-being* p.171). We are on a paradoxical crash-course to destroying ourselves in our quest to feel better – quite a dilemma! Even though we know these facts, can see our behaviour is illogical and dangerous, and, what's more, *can choose to do differently*, we keep on the same path anyway. Like addicts, we are fixated and obsessed with our false beliefs. And, like any addict, it is nigh impossible to contemplate giving them up. Without them, it feels that life will lose meaning and purpose. Threats to this are inevitably resisted.

Resistance is a powerful force. So is the force of cultural habits which protect us from the difficult emotions we feel threatened by. Even if I do *experience* something else as true, I may also feel huge social pressure *not* to believe it when this would threaten the belief-habits of my collective peer group. I might be excluded, marginalised. Besides, even if I don't go along with what's deemed to be true, then how am I to make sense of my experience? What belief frameworks am I to use to make sense of my self and life, if not those that are culturally acceptable and to which I've become habituated?

More and more people – through empirical evidence of their own first-hand experience – are, however, recognising that their belief-habits both fail to live up to their promise of satisfaction and are gravely dangerous ecologically. Decades of analysis back this up, but by writers who have been ostracised as prophets of doom by mainstream society because too challenging to accept. See, for example, Paul Ehrlich (e.g. 1971), Donella Meadows et al. (1972, 1992), Geoffrey Vickers (1968), Herman Daly and John Cobb (1989), James Lovelock (1979), Edward Goldsmith, founder of *The Ecologist* magazine (1992), Erich Fromm

(1978), Ervin Laszlo (1989), Roy Rappaport (1979), and many others including those cited in these authors' works.

So why is it so hard to find convincing alternatives to our cultural habit of seeking satisfaction and life-meaning through material possession and consumption? We have made other alternatives unacceptable. Dominant culture has effectively de-legitimised any explanations or possibilities for meaningful life that do not have a materialistic basis. This is in spite of the logical contradiction in insisting that non-material desires can be satisfied through material means.

Most cultures in human history have had non-material options for satisfying non-material needs, usually through some form of belief, based on empirical observation, that humans exist within a context that is bigger than them, encompasses them, and that they can experience themselves as having a meaningful role or niche to play within it (Maiteny 2004). Today, such spiritual or religious-type belief is popularly dismissed as ignorant superstition at best, and as mad delusion at worst. This is despite the fact that many people continue to find life-meaning in such convictions, and in ways that are more sustained and long-lasting than purely materialistic beliefs can generate (see Maiteny 2002, 2008).

The context-based mode of meaningfulness can be compared with fitting a niche in an ecosystem, or with the notion of Gaia, the planet as living organism, where all aspects play a part in the healthy functioning of the whole (Lovelock 1979, also see *Gaia Awareness*, p.89). But it contrasts markedly with the consumption-based mode of meaning-making which can never succeed and results in an ecologically destructive need for constant, addiction-like replenishment.

Meaningfulness through the contextual, relational mode (see *Ecological Intelligence*, p.77) does not depend on consumption, material or otherwise. On the contrary, it depends on persons and groups *experiencing* themselves as part of the bigger ecological whole, with a role to play within it, and in service to it. This is *contextual* awareness. It puts people in touch with non-material wealth, enabling them to go beyond the cognitive skills of *thinking* systemically or relationally to actually *feeling* ecologically embedded and related in ways that generate meaning, purpose and satisfaction through non-material means. As humans, we do not 'fit into' the ecological whole like this as unconsciously and instinctively as do non-humans, although we might find we feel an instinctive truth in such a perspective. No: for us humans, finding our role within the ecological scheme of things has to be a more *conscious process of inner inquiry* and discovery. We have to choose the contextual over the consumptive mode. In this sense, it is akin to a spiritual or quasi-religious process (the word 'religion' deriving etymologically from 'to re-bond' or 're-connect'), but in a modern, scientifically informed way.

There is, in fact, a stream of evolutionary thought, ignored by neo-Darwinists, that is concerned with *future* evolution through human psycho-social development (see *A Learning Society*, p.215). Sir Julian Huxley, zoologist, founder of the International Union for the Conservation of Nature, first Director-General of UNESCO, and brother of Aldous, was a high-profile researcher in this field. So was Sir Alister Hardy (1975), Professor of Zoology at Oxford University. He considered it perfectly logical that *all* human capacities must have significance for human evolution and adaptation. This, of course, includes being able to experience oneself as embedded in a bigger context, and to imagine and conceptualise this in symbolic, religio-spiritual forms. Huxley (1957) put it like this:

> As a result of a thousand years of evolution, the universe is becoming conscious of itself, able to understand something of its past history and its possible future. This cosmic self-awareness is being realised in one tiny fragment of the universe – in a few of us human beings. Perhaps it has been realised elsewhere too, through the evolution of conscious living creatures on the planets of other stars. But on this, our planet, it has never happened before. . . . It is thus part of human destiny to be the necessary agent of the cosmos in understanding more of itself, in bearing witness to its wonder, beauty, and interest. . . .

Amongst other things, this is a poetic way of saying that the human species has a special part to play in nature by virtue of the capacities we have evolved that we do *not* share with other species. These include, of course, our capacity to symbolise and having a greater degree of free choice than other animals.

One application of choice is, as mentioned, to see 'others' – nature, people, the world – as *ours* to consume as we want, pursuing only our basic instinctive needs, as other animals do, but using our ingenuity to consume it far more intensively than they ever could. Religious teachings have, of course, consistently been distorted to justify and reinforce such self-interested, materialistic aims. Their true message is contrary to this, being concerned with finding one's niche in the encompassing Whole.

At a day-to-day level, this consuming and possessing orientation tends to mean seeking happiness by using things and people to fill up an emotional hole of dissatisfaction or inner emptiness. It means people seeing themselves as being, as it were, at the centre of the universe. It is as if everything else exists to serve them with material to consume. This, of course, can never ultimately satisfy. It's not actually the *thing-in-itself* that we desire but the feeling-experience we *believe* it will bring us. We project the desire onto the object and the object therefore comes to represent satisfaction of the desire. We confuse the thing for the desire and the hoped-for satisfaction it symbolises in our imagination. Shopping is a good example. Once people have got what they wanted, the satisfaction soon disappears ('the novelty wears off') and their desire moves on to seek something or someone new they believe will satisfy them instead. It sets up an addictive and constant cycle of gasping-grasping-gasping for more and more. *It's the non-material experience that people seek.* The 'thing' simply symbolises that. Emotions are non-material. People cannot ultimately satisfy them by consuming and possessing things (or people). But they can choose to *believe* they can. Unfortunately, as we're beginning to experience, this belief eventually puts our life-support systems – and hence ourselves – in grave danger.

The other application of our capacity for choice and self-awareness is to see ourselves as *part of* the ecological scheme of things, bound up within it, with a unique part to contribute in its further evolution, as Huxley describes above. He sees humans as having the *possibility* of generating the next phase of evolution – through psycho-social development, not biological. It would mean harnessing all our unique capacities to this purpose – but we have to choose to do it.

This orientation entails finding a role to take in the ecological scheme of things, in the body of Planet Earth, linked with other 'organs' playing their parts too in a great complex web (see *Being-in-the-World* p.185 and *Gaia Awareness* p.89). Experientially, learners find meaning and satisfaction from *feeling* and *believing* they have a purpose to serve and *role* to play in the 'ecological scheme of things', and in trying to work out for themselves what that might be. Interestingly, the purpose of the great spiritual traditions has always been to help guide learners in a process such as this. Ecological experience and thinking is a new way of expressing it.

When learners find meaning and purpose in 'fitting' themselves to planetary ecology rather than seeking to 'fill themselves up' by consuming it, bio-ecological sustainability will start happening as an *inevitable* consequence of reduced consumption. It will start happening almost without trying. Physical pressures put on resources and ecological systems by consumption will simply lift when satisfaction-seeking shifts away from consumption.

Materialistic culture has denied ecological experience more than most others in human history. And it is no coincidence that this has gone hand-in-hand both with growing numbers of people experiencing emotional unsustainability of meaning in life, and with being the first species in the history of Planet Earth to have had such a suicidal impact on the global ecosystem on which its existence depends. Odd and contradictory though it is, we have 'achieved' breakdown – ecological and emotional – by consuming in pursuit of happiness and meaningfulness. We have the possibility of evolving and the capacity to do so.

Activity

The following activity is designed to engage learners in investigating how they live through reflection on consuming and contextualising orientations in their own lives, as a step towards finding meaning through non-material wealth.

Firstly, list ways in which you consume to satisfy your basic material needs such as hunger, thirst, shelter, clothing, warmth, exercise. . . . Like everything else in nature, satisfying material needs by material means is essential and inevitable. It is when we feel moved to try to satisfy non-material needs in this way that contradictions emerge.

The next step is to list ways in which you try to satisfy non-material needs through consuming or possessing. Obviously this applies to material things, but you might also consider ways in which you take a consuming or possessive *orientation*, say towards other people or ideas. It might, for example, feel as though something of yourself feels lost or empty without these people or things. What do you do when you feel this? Do you look for something more to fill the 'gap'? How long does that satisfy you for before you feel a need to look for something new again? This is the gasping-grasping-gasping vicious circle that is similar to addiction.

Now think of times you have felt a sense of meaningfulness, purpose, beauty, love, joy or similar emotion that feels satisfying or nourishing. Give yourself time and space to bring the experience back. Allow yourself to *feel* it again. To what extent does this feeling *depend* on consuming or possessing something or someone. Chances are that when you try to grab it, to have it, the feeling dissipates, whereas feeling absorbed *within* it allows it to remain more readily. To what extent does the feeling depend on feeling connected or part of something bigger?

You might also like to think about your 'life's big questions'. What's it all about? What are you here for? What role can you find for yourself? And many other such questions. They might seem embarrassing or 'too big'. But this is, at least partly, a response conditioned by current cultural embarrassment with them. It can be well worth sitting that out and pondering the questions anyway. They can help develop that contextualising and relating orientation towards finding meaning, purpose and satisfaction in life. I wish you well on your journey.

References and resources

Daly, Herman and Cobb, John (1989) *For the Common Good: Redirecting the economy towards community, the environment and a sustainable future.* London: Green Print.

Ehrlich, Paul and Harriman, Richard (1971) *How to be a Survivor: A plan to save spaceship Earth.* London: Ballantyne.

Fromm, Erich (1978) *To Have or to Be?* London: Jonathan Cape.

Goldsmith, Edward (1992) *The Way: An ecological worldview.* Dartington: Green Books.

Hardy, Alister (1975) *The Biology of God: A scientist's study of man the religious animal.* London: Jonathan Cape.

Huxley, Julian (1957) *New Bottles for New Wine.* London: Harper and Row.

Laszlo, Ervin (1989) *The Inner Limits of Mankind: Heretical reflections on today's values, culture and politics*. Oxford: One World Publications.

Lovelock, James (1979) *Gaia: A new look at life on Earth*. Oxford: Oxford University Press.

Maiteny, Paul (2002) 'Mind in the gap: summary of research exploring "inner" influences on pro-sustainability learning and behaviour'. *Environmental Education Research*, 8:3.

Maiteny, Paul (2004) 'Perceptions of Nature by Indigenous Communities' in J. Burley, J. Evans and J. Youngquist (eds.) *Encyclopedia of Forest Sciences* (Landscape & Planning section). Oxford: Elsevier. pp. 462-471.

Maiteny, Paul (2008) 'The importance of psychotherapy as an eco-systemic activity'. *The Psychotherapist*, 40 (Winter 2008).

Meadows, Donella; Meadows, Dennis; Randers, Jørgen and Behrens, William (1972) *The Limits to Growth*. New York: Universe Books.

Meadows, Donella; Meadows, Dennis and Randers, Jørgen (1992) *Beyond the Limits: Global Collapse or a sustainable future*. London: Earthscan.

Rappaport, Roy (1979) *Ecology, Meaning and Religion*. Berkeley: North Atlantic Books.

Vickers, Geoffrey (1968) *Value Systems and Social Process*. London: Tavistock.

Chapter 27

Being-in-the-World

*The ability to think about the self in interconnection
and interdependence with the surrounding world*

John Danvers

Author of *Picturing Mind*

If we are to develop sustainable ways of interacting with, and making use of, the world's material and immaterial resources, we have to change the way we think about ourselves and to develop more sustainable ways of being-in-the-world. We have to re-orientate and re-educate ourselves as beings *in*, and *of*, the world, as embodied fields of consciousness participating in an indeterminate flux of chemical, biological and cultural interactions.

* * *

Since at least the seventeenth century in the West there has been, and perhaps there still is, a tendency to view the self and its relation to the world in what might be labelled Cartesian or Newtonian terms (though this over-simplifies the thinking of both Descartes and Newton). While Newton argued for a model of the world as a clockwork machine-like system composed of distinct and solid bodies that interact according to deterministic processes and laws, Descartes emphasised the separateness of things and the importance of rational thought as a way of understanding the world, a form of understanding that is analytical and 'objective'. Descartes believed that the mind is a non-physical substance wholly distinct from the physical body. This separation of mind and body, aligned with Christian dualisms such as God/humanity, spirit/matter, heaven/earth, has been one of the foundations of scientific and philosophical thinking in the West. As Mary Midgley argues:

> The notion of our selves – our minds – as detached observers or colonists, separate from the physical world and therefore from each other, watching and exploiting a lifeless mechanism, has been with us since the dawn of modern science. (Midgley, 2001, p. 19)

From this perspective, the Earth and the natural world become a largely inanimate resource to be exploited for the 'benefit' of mankind – a vast bank of materials to be converted into energy and goods for trade and use.

* * *

We can look at this from another, very different, perspective. In the reductive search for the ultimate 'substance', which was once a goal for the 'hard' sciences, the atom was posited as the building-block out of which the universe was built. Democritus, the Greek (*c*.460-*c*.370BC), was one of the first to believe this. But as the atom was 'mapped' in the early part of the twentieth century, researchers realised that the atom itself was more like a cloud than a speck of dust, a cloud that was largely empty space – a tiny field of energy bounded by the shifting trajectories of electrons, neutrons, protons and other subatomic forces. It is this concrete emptiness which lies at the paradoxical heart of our solid world. The things we bump into, the hammer that hits the nail (or my thumb) and the chair I sit on, are quite literally condensations of space that happen to reflect, refract or transmit light, and thus be visible to one apparatus or another, including the human eye.

The other paradoxical feature of atoms, hardly believable, is that despite their smallness and delicate cloud-like fuzziness, they are remarkably durable. It is almost certainly the case that every atom in my body, or yours, has passed through many stars and been part of millions of other organisms before becoming me or you and passing on to be part of countless other entities. In his inimitable way, Bryson (2004: 176) points out that atoms are so numerous and so enduring, that any or all of us may now be composed of atoms that were once part of Shakespeare, or Hildegard of Bingen, or, spare the thought, Attila the Hun.

These characteristics of atoms and their subatomic constituents raise obvious questions about our own sense of self-ownership, self-identity and solidity. We are all atomic cousins, and we need to be mindful of the long-dead ancestors whose atoms we may share – constituent parts of this temporary atomic structure we call 'our' body or 'our' self. And we should keep in mind that atoms are utterly indifferent to the race or religion of the so-called 'individuals' to whose lives they give form and temporary shelter. These intermingled atoms do not recognise bodily boundaries, national boundaries, political differences, or any of the petty conflicts that arise from notions of 'purity', autonomy or exclusivity. The most fanatical ideas of ethnic and religious difference arise in brains that share a common and universal atomic ancestry.

* * *

Inside every apparently solid object there is an infinity of space, just as in every mind there is an imaginative infinity – though can we really speak of '*a* mind' (for where are its boundaries) and can a mind (which is an indeterminate field of energies, firing at great speed and unfathomable complexity) have an 'inside'? Where is the boundary of my bodymind? And how can I disentangle *my* thinking, sensing, hoping and believing from yours? Are we not all more like a forest, a patch of brambles, or a confluence of trickles of rainwater merging into a stream, a river and a sea, or an intermingling of clouds?

As a metaphor for this intermingling of minds, and of chemical and biological processes, it may be useful to think of the mycelium of a fungus: the mass of thread-like filaments that exists below the ground, through which the fungus absorbs and processes nutrients. Mycelia often spread over large areas, interconnecting and interweaving with each other. The apparently *individual* mushroom or toadstool is only a part, the fruiting body, of a much larger and more indeterminate organism. Maybe *we* are only the fruiting bodies of networks of thoughts and signs, imaginations and constructions – networks that we refer to as cultures.

Body as gathering-place, mind of the many

If we are all manifestations of the mutuality of existence, participating in the interpenetration of all things, how does this impact upon the way we think about ourselves? Our human 'skin' can be seen as a porous zone through which we interact with everything that surrounds us. There is a unity of inside and outside. At the chemical, micro-biological and quantum levels there are no easy and obvious distinctions between one organism and another, or between organism and environment, subject and object, observer and observed. We are all implicated in the whole of existence, participants in the web of being and becoming.

A vivid description of this interdependence is given by Lewis Thomas. He describes how each of us provides, in each of our bodies, a habitat for other organisms.

> There they are, moving about in my cytoplasm. . . . They are much less closely related to me than to each other and to the free-living bacteria out under the hill. They feel like strangers, but the thought comes that the same creatures, precisely the same, are out there in the cells of seagulls, and whales, and dune grass, and seaweed . . . and even in that fly on the window. (in Capra, 1990, p.294)

Given the ways in which organisms and ecosystems are woven into each other, how are we to refer to ourselves? When I say 'me', am I really referring to a whole community of organisms of which 'me' is the collective title? Am 'I' an assembly of immigrants, a place in which many organisms reside? How can I call this body 'mine' when it is a gathering-place of creatures, all of whom are tenants, residents, citizens? Are 'my' thoughts and feelings not as much 'theirs'? Is the consciousness that arises in this body a collective consciousness? Whose is this mind I treat as if it were mine? Shouldn't the term 'I' be replaced by 'we' and 'mine' by 'ours'?

* * *

One consequence of the coming together of these strands of thought is the real-isation that incompleteness, instability and openness are characteristics of the *self as open-work*. The self as process, rather than as object, is in continuous construction. We weave and compose as we are woven and composed. There is no end to self-construction except in death, and even then we might consider the finite ego-self as being dissolved into the network of objects, memories and stories made by ourselves and by others, and into the atoms we return to the atomic storehouse. In this sense our artefacts and stories, our bodymind, are continued, revised and absorbed into the collective stories of a culture, into the unfolding communal mind (Danvers 2006: 157).

* * *

To sum up, I have been trying to suggest that we are participants in the mutuality of existence, embodied manifestations of the chemical, biological and cultural processes that constitute the world we inhabit. I have suggested that there are no 'things' in the world, in the sense of objects with separate fixed essences. What we call 'objects' and 'things', or apples, or beings like mosquitoes and John Danvers, are only conventional labels for states of relationship and interdependence. The skin of the apple, or 'my' skin, is as much the skin of the surrounding space. At the sub-atomic level there is no separation between apple, skin and the rest of the world. All 'things' are permeable and in flux. We are all endlessly exchanging energies with everything that is around us. We are transparent vessels through which pass waves of sound, cosmic radiation and light. There is no clear boundary between inside and outside. But most of the time we think and act as if there is.

The word *sustain* carries both the sense of enduring and the sense of giving nourishment to or supporting. In both these senses cultural diversity across all life forms is as important as biological and chemical diversity. Sustainability literacy requires an education in the arts and the sciences to help gain a more durable, sustainable understanding and kinship, grounded in a multi-perspectival view, a gathering of learnings from all quarters, from many minds and from many modes of being.

The term *sustainability* also implies that the use of resources is conducted in a manner that protects the resource base for use by future generations. An important part of that 'resource base' is the polyphony of cultures and languages, human and non-human, which speaks to us *of* ourselves and *about* the world we inhabit. Sustaining this polyphony, the cultural music of fibre, flesh and bone becomes a necessity if our view of ourselves is rooted in a deep sense of kinship and mutuality with all forms of existence. It is this self-reorientation that enables us to look both to our feet and to the horizon, to combine a buzzard's eye view with a worm's touch, to re-vision ourselves as porous and permeable, in interdependent co-relation with all entities – sensitive to the polyphony of the many, rather than to the monologues of the few. Maybe we can also extend our appreciation of human cultures to include the arts and cultures of animals and birds, of deserts and ponds – to learn from, and to help sustain, both the swallow's pirouetting flight and the slow movement of the lichen that grows millimetre by millimetre over hundreds of years on a rough patch of Dartmoor stone.

* * *

Learning how to realise being-in-the-world, rather than thinking of ourselves as being-apart-from-the-world, is not easy and takes time. Educators can help themselves and students begin this work of reorientation in a number of ways. Firstly, it is important to realise that in most circumstances the use of verbal language reinforces our sense of separation from the world because we tend to use words to divide and categorise experience, disconnecting us from ourselves and from the world. Although we need to think verbally in order to develop a strategy for being-in-the-world and for reflecting critically upon our progress, we need to engage directly with experience, to *enact* change rather than to *think* about change (see *Beauty as a Way of Knowing*, p.191).

There are many ways to bring about change; here are two exercises that highlight some of the issues and possibilities.

Firstly, here is a suggestion in the form of a poem by the American poet, Lew Welch, from his Hermit Poems sequence, (1973: 73):

Step out onto the Planet.
Draw a circle a hundred feet round.

Inside the circle are
300 things nobody understands, and, maybe
nobody's ever really seen.

How many can you find?

This poem-as-instruction combines two important threads of being-in-the-world: on the one hand, attentiveness to the here-and-now, that is, developing a clear and unbiased awareness of our immediate surroundings – experiencing what *is*, rather than what we *think* there is; and, on the other hand, learning to live with uncertainty and not-understanding – recognising the importance of 'unknowing' as a complement to 'knowing'; unknowing as a state of open ecological attention uninflected by desire, intention and linguistic categorisation.

The second exercise focuses on another aspect of awareness. Notice how, when you pay attention to a particular object or sound or feeling, other objects, sounds or feelings, recede into the background – to the point that we often forget that they are there. This can lead us to suppose that the world is broken up into separate objects, sounds and feelings. But if we shift our awareness very slightly, we can attend to objects *and* their immediate surroundings, we can see where objects *meet* their surroundings, how the apparent shape and colour of an object is always determined by the shape and colour of its surroundings. As we look at an apple in a bowl, we notice how there are no edges to the apple in the shadows beneath it. We also notice, if we look very closely, that the apparently static apple and bowl are always moving very slightly as we breathe in and out, and as our eyes constantly scan the field of vision. They are actually constantly shifting zones of interrelated colours, tones, surfaces and reflections that for reasons of language and convention we treat as separate entities. If we practise this kind of attention in different contexts, we become more and more aware of the fields of relationship and interconnection that constitute the world. We also notice how we are ourselves ever-changing streams of sensations, thoughts, memories and feelings interacting with everything that is about us.

Visual images can be used to overcome the limitations of linear verbal narratives and explanations. Close observation of the paintings and drawings of Leonardo da Vinci, for instance, can provide learners with a vivid manifestation of this mode of attention. The realisation that there are no boundaries around things was one of Leonardo's key insights. He used the term *sfumato* (from the Italian, *fumo*, meaning smoke) to refer to this absence of boundaries, and he applied his understanding not only in paintings and drawings (in which objects are depicted as having no percep- tible edge or limit) but also in highly creative, inter-disciplinary thinking about the world – a world of process, change and interconnectedness.

By paying close attention to the sensual world around us, and by observing the work of artists and poets who have paid similar attention, learners can begin to grasp the unboundedness of being-in-the-world – a mode of being that could help us achieve a sustainable future.

References and resources

Bryson, Bill (2004) *A Short History of Nearly Everything*. London: Black Swan.

Capra, Fritjof (1990) *The Turning Point*. London: Fontana.

Danvers, John (2006) *Picturing Mind: Paradox, indeterminacy and consciousness in art and poetry*. New York: Rodopi.

Midgley, Mary (2001) *Gaia: The next big idea*. London: Demos.

Welch, Lew (1973) *Ring of Bone: Collected poems 1950-1971*. Bolinas California: Grey Fox Press.

Chapter 28

Beauty as a Way of Knowing

*The redemption of knowing through
the experience of beauty*

Barry Bignell

Victorian College of the Arts, University of Melbourne

Progress in human affairs is most often gauged by the expansion of knowledge. Yet despite the enormous expansion of knowledge in the twentieth century, it is fair to say that we are more than ever aware of what we do *not* know, if knowledge can be defined as the relation of human beings to themselves and to the world.

There has been in recent decades a growing concern for the fate of the natural world; a fate, it would seem, that is contingent on the direction taken by human intelligence. What kind of intelligence, and what direction? The question begs the whole point of this chapter, which is that the same intelligence that gave rise to an ecological crisis of unprecedented magnitude will prove spectacularly impotent in grappling with the crisis it has created, and that to avert the crisis, it must learn to know *itself*, a different thing from knowing *about* itself.

"*Homo sapiens*", writes scientist Edward O. Wilson, "is the only species to suffer psychological exile" (1998:243). The reference here is to that aspect of the human condition known as self-consciousness, the awareness of oneself and of the *distinction* between oneself and the external world (see *Being-in-the-World*, p.185). Self-consciousness as a fact of our existence means that all our knowledge is generated from a perspective on, above, or over against things, that is, as *outsiders*. While self-consciousness may be seen as an evolutionary gain in that it eliminated medieval superstition and bondage to the will of Nature, and made possible the conquest of the physical world which resulted in the many technological and medical benefits we now enjoy, it has been won at a cost: disconnection from the source of experience. It may be said that we know, but without experiencing or living that knowledge. Most of our knowledge is abstracted *from* experience. (How many experience the sounds of the words they speak, for example?) In knowing a thing, we affirm our own separate existence as a subject distinct from the thing known; but at the same time we exclude from our consciousness the *life* of the thing. For example, one can learn many things about a butterfly by pinning it to a board, except what makes it a butterfly: life.

Our status as knowers makes us cognitively privileged beings; for, to know is to *take possession* of a world. Knowing sets us apart from that world, as Owen Barfield explains:

> The real world, the *whole* world, does not consist only of the things *of* which we are conscious; it consists also of the consciousness and subconsciousness that are correlative to them. They are the immaterial component of the world. But today the only immaterial element our mental habit acknowledges is our own little spark of self-consciousness. That is why we feel detached, isolated, cut off not only from the world as it really is, but also from those other little sparks of detached self-consciousness we acknowledge in our fellow human beings. (1987:71-72)

'Psychological exile' is not, however, a permanent condition to which we are irrevocably condemned. Barfield (1967:169) points out, on the contrary, that although self-consciousness is "an obvious and early fact of experience to every one of us, a fundamental starting-point of our life as conscious beings, we can see from the history of our words that this form of experience, far from being eternal, is quite a recent achievement of the human spirit." It is only from around the time of the Reformation that a crop of words prefaced with self (e.g., self-conceit, self-liking) appeared in the English language (Barfield 1967:170).

If we are to take our potential as self-conscious knowers to a deeper level, the first step is to acknowledge our cognitive cut-offness, if I may use that term, and the suffering it can provoke, a sense of which is conveyed in this passage by the poet Paul Matthews (1994:17):

> Many people today have developed a deep concern for the Earth, and feel Nature's wounds as their own, but how many realise that language too is involved in this ecology (this 'house-logos')? (1994:17)

The wound manifests as a kind of longing, a yearning for something lost, a vacuum where something else should be. Although we each feel this longing as our own (for that is what *self*-consciousness implies), we find, if we look closely, that it is there in the world. Can we not see a stone released from the hand as exhibiting longing in its fall to the earth, where it belongs? Does a plant, in reaching upwards to the light, not reveal its affinity for the sun? Does the heart not pulse in its yearning for more blood? (To offer explanations of gravity, photosynthesis and blood circulation respectively to a child too young to handle abstraction will no doubt result in a blank, if not resentful, stare.) Can the consonant not be seen as longing for the vowel? Does the caged bird not long to fly? There are many such examples, but in every case the longing is a desire of the thing to be itself.

Can we say, then, that the loss of which we are vaguely aware is the loss of ourselves, our essential nature, and that the longing we feel is a desire to be more than we are, to be more fully human? Is our empathy, another name for which is un-selfing, not telling us that, although as outsiders we are able to identify things, in that very act of identification – that is, in naming them – we ignore them, and therefore cease to identify *with* them? The longing, then, is a yearning *to be*, nostalgia for home, to which the French give the term *Nostalgie du Paradis*. Occasionally, in unguarded moments, we catch a glimpse of home across the gap isolating us from the other, and it can move us to tears. We are, for a time, transformed; we become different people, people who have found our natural epistemological condition. This "felt change of consciousness", as Barfield (1984:48) calls it, is what I am calling the experience of beauty.

I am acutely aware that the formal discourse on beauty (aesthetics) is concerned, for the most part, with the beautiful object. This approach seems to me to take the subject/object binary as an irreconcilable given. The "felt change of consciousness" I am speaking about here has nothing to do with seeing beauty *in* something (as in the cliché, 'Beauty is in the eye of the beholder') nor with beauty as some kind of value-adding. Rather, it is about entering, in full consciousness, the experience of knowing and, *in* the experience, seeing the known and ourselves in a new light. Beauty is not the exclusive province of aesthetics; the *experience* is available to all.

Philosopher John Armstrong (2005:74) says something of the experience as developed by the Greek scholar Plotinus (AD 204-270):

> The pain of beauty occurs because it puts us in touch with an aspect of ourselves that we value highly (our 'true home'), an aspect of existence in which, for a while, we feel that we are what we should be. An order of value is made apparent to us. But we also see, also feel, that very much of the time, nearly all of the time, we neglect and disown this part of ourselves, or feel that we have to smother it in order to get on with the business of living. Thus we feel that we have betrayed or lost what should have been the most precious aspect of ourselves. It has become marginal; we have disowned ourselves.

Can we make the experience more than a chance occurrence? Can we, in full awareness inhabit the threshold, the space between knowledge and experience? Can we, in fact, raise ourselves to knowing *as* experience, to a kind of knowing that comes before words? For 'being outside' is a prerequisite for a language of the already formed, the abstract, which cuts us off from the source of experience. The possibility is already given in the fact of self-consciousness, but is conditional on our having "enough imagination, and enough power of detachment from the established meanings or thought-forms of [our] own civilisation . . . the power not only of thinking, but of *unthinking* . . ." (Barfield 1984:133). It requires that we can picture reality, not as objects, but as image, figure and motion.

To conclude, underlying the most pressing issues facing us today is the trivialisation of human intelligence, by which I mean the assumption that the future of civilisation consists in more knowledge, rather than better knowing. Direct knowing and participation in the world through the experience of beauty can help fill the emptiness, heal the wounds, reduce the separation, ease the alienation, fulfil the longing, and satisfy the yearning in ways that do not rely on the false promises of consumerism and technological progress. The more learners can become fully themselves through developing a sense of beauty in being-in-the-world, the less likely they are to destroy that world, since they would know that they are destroying themselves. The changes that sustainability demands go beyond material changes in our surroundings, to cognitive change, or more simply, a change of mind, upon which the psychological and spiritual health, the very sanity of humanity as well as its future survival depends.

Activity

The following activity is designed to help learners transform abstract, verbally generated knowledge into experiential knowing by developing their powers of pictorial and kinaesthetic imagination.

Stand before, say, a yew tree. You know it *as* a yew tree because you can identify it. What you may not realise is that your knowledge is dependent on your mental activity, which consists in your meeting what is there before you with the learned concepts encapsulated in the words trunk, bark, branch, leaf, growth, physical space, stability, uprightness, green, and, of course, yew or conifer, all of which combine to allow you to make the judgement: yew tree. Further, you know this tree only because you inwardly compare it with all other species of tree. All this happens outside your awareness.

Now, imagine that the tree is new to you, *as if* you have not seen it before, as if you do not know the word 'tree' – which is a generalisation in any case – as if you cannot even speak its name. Ask yourself: What is the gesture of this *particular* tree. How does it express *itself*? What does *it* say to me of its becoming and its form, of its unfolding from the womb of the earth? Go to the beginning of language, rather than the end. Let your arms and hands rather than your larynx do the talking; for the larynx, in evolutionary terms, is really a condensed form of the speaking and simultaneously spoken body. Go to the invisible *movement* of speech, the vestiges of which are still there in your hands when you speak to others in ordinary conversation. Become the tree. Find a gesture for it. Per-form it. *This* is speaking. This *is* naming. It is just that it is speaking in order to disclose, not to represent, symbolise, signify, label, or even to communicate.

You will discover immediately how difficult it is to avoid thinking old concepts. But abstraction is the habit of a lifetime, and an extraordinarily difficult one to break. You may feel that your first efforts are somewhat unreal, shadowy, or empty. With the *will* to practise, however, and applying it to all percepts, including your own longing, you will find in time that you become *inwardly* articulate. You are participating in your own knowing process, rather than substituting familiar words for it. You are practising responsible knowledge. Bear in mind that your aim is not to be correct; for truth today has come to mean the correctness of statements as expressed in the precise meanings of words, as these *correspond* to things and events in the external world. The 'truth' you are living is an ancient one, to which the Greeks gave the name *aletheia*, unhiddenness, as a thing uncovering or revealing itself. We can ponder John Keats on this: "What the imagination seizes as Beauty must be truth" (1979:36f). In your attempt to reveal the tree-ness of the tree, which can never be more than itself, *you* are yourself by being *more* than yourself.

References and resources

Armstrong, John (2005) *The Secret Power of Beauty*. London: Penguin Books.

Barfield, Owen (1967) *History in English Words*. Great Barrington, MA: Lindisfarne Books.

Barfield, Owen (1984) *Poetic Diction: A study in meaning*. Hanover: Wesleyan University Press.

Barfield, Owen (1987) *History, Guilt and Habit*. Middletown: Wesleyan University.

Bortoft, Henri (1996) *The Wholeness of Nature: Goethe's way toward a science of conscious participation in nature*. New York: Lindisfarne Press (this text contains a very detailed discussion of the role played by language in perception and cognition).

Giannetti, Eduardo (2001) *Lies We Live By: The art of self-deception* (trans. by John Gledson). London: Bloomsbury.

Johnston, Caryl (2000) *Consecrated Venom: The serpent and the tree of knowledge*. Edinburgh: Floris Books.

Keats, John (1979) *Letters of John Keats*. London: Oxford University Press.

Matthews, Paul (1994) *Sing Me the Creation*. Stroud: Hawthorn Press (a treasure-trove of exercises designed to resuscitate the living quality of language in the individual and in the world).

Neville, Robert (1981) *Reconstruction of Thinking*. Albany: State University of New York Press.

Wilson, Edward O. (1998) *Consilience: The unity of knowledge*. London: Abacus.

Part 2

Educational Transformation
for Sustainability Literacy

Chapter 29

Citizen Engagement

Geoff Fagan

Director, CADISPA at the University of Strathclyde

It is hard to imagine what a 'sustainable community' would look like at a time when, through no fault of their own, people are losing jobs, identity and quality of life. It is especially hard for ordinary people to adopt behaviours and practices that encourage a commitment to a lighter environmental footprint when system-abuse by the economically powerful results in hardship for the many. Had the institutions for which these players worked been grounded in the reality of everyday life, and had there been a connection between those large institutions and ordinary people, there is a real chance that behaviours would have been modified and a world crisis avoided. The time has come to create a shared common space in education between people and professionals, and between traditional and non-traditional learners.

When Hopkins (2008) talks of Transition Communities and the Great Re-skilling, he is advocating a fundamental shift in the way that we understand and engage in our society, and the development of a new skill set across that society (see *Transition Skills*, p.43). This means enabling more people to become skilled in reinventing society based on a fundamental reassessment of the values and principles that underpin it. David Orr (1994) asks the inconvenient question: "Why make formal education more efficient when we know that it is not the inefficiency of the structure that is at fault – but the education system itself?" If we do not change the education system in a fundamental way, we will, by making it more efficient and fit-for-purpose, support and encourage unsustainable practices.

New educational programmes are needed which are based on different values and a process of learning based on ethical principles, ecological values and with the inclusion of ordinary people. The crisis that the world faces is too large to be addressed by focusing education on a narrow range of learners: educational institutions need to reach out to provide opportunities for a diverse cross-section of the local community to gain sustainability literacy skills. At the same time, there are important skills and knowledge about living sustainably which are embedded in the traditions of local communities, and can be shared with both learners and educators alike if educational institutions become more inclusive. The question is 'how?': what would this new contract look like?

The change required is profound, and is based on an acceptance that learning from within the old paradigms will lead to the perpetuation of that which has led to the current crisis. The reskilling of the population that Hopkins (2008) calls for means the adoption of new definitions of what constitutes 'worthwhile knowledge' and new partnerships for learning. It means ensuring that sustainability literacy permeates through every learning programme so that entire populations become sustainability literate and use their skills within local communities, nationally and globally. It also, necessarily, means that learning institutions relocate from their campus fortresses to places that are geographically and philosophically accessible and open.

Probably the greatest change, however, is in reassessing the assumptions that underpin the generation and transmission of knowledge and its ownership by an intellectual elite. The skills necessary to survive in the twenty-first century are in existence already – they are demonstrated every day by those in the most disadvantaged circumstances. How they live within their means, balance and define priorities, protect the powerless, problem-solve and share knowledge are lessons that have their location in everyday living. However, this kind of practical wisdom for making skilful use of local social and physical resources is exactly the kind of knowledge that is devalued by a formal education system which favours abstract, generalisable or technical knowledge.

Somehow, a common space of learning has to be created that flattens the intellectual playing-field and creates porous, permeable boundaries between those who know (in whatever situation) and those who would wish to know. The university professor, in this circumstance, would truly become the novice learner, and the community activist who left school at fifteen and yet who knows in fervent detail the skills of political engagement and local sustainability becomes the expert. After all, many 'lecturers' are from a generation responsible for immense environmental destruction, so it is questionable whether they should 'lecture' those who will be facing the consequences of that destruction. This fluidity of role, its challenge to the assumption of who might know, and the permeability of the boundaries between learners and facilitators is the critical change for the foreseeable future. But what does this mean for institutions and the role of the educational facilitator?

First, ordinary people need to be welcomed into an institutional learning community as equals. Without this, they will be without status and unable to contribute to the generation of knowledge for building a sustainable society. This connection of education to living experience is not as strange as it seems – nor as radical. One of the purposes of education is to serve the common good. It belongs to the people. It stems from them; it is financially supported by them and, however indirectly, it must service their human needs. If education exists for the common good, it must be seen to belong to the people and be allowed to serve the learning needs of all. If people from a wide range of social and economic circumstance are welcomed into the decision-making heart of any learning institution, the institution will inevitably influence (for the better) the communities it serves.

An open, inclusive partnership between a host community and an institution would mean learners have the opportunity to interact with people whose life experiences more than qualify them to sit and debate, to wrestle and defend and eventually to decide on the future direction of their place. The effect on all learners would be profound. This injection and grounding of reality into what was once cloistered lecture theatres could be central to the new paradigm of learning.

The new partnership also demands change in the way that learning institutions structure themselves. Discipline silos have no place in twenty-first-century education. The world today presents itself as a set of complex and interconnected problems, and this is how learning institutions must help us solve those problems. Complexity is at the very core of sustainability, and dealing with complexity an essential sustainability literacy skill (see *Coping with Complexity*, p.165). To deny that, and to tackle problems as though they can be successfully distilled to their elemental parts – siloed and then solved – will not help learners gain the essential skills they need to navigate their lives in a complex world (see *Ecological Intelligence*, p.77). This change is perhaps the hardest lesson for traditional learning institutions to accommodate. They will need to accept that they are no longer the sole purveyors of worthwhile knowledge, the owners of a knowledge depository to which only the privileged can get access – at a price. Knowledge itself must come to be recognised as dynamic, related and positional – and not a possession. It will soon become more appropriate to talk of knowledges, and in so doing recognise and celebrate different interpretations of situations, and the many ways in which those interpretations can be applied with equal ethical merit in a world of competing cultural differences.

Learning facilitators have a critical role to play in this new 'education of the future'. What is described here is a new educational discourse based on different values. It seeks a learner's involvement in a new power relationship to their subject and towards their co-learners. It seeks to diminish the pseudo-expert role so comfortable to many teachers (yet so wafer-thin in reality) as unnecessary and obstructive. Learners need facilitators – not Educational Horticulturists or Priests (Brookfield 1983). The learners of tomorrow need help in eliciting information from a wide variety of sources, sifting it, understanding it and, importantly, taking a critical relationship to what it is telling them. They need help in understanding the political dimensions of knowledge creation, the social construction of society, and what that might mean when applied to their circumstances. They need to value a range of different forms of knowledge, including the traditional knowledge of living sustainably within the local environment that is embedded within indigenous and local communities – the kind of knowledge that is passed down inter-generationally rather than through textbooks. The role of the learning facilitator and local community is therefore of great importance if education is to provide learners with sustainability literacy skills.

With peak oil and constraints on fossil-fuel use threatening intensive farming as well as mass production, transport and long distance supply lines, the twenty-first century is likely to see a great deal of relocalisation and participatory democracy. Learners eventually will demand, as will entire populations, a much greater engagement in the affairs that concern them (IAP2 2009). The days when institutions of all kinds could rely on hierarchical structures, opaque decision-making processes and the strict and elitist control of access to information and critical debate are fast disappearing. Community participation and engagement with shared decision-making, and a consequential ownership of outcome, is the way the future will inevitably be constructed. This new intellectual democracy holds immense potential for change, accountability and transparency when applied to educational institutions.

The new educational era brings together learning facilitation, participatory curriculum planning and citizen engagement in the affairs of all learning institutions and in knowledge generation. It ushers in a time when collections of learners will focus on gaining the sustainability literacy skills that are essential for dealing with the new and unique challenges ahead, and using those challenges as a central focus for learning. The institution itself will, in embracing this new era, liberate itself from the constraints of elitism, selection and exclusion, and embrace its core and historical purpose – that of serving the common good. Local communities in this new era will be recognised as a rich depository and generator of knowledge and skills for sustainable living, and will be openly welcomed as equal partners in the processes of learning.

So, when we ask the question about how education will change in the future, how it will adapt to the threats and opportunities of the twenty-first century and provide learners with the sustainability literacy skills they so urgently need, there are a number of possible directions:

- Institutions will do what they demand of others: become open, transparent, participatory and inclusive – and demonstrate a commitment to intellectual and ethical sustainability that embraces both behaviour and systems. But also, and much more profoundly, they will alter their relationship to knowledge generation, learners and facilitators, changing the perception that worthwhile knowledge belongs exclusively to them.

- Educators will undergo professional development to become facilitators of learning, and in the process liberate themselves from discipline silos, instead sharing learning and teaching, knowledge and power. The learners will then begin to take the responsibility for their own learning in partnership with members of the local community and educational facilitators, in classes which reflect the problems of the world. Place-based learning will not be an after-thought but integral to the framework within which learning takes place (see *A Learning Society*, p.215). This will provide the basis for the Great Reskilling.

- Educational institutions in the future will not be campus-based, but will reach far into the hinterland of local and national communities and into the minds of learners everywhere. The days when education could be separated from the vast majority of the citizenry are disappearing. Its knowledge banks, so long the inaccessible domain of just the few, will continue to be drilled deeply but, and at the same time, will apply the learning gained so that it flows widely and usefully into the communities it serves.

- Education will be integral to the Democratic Project. It will demonstrate its commitment daily to negotiated learning and help ordinary people as well as emergent young professionals make sense of their world and act upon it. It will also, in part, continue the tradition of solitary and rarefied research but not, as now, in an institution set aside from life.

Education will be able to contribute most to sustainability literacy when it is able to coalesce around a new set of inclusive values that celebrate the potentiality in all people. Sharing power, giving access freely, listening actively to people with a diverse set of skills is just the start. This is a new paradigm of education that is grounded in reality and will promote a knowledge exchange that not only helps learners gain skills for life in the twenty-first century but is also life-enhancing for all involved.

References and resources

Brookfield, Stephen (1983) *Adult Learners, Adult Education and the Community.* Milton Keynes: Open University Press.

Conservation and Development in Sparsely Populated Areas. www.CADISPA.org.

Hopkins, Rob (2008) *The Transition Handbook: From oil dependency to local resilience.* Dartington: Green Books.

International Association for Public Participation (IAP2). www.iap2.org.

Orr, David (1994) *Earth in Mind: On education, environment and the human prospect.* Washington: Island Press.

Quest University Squamish BC Canada. www.questu.ca (an example of a university that goes beyond the boundaries of academic disciplines and geographic borders in the pursuit of knowledge and global understanding).

Sterling, Stephen (2001) *Sustainable Education.* Dartington: Green Books.

Chapter 30

Re-educating the Person

Karen Blincoe

Director of International Centre for Creativity,
Innovation and Sustainability, Denmark
Director of Schumacher College 2006-2009

Having been part of the sustainability movement since the late 1980s, having witnessed the increasing environmental interest, research and expertise arising out of the Rio Conference in 1992, and having observed attempts by pioneers, experts, researchers, leaders, governments, businesses and educational institutions to try to inform people of the imminent and serious threat of global warming, I have often wondered why the message has not been getting across.

We know that what we do and the way we live have serious consequences for the future of humankind. Those of us with children can imagine the challenges they will meet, and wonder whether they will be able to live as fully as we have had the privilege of doing, or whether indeed, they will have a life at all. Yet we have been behaving as in the story of the frog in the pot of water. As the water gradually gets warmer and warmer, the frog does not jump out but stays until she dies. In our situation, the repercussions go further. Our entire species is at risk and still we haven't jumped out, even though we have the research, technological solutions, methodologies and the know-how to mitigate global warming, adapt to changing climate and to live sustainably. Somehow, though, we have lacked the will, the impetus, the desire and the ability to do what it takes.

The excuse for not taking personal action is often that there is a lack of leadership. People frequently say something along the lines of "I'm willing to take action, but only if government legislation forces everyone else to do likewise." In the field of design, where I operate, the response from designers to issues of sustainability is frequently "When businesses require that I know how to undertake life-cycle analysis or adopt the cradle-to-cradle approach, then I'll take action". Businesses, likewise, have been saying: "When the consumers want goods that are sustainable, then we'll start producing them". We have been waiting for someone else to take the lead, to start, to show us what to do and even to demand and require that we do it. No one wants to take the responsibility for starting the process (Blincoe and Spangenberg 2009).

The failure by environmentalists seems to have been the inability to explain and demonstrate both the immediate as well as long-term gains of sustainable living. We have not been able to convey the life-enhancing benefits of engaging in more sustainable practices (Blincoe and Spangenberg 2009). We have not been able to engage and stimulate people's imagination of a worthwhile future (see *Futures Thinking*, p.94). The negative and apocalyptic scenarios of the future created by the film industry are powerful: *Soylent Green, Waterworld, The End of the World, The Day After Tomorrow* and *The Age of Stupid* have captured people's imagination. Where are the visual artistic scenarios of a sustainable, beautiful world, a world in equity, a world for everyone? People need dreams. They need the carrot. Until now all that has been flagged is the stick: "Unless you change your ways . . ." "see what you have done . . ." are the mantras, even though the dream of a meaningful life and better future is what motivates most of us.

It seems then that a different, more positive way of communicating the need for a sustainable world could inspire people into action. We need to be able to demonstrate what 'a better life' might look like and feel like, within a paradigm of a new set of values and principles. We need to be able to demonstrate how this can be achieved, what to do, and what both the immediate as well as long-term gains are for the individual as well as for the community at large.

It is also apparent that some retraining and disciplining of our minds need to take place, together with a revision of our values and belief patterns. We need to learn to live from a place beyond our feelings of greed, and understand at an emotional level that instant gratification has no lasting value.

Inspiration for more sustainable ways of living comes from many sources, including Buddhist beliefs and practices and the philosophical principles of Taoism (Dyer 2008, and see *Effortless Action*, p.58). These are spiritual beliefs where humans and nature coexist in harmony, where people are seen as an integral part of nature, and part of the universal ebb and flow of life. Everything is seen as interconnected, a matrix, or concentric circles overlapping, and nothing stands alone. Buddhism provides a whole series of meditative exercises for experiencing interconnection and directly perceiving the world we are part of. The exercises help to temporarily quieten the reductionist, rational side of the mind that is so quick to form abstractions, and reduce the constant internal mental chatter, opening up new ways of being in the world (see *Being-in-the-World*, p.185). The teachings provide wisdom which we recognise (on reflection) but which we, through our current living patterns, have suppressed, denied or simply forgotten.

Mainstream education can help correct the current imbalances, help learners gain a sense of interconnection, and educate the next generation for a sustainable life even in the midst of climate change. To teach competences, tools and skills with this in mind, new educational principles have to take the place of current practices. The Western educational system has become as rigid as the development, production and economic infrastructures that it has both shaped and been shaped by. The wheels can only turn one way, and cannot solve the problems we are faced with.

From an early age, learners are being taught in a chronological and linear fashion. Current schooling uses teaching and learning methodologies which are based on a left brain, technical, reductionist and atomistic belief system. As this belief system is the platform on which Western society rests and from which globalisation and development problems like global warming derive, it is a platform which needs reshaping in order to effect change.

Teaching is currently focused on giving learners the tools and skills to get along in a market-orientated world (see *A Learning Society*, p.215). They are taught about a world where winning and losing are important, where being good and clever is measured against a standard based on competition. Education passes the old materialist dream on to learners time and time again, and we are all reaping what it has sown. The seeds and the method of sowing need changing.

We could start by rethinking our educational platform to include intuition, imagining, wisdom, spirituality and holism, as well as basic knowledge of the interdependence and interconnectedness of all things. We could teach the next generation of learners skills in how to relate to other people, how to be part of a community, how to go beyond winning or being first (see *Effortless Action*, p.58). We could help them gain the attributes of being true, authentic and content with who they are, at any time and in any place (see *Emotional Well-being*, p.171). Learners could 'go walk-about' as the aborigines in Australia do, in order to learn to communicate with their natural environment, expand their senses and increase their intuitive powers, and gain storytelling skills to share their experience.

Learners would then learn the difference between knowledge and knowing, between science and wisdom, between religion and spirituality, between doing and being, between being disconnected and connected, between being fragmented and being whole, between the 'me' and the 'us'. All contain constructive as well as destructive elements. The education would be in learning balance and the wise use of all of the above.

A glance into the past can bring inspiration to learn from. When lecturing on education for sustainability I often look back at the events that changed Danish society in the mid 1800s, and wish we had retained some of the qualities from that period. When Denmark went bankrupt in 1813 following a period of corrupt government, the country changed beyond recognition. Feudal rule was abolished, and the country got a constitution and a parliament. Danish democracy was founded on thoughts of seeds sown in Europe during the 18th century as a reaction against royal absolutism. Change became a way of life in Denmark after the bankruptcy. Change agents and pioneers emerged from the church, the fields of literature, philosophy, politics, law and the arts, and together they created the platform on which the future of the country was based. The co-operative movement flourished, and farming became the main area of development. The Education Act of 1814 introduced schooling for everyone, with the aim of lifelong learning for ordinary people as well as a radically different approach to teaching and learning.

It is interesting to look at some of the new principles for education that were being put forward at that time. Some of the most profound concepts were based on the following ideas:

- A person can find her/his uniqueness in his/her reflection from the community. We must seek others as others must seek us. We must be each other's mirrors, and be inclusive.

- Education must be lifelong education/enlightenment/information. Education must address learners' lives here and now – and not be aimed solely at some future career.

- The purpose of education is to make the students wiser and more knowledgeable regarding the meaningfulness of their lives. Through lifelong learning, the mystery of life will slowly unravel.

- Education must be for the 'whole' person, using imagination, feelings and intuition in order to keep the mind 'in place'. There must be a balance between mind, body and spirit.

- Taught subjects must bring life to words through dialogue and discussion.

- Education must be both historic and poetic: education should give learners knowledge of the history they share with others (historic) and motivate them to find their dreams and hopes in life (poetic).

- Learners and educators must learn from each other, since both are equal when it comes to the wisdom of life.

- Educational institutions should give information, knowledge, tools and skills. However, they must also inspire. Learners should love life as well as learning.

The educational philosophy from that time contributed to creating a socially and environmentally aware nation, which Denmark was more or less until the last decade, when materialism and right-wing policies took the lead and drove the country into a period of primitive and aggressive materialism and intolerance, which I sincerely hope will be short-lived.

Whilst I am not advocating applying old principles to a new educational philosophy for sustainability literacy, I do believe that some of the principles are valid and could be mixed with new ones based on what we now know. What I also have learned from looking back into history is the fact that people seem to need crises to radically rethink their behaviour. If Denmark had not gone bankrupt, then radical change would not have come about. There are many other examples from history of societies changing when a crisis looms, sometimes in time to avoid collapse or disaster. We currently have the ideal environment for radical change – change that could bring about sustainability worldwide. Even if governments are fixed in old thought patterns, there is now room for visionaries, radicals and pioneers from all fields to change our societies.

One first glimmer of a positive outcome from the current economic crisis is a new mainstream trend towards serving others, rather than wanting to be served. There is a move from the focus on ego towards wanting to become part of communities and make a difference for others (van Hauen 2009, Hopkins 2008). There is a greater move towards philanthropic actions, wanting to give rather than take. This is quite extraordinary, and people who push these boundaries, the pioneers and new thinkers in the forefront of change, are the ones we should write about and create films about.

We live in an extraordinary time on the planet. What we do now and how we act will have a determining effect on humankind and countless other species. We are the stewards, and responsible for not just ourselves but also each other, our environment and future generations. If learners are provided with an environment that allows them to gain sustainability literacy skills, then they could contribute to a collective leap beyond instant gratification to the creation – and more importantly, the implementation – of a framework for a sustainable future.

References and resources

Blincoe, Karen (2009) *Lifelong Learning*. Schumacher Lecture. www.schumacher.org.uk/schumacher_lectures.htm.

Blincoe, Karen and Spangenberg, Joachim (2009) 'DEEDS: A teaching and learning resource to help implement sustainability into everyday design and professional practice'. *International Journal of Innovation and Sustainable Development*, 10.

Design Education and Sustainability (DEEDS). www.deedsproject.org (a project seeking to integrate sustainability into design education and the design industry in the EU).

Dyer, Wayne (2008) *Living the Wisdom of the Tao*. London: Hayhouse.

Hopkins, Rob (2008) *The Transition Handbook: From oil dependency to local resilience*. Dartington: Green Books.

Lehrer, Jonah (2009) *How we Decide*. Powells Books.

van Hauen, Emilia (2009) *Farvel Egofest: Og goddag til formål og fællesskaber* [*Farewell Egofest: And hello to purpose and community*]. Copenhagen: Akademisk Forlag.

Chapter 31

Institutional Transformation

Anne Phillips

Director of Schumacher College 1993-2006
Author of *Holistic Education: learning from Schumacher College*

The purpose of this chapter is to look at some of the changes that educational institutions will need to make if their learners are to acquire sustainability literacy skills for life in the twenty-first century. Instead of providing a blueprint for institutions which focuses on a particular form, I am advocating an education system where *process* is paramount and itself becomes the change that will take us through sustainability literacy towards sustainability. My work at Schumacher College was to translate the new worldview into both an overt and a hidden curriculum. For me, therefore, the really interesting question is how institutions can transform themselves so they are ready and willing to embrace such a process. As we begin to see the unprecedented disruption of the life systems that have sustained us, it is clear that the need is urgent and unavoidable.

The educational system, of course, is at the heart of our current unsustainable society, being both its product and its creator. Embodied in all its aspects, from the buildings to staff selection and from catering to curriculum planning, are values and assumptions which are in themselves unsustainable. In theory, this is widely recognised and accepted. Awareness of the current ecological and environmental crises – and the risks of not addressing them – has been with us for decades, yet the international community, despite applying some of the most highly educated minds, shows no sign of being able to avoid the disaster that is forecast. It is axiomatic that effective action is unlikely to come from people whose training has been within, and whose loyalty is to, the unsustainable paradigm the current education system reflects. Further, 'more of the same' educational approaches will surely create 'more of the same' outcomes: graduates incapable of developing effective strategies for building a sustainable society.

As an example of the incapacity of the education system to produce an adequate response to the challenges of sustainability, it might be useful to reflect on the response of governments worldwide to the current recession. The response so far has been to encourage consumers to buy more, to encourage banks to lend more, and for governments to throw money into propping up failing industries such as the car industry, all to keep the wheels of commerce turning and people in jobs. In other words, the aim is to return to exactly the same unsustainable system which caused the economic collapse in the first place. The response also ignores the lessons of history, where recession and reinvestment have been linked with war.

It is probable that the people taking the decisions that determine the trajectory of our global and local development are generally themselves the most successful products of what we might agree is a flawed educational system. Their academic achievements reflect its most highly prized values, though clearly many of those values can now be seen as contributing to unsustainable practices (see *Values Reflection and the Earth Charter*, p.99). Rather than people such as this, it will probably be courageous individuals who have experience of and success in real-life problem-solving who will help point us towards a more sustainable future. They will most likely be flexible, imaginative and co-operative people, able to talk with others outside their narrow disciplines and personally committed to the need for social transformation. All educational institutions will have to respond to the imperative to nurture such inspiring individuals within the communities they serve, and to incorporate them at the heart of decision-making.

Stephen Sterling (2004) has described three possible levels/orders of institutional response to the challenge:

1. There are places which respond by educating *about* sustainability. This content and/or skills emphasis in the curriculum is fairly easily accommodated into the existing system, often by 'bolting-on' modules about sustainability. The learning is *about* change. He describes this first level as an accommodative response.

2. Education *for* sustainability has an additional values emphasis and thus involves the greening of the institution itself. It necessitates deeper questioning and reform of the institution's purpose, policy and practice, so that learning *for* change takes place. This is the reformative response.

3. At its most demanding and thorough-going, education that can equip learners with sustainability literacy skills is about *capacity building* and has an emphasis on action. In this transformative response, a 'living' inquiry-based curriculum is developed. The focus is on becoming permeable, experiential learning communities and organisations. The learning *is* the change. It is only through this type of response that education can provide an environment where learners can transcend the limited set of skills offered by traditional education and gain the skills they will need to contribute to a more sustainable society.

The carrots and sticks used to control our educational institutions instil in them an aversion to risk. Even so, their leaders make space for innovation, if only to get a competitive edge over rivals, as long as the attendant risks are relatively small and the rewards sufficiently attractive. Thus forward-thinking senior management already does promote first or second order change by embracing experimentation in education about, or even for, sustainability. It is less likely that an institution will opt for the third order of change, with its emphasis on growing permeable, experiential learning communities. But since conditions arising from climate change, peak oil, economic instability and ecosystem degradation look set to result in global conflicts and disruption of current systems, it will not be sufficient to respond with anything less than third order change. Our places of learning have to become places of transformation and enquiry.

How are our educational institutions to be encouraged to pursue this third level transformation? To be fair, none of us is certain what a sustainable society will look like (although some of us like to think we have some ideas), so precisely *what* form of education will help students deal with the challenges ahead is unproven. We can be sure that all individuals, whether leaders or not, have to learn to be adaptable and take the risks which will help wider society draw up a map to sustainability, because the risks of doing nothing are immense. This volume gives numerous examples of what sustainability literacy might include. Certainly, followers and leaders alike will have to develop their imaginations, and learn to live with the uncertainty, setbacks and the potential failures that such risk-taking will inevitably entail. They will turn their backs on the greed and profligacy which brought us to where we are now and recognise a need to alter our relationships with each other, with the planet and the other beings with whom we share it.

Embarking on the journey of transition, each institution will have to examine the very basic assumptions it is founded on. At the heart of their questions, they will need to consider what is required of us as sane creatures living on a fragile planet. They must recognise that the world we live in now is both orderly and predictable *and* unpredictable and chaotic, and demands from us a model of education different from that which gave us the modern unsustainable industrial society. They must accept that any educational system should aim to demonstrate interconnectedness and interdependence if it is to offer a helpful model for living in a sustainable world. In their programmes they will need to create a balance between on the one hand the rational and scientific, and on the other the intuitive, qualitative and creative dimensions of education. They will need to accept that for a more sustainable world, social, environmental and economic well-being must *all* be nurtured, and that means helping learners to appreciate interconnections between human systems and natural systems, and to develop skills in working across disciplines. There are new principles that institutions of higher learning will have to welcome. Working in a different paradigm from the old mechanistic one, they will need to embrace uncertainty, constant change, paradoxes, contradictions and ambiguity. All will come to be seen as opportunities to develop our own understandings as we grope towards sustainability. For example, instead of U-turns being occasions for condemnation, changing our minds will be applauded as circumstances change and new information becomes available.

There will have to be a recognition and an acceptance that the time available to shift our direction is short, so speed is of the essence. On the other hand, practices to promote mindfulness and deep reflection rather than formulaic responses to sustainability issues will have to be encouraged. 'Slow thinking', like slow food, will be a badge of quality.

Each organisation may need to sweep away many of the day-to-day rules which govern members' lives, upgrading expectations of behaviour and encouraging personal responsibility. Current regulations often assume the lowest common standards and therefore bring forth the least responsible behaviour and a breakdown of relationships.

Society will be searching for new models for learning. Learners will be seeking a combination of intellectual study and active engagement in societal change processes. In time, instead of going away to large-scale centres of learning, many young people will choose to remain in their local community to work on its adaptation to the harsh conditions it finds itself in. 'Community' will become a more central notion, a place where communal work/service makes a person feel at home and fulfilled, a place to bond across generations (see *Citizen Engagement*, p.199). Our localised places of learning will be places of human scale, beauty, joy and fun, of routines and rituals which make people feel at home, and where the focus is on facilitating the learning process.

At present, educational establishments are often monocultural and monogenerational. Recognising that living and working in community creates the need and opportunity for all kinds of problem-solving, institutions must devise strategies to enable different groups in the community, people of all generations and those with different life experiences, to work together on real-life projects. Interdisciplinarity will be an important vehicle for driving transformation and will demonstrate that success does not simply derive from specialisation and narrowness.

Here are a few practical suggestions about where the iterative processes leading to transformation of the existing system may begin.

If learners are to gain sustainability skills through tackling real-world problems, a good place to start would be in the places they are studying. At the moment the physical buildings and campuses of schools and universities manifest unsustainability, whatever their courses say about sustainability. The hidden and overt curricula are at odds. If administrators are to make their organisations genuine learning institutions, they must start on their redesign so as to involve users in as many aspects of their development and maintenance as possible. In embracing a transformative agenda, institutions will be modelling the need and capacity to live with ambiguity and uncertainty.

Students, staff and community could gain sustainability literacy skills through engaging in both policy-making and management decisions about campus and community transformation. For example, food – its growing, sourcing and cooking – offers limitless opportunities for both real-life learning and promoting the resilience of the local community. Staff selection and recruitment, campus traffic management, building maintenance and estate management, energy provision and security are critical areas in which everyone can engage and learn through the institutional transformation process.

A root and branch review of facilities could lead to a gradual retro-fit using more sustainable technologies. In this, learners can gain skills in ecological design, getting a practical understanding of principles such as adaptation rather than replacement, reducing use of resources, diversity rather than uniformity, feedback, relationships, connectedness, and so on.

Appropriate assessment procedures will have to be devised to ensure that sustainability literacy is centrally valued. This may involve a shift away from the kind of marks-orientated summative assessment that is currently dominant within the education system, towards formative assessment and assessment for learning (Broadfoot 2007). Quality assurance procedures can nurture the context which enables individual learners to acquire a broad and diverse range of skills and attributes for sustainable living, such as the courage to take risks; the capacity to work hard under pressure; the willingness to deal with setbacks; intellectual flexibility and innovative thinking; confidence to work when there are no 'right' answers; co-operation as well as competition; and understanding of social, environmental and economic well-being. At the same time, procedures requiring the constant review of plans and policies need to be incorporated into organisational practices. For example, more flexibility has to be designed into programme planning so real-life learning opportunities can be seized as they arise.

All aspects of both the overt and hidden curricula will have to be revisited time and again, and re-examined to see whether and how they contribute to the critically important agenda of reorientating education towards sustainability. A fearless and ongoing scrutiny of institutional plans, practices and policies must be welcomed in the spirit of identifying what will promote transformation. And, on the journey, we shall have to identify between us what seems to work, sharing good practice across institutions. Administrators will have to let go the desire to keep control, because the speed of the transformation required is such that traditional planning methodologies just will not deliver. Change agents may be anywhere and everywhere in the institution, and transformation will be bottom up, top down and middle out.

Predictions of irreversible climate change, the urgency of learning low-carbon lifestyles, the unacceptable disparity between global rich and poor – all these demand that there can be no further procrastination. We might fear that achieving sustainability is impossible. Yet, given that in our own various ways we have all contributed to the problem, perhaps our shared steps in a new direction might lead us on a more constructive path. Learning institutions are uniquely well placed to represent an attractive and positive set of values aligned with humans' best aspirations, and to rise to our most demanding and potentially most rewarding remit: of helping learners develop the skills to survive and thrive in the challenging conditions of the twenty-first century, and contribute to a more sustainable future.

References and resources

Berry, Thomas (1999) *The Great Work*. Hollingbourne: Bell Tower.

Broadfoot, Patricia (2007) *An Introduction to Assessment*. London: Continuum International (describes how assessment needs to change in response to the new realities of the twenty-first century).

Orr, David (2004) *Earth in Mind: On education, environment and the human prospect* (revised edn). Washington: Island Press.

Phillips, Anne (2008) *Holistic Education: Learning from Schumacher College*. Dartington: Green Books.

Sterling, Stephen (2004) 'Higher education, sustainability and the role of systemic learning', in Corcoran, Peter and Wals, Arjen (eds.) *Higher Education and the Challenge of Sustainability: Contestation, critique, practice, and promise*. Dordrecht: Kluwer Academic.

Stone, Michael and Barlow, Zenobia (2005) *Ecological Literacy: Educating our children for a sustainable world*. San Francisco: Sierra Club Books.

Chapter 32

A Learning Society

Kate Davies

Director, Center for Creative Change, Antioch University Seattle

*The next step in human evolution depends on developing a society
that can learn to live sustainably on the Earth*

Human evolution has always depended on the ability of communities and groups to learn. In prehistoric times, bands of early hominids survived by learning how to work together to find food. The Agricultural Revolution was only possible because hunter-gatherers shared information about how to cultivate seeds and domesticate animals. In the eighteenth century, the Industrial Revolution was built on a partnership between scientists and capitalists. These and many other advances depended on collaborative learning. Now, in our time, we need to develop an entire learning society so humankind can take the next step in its evolution.

To continue our evolutionary journey, *Homo sapiens* needs to learn how to live sustainably on the Earth (see *Finding Meaning Without Consuming*, p.178). Previous advances, while bringing many gains, have led to an ecological crisis of unprecedented proportions that threatens our well-being, and perhaps our very survival. Created by Western culture's addiction to economic growth and consumerism, the crisis is comprised of many interconnected facets including climate change, the depletion of natural resources, the loss of biodiversity, and increasing pollution and toxic wastes. Looking at the whole picture, it is easy to see that human health and the health of the ecosystems which support life are in jeopardy. Unless our species can take the next step and learn to think and act sustainably, the future appears grim.

If learners are to gain the sustainability literacy skills necessary for life in the twenty-first century, there will need to be a fundamental reform of the education system. Today's schools, colleges and universities serve the needs of the industrial society, fostering consumerism, over-reliance on technical solutions, competition and individualism. They prepare students to become willing cogs in a vast dysfunctional economic machine. Their approach to learning emphasises theories over ethics, detachment over relationship, and immediate answers over thoughtful inquiry. Based on a worldview that asserts the superiority of our species above all others, mainstream education perpetuates the patterns of thinking and behaving that have caused the ecological crisis.

Among those who have called for a radical transformation of education are David Orr and Fritjof Capra. They have suggested that the purpose of education is to develop an ecologically literate society – one that understands the principles of ecological systems and uses them to design sustainable human systems. David Orr's (1992) book *Ecological Literacy* developed this idea and laid out an entire educational agenda based on the belief that "all education is environmental education". At about the same time, New England educators and environmentalists Laurie Lane-Zucker, John Elder and David Sobel coined the phrase "place-based education". This form of education is based on the proposition that the best learning happens when it is grounded in familiar local communities and ecosystems (Sobel 2004, Elder 1998). Then in 1999 Ed O'Sullivan went to the other end of the spatial scale and advocated a cosmological approach to education. In his book *Transformative Learning* (O'Sullivan 1999), he suggested that education should be based on the "universe story", the grand narrative of the cosmos originally developed by Brian Swimme and Thomas Berry (1992).

Ecological literacy, place-based education and a cosmological approach to education are excellent suggestions. But they do not fully recognise that the transition to sustainability will require creating an entire learning society where people gain sustainability literacy skills together. Just as it 'takes a village to raise a child', it will take human society as a whole to learn how to live lightly on the Earth. No one person or group of people has all the answers. We need the knowledge of indigenous peoples, the expertise of people who work on the land, the curiosity of children, and the wisdom of the elders. We need artists, scientists, poets, engineers, spiritual leaders and film stars. In short, we need everyone's creativity and ingenuity. Only by listening to each other and sharing what we know will humankind be capable of evolving truly sustainable societies.

Active listening and authentic sharing are essential, not only because they encourage the exchange of ideas, but because they make collaborative learning possible. Like a synergistic chemical reaction in which substances interact to create new ones, collaborative learning is a powerful way of creating new knowledge. When individuals share their thoughts and experiences about a mutual problem, new and better solutions emerge. The collective creativity often generated in groups leads to fresh perspectives and innovative thinking. Recognising that 'the whole is greater than the sum of the parts', collaborative learning views learning as a social process as well as an individual one.

If learning is a social phenomenon, education cannot be limited to schools, colleges and universities. It becomes a lifelong active learning process that can occur anywhere, any time, with anyone, no matter how young or old. Learning is not a segregated set of activities, conducted at specific times of the day, in specific places, and at a specific stage of life. Instead, it is integrated into the fabric of everyday living. As singer and actress Eartha Kitt once said, "I am learning all the time. The tombstone will be my diploma." And understanding education as an active, lifelong, collaborative process is at the heart of a learning society.

The idea of a learning society was first proposed by American educational philosopher Robert Hutchins. In a 1968 book called *The Learning Society*, he advocated a society whose primary goals were continuous learning, active citizenship and social well-being. According to Hutchins (1953:3), "The object of the educational system, taken as a whole, is not to produce hands for industry or to teach the young how to make a living. It is to produce responsible citizens." His idea of a learning society was based on the belief that education should improve society by helping learners understand, participate in, and change the world around them.

Sadly, Hutchins' original idea has been turned on its head. Since the mid-1970s, governments and businesses have used the phrase 'a learning society' to mean the opposite of what he intended. Arguing that its purpose is to continuously update workers' skills, they are using this idea to enhance national competitiveness and economic growth. For instance, in 1998 the UK government published a Green Paper called *The Learning Age* which stated that a learning society could help ensure a well-trained and adaptable labour force. The paper calls for the UK to be re-skilled to create a repeat of the industrial revolution, with a nod towards social justice in the limited sense of more people having the opportunity to get rich, but without considering the disastrous impact of the previous industrial revolution on the systems which support life. The introduction to the paper states that:

> The Industrial Revolution was built on capital investment in plant and machinery, skills and hard physical labour. . . . We will succeed by transforming inventions into new wealth, just as we did a hundred years ago. But unlike then, everyone must have the opportunity to innovate and to gain reward – not just in research laboratories, but on the production line, in design studios, in retail outlets, and in providing services. (*The Learning Age* 1998: introduction section 1)

The more recent Leitch Review of Skills (2006) is entitled *Prosperity for all in the global economy: world-class skills*, and echoes exactly the same sentiments:

> In the 19th century, the UK had the natural resources, the labour force and the inspiration to lead the world into the Industrial Revolution. Today, we are witnessing a different type of revolution. For developed countries who cannot compete on natural resources and low labour costs, success demands a more service-led economy and high value-added industry. . . . The prize for our country will be enormous – higher productivity, the creation of wealth and social justice. (Leitch Review of Skills 2006:1)

The thought that a learning society should produce engaged citizens with the capacity to lead social change has all but disappeared from public discourse.

So how can we revive Hutchins' original idea and develop a learning society to assist humankind's evolution towards sustainability? How can we help learners of all kinds gain the sustainability literacy skills they will need to survive and thrive in the twenty-first century while building a more sustainable world? A good start may be to explore how a learning society can support ecological literacy, place-based education and a cosmological approach to learning. Let me suggest six strategies:

1. Creating Learning Communities

Collaborative learning happens best in communities, so it makes sense to create learning communities for sustainability throughout society. First developed in higher education, there are now many types of learning communities, including professional, online, spiritual and neighbourhood ones. A learning community is any group of people who share a common purpose and who are engaged in learning from each other. Conversation Cafés and World Cafés are other forms of learning community that can bring a diverse range of participants together to share perspectives on sustainability issues. Involvement in practical shared tasks such as creating community gardens or building a transition town can stimulate active learning and the sharing of skills.

2. Learning from Experience

Experience is an important guide to living sustainably. Books and experts can be helpful, but our own lived experience is a powerful teacher. Through experimentation and critical thinking we can learn what works and what does not. John Dewey, the father of experiential education, claimed that learning from experience can equip students to become better citizens. By developing knowledge based on their own experiences of the world, they become responsible and engaged members of society. This form of active learning is obviously very different from conventional educational practices which deliver a predetermined body of information to passive learners. Experience does not just have to be personal, however. It is also possible to learn from the historical, place-based experience of living sustainably in the local environment which exists within local communities and is passed on through the generations (Bowers 2006).

3. Fostering a New Cultural Worldview:

A learning society for sustainability could foster the development of a new cultural worldview – one that is based on respect for the Earth and the great diversity of life that humans depend on both for meaning and for continued existence (see *Values Reflection and the Earth Charter*, p.99). With its presumption of human superiority, the dominant Western worldview is based on disrespect and arrogance. It assumes humankind has the inherent right to over-exploit other species and exhaust the planet's resources, sawing away at the branch that we and countless other species are standing on. Developing values and beliefs consistent with sustainability will require a shared understanding of the destructive consequences of the old worldview, as well as a widely-held desire to create a respectful, long-term relationship with the Earth.

4. Thinking Systemically

A learning society must be able to think systemically. Based on the belief that the parts of a system can best be understood in the context of their relationships with each other, systemic thinking emphasises patterns, trends and feedback loops (see *Systems Thinking* p.84, and *Gaia Awareness* p.89). Within a learning society, systemic thinking would focus on understanding the interactions between human and ecological systems, and restructuring human systems to be more sustainable. Without systemic thinking, society will continue to apply ineffective band-aid solutions that do little to resolve underlying problems.

5. Embracing Diversity

A learning society would embrace diversity – not only different cultures and ethnicities, but also different ideas, beliefs, and ways of knowing. A diverse learning society is important because it demonstrates a commitment to a democracy based on inclusion, equality and respect. It is also important because differences are a source of learning. We can learn from people who do not think like us because they challenge our assumptions, beliefs and expectations. We can learn from the wisdom of peoples and communities around the world that have proved their sustainability over hundreds or thousands of years, who have found ways to live in a great diversity of local environments and conditions. In the same way that the health of an ecosystem depends on its biodiversity, the sustainability of human systems depends on cultural diversity and a diversity of ideas and practices.

6. Whole Person Learning

A learning society could foster the development of whole human beings, who are able to think critically, respond compassionately and act ethically. Whole person learning enables students to grow as authentic human beings. It develops their personhood. This is very different from contemporary education, which focuses on the intellect while ignoring ethical values, emotions, embodied experience and the grounded experience of place. Contemporary education leaves learners with few practical skills for sensitive engagement with those around them, for interacting with their local environment, or for navigating the complex world around them. We need a learning society that engages and integrates people's hearts, minds, hands and spirits.

These six strategies are a beginning, but there is not much time. The task of developing a learning society to facilitate humankind's evolution towards sustainability is urgent. Given current trends, our species will need to learn and change more in the next 50 years than it has in the past 50,000. The Agricultural Revolution took thousands of years, and the Industrial Revolution took 200. We have so much less time to achieve the massive social changes needed for survival. While governments are urging us towards another, even more intensified Industrial Revolution through their skills agendas, it is urgent for us to step back, look at the larger picture, and ask what skills it will take for people to be able to contribute to thriving, flourishing and, above all, sustainable societies. Let us hope that the urgency of the global situation catalyses the creation of a learning society where people can gain sustainability literacy skills and dramatically enhance *Homo sapiens'* ability both to survive and evolve.

References and resources

Berry, Thomas (2000) *The Great Work: Our way into the future.* New York: Bell Tower.

Berry, Thomas and Swimme, Brian (1992) *The Universe Story: A celebration of the unfolding of the cosmos.* New York: HarperCollins.

Bowers, Chet (2006) 'Silences and double binds: why the theories of John Dewey and Paulo Freire cannot contribute to revitalizing the commons'. *Capitalism, Nature, Socialism,* 17:3, 71-87.

Capra, Fritjof (2004) *The Hidden Connections: A science for sustainable living.* New York: Anchor.

Department for Education and Employment (DfEE) (1998) *The learning age: a renaissance for a new Britain.* UK Government Green Paper. www.lifelonglearning.co.uk/greenpaper.

Elder, John (1998) *Stories in the Land: A place-based environmental education anthology.* Massachusetts: Orion Society.

Hutchins, Robert (1953) *The University of Utopia.* University of Chicago Press.

Hutchins, Robert (1968). *The Learning Society.* University of Chicago Press.

Leitch Review of Skills (2006) *Prosperity for all in the global economy: world-class skills.* http://hm-treasury.gov.uk/leitch.

Orr, David (1992) *Ecological Literacy: Education and the transition to a postmodern world.* Albany: State University of New York Press.

O'Sullivan, Edmund (1999) *Transformative Learning: Educational vision for the 21st century.* London: Zed Books.

Sobel, David (2004) *Place-based Education: Connecting classrooms and communities.* Massachusetts: Orion Society.

Other books by these authors available from Green Books:

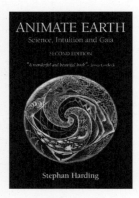

ANIMATE EARTH
Science, Intuition and Gaia

Stephan Harding

"*Animate Earth* represents systems science at its best . . . gives a whole new dimension to what 'environment-friendly' really means." – Jonathon Porritt

In *Animate Earth* Stephan Harding explores how Gaian science can help us to develop a sense of connectedness with the 'more-than-human' world. His work is based on a careful integration of rational scientific analysis with our intuition, sensing and feeling – a vitally important task at this time of severe ecological and climate crisis. This expanded second edition includes a new chapter on fungi, new contemplative exercises and an update on the global climate situation. ISBN 978 1 900322 54 6, 224pp with illustrations, charts and diagrams, £12.95 pb.

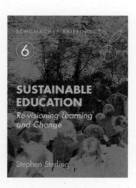

SUSTAINABLE EDUCATION
Re-visioning Learning and Change
Schumacher Briefing No. 6

Stephen Sterling

"I've read no clearer or more concise description of the need for authentic education than that given here . . . The stakes have never been higher." – David Orr

Since its publication in 2001, *Sustainable Education* has become a recognised classic in the field of education for sustainability. This Briefing critiques the prevailing managerial and mechanistic paradigm in education, and argues that an ecological view of educational theory, practice and policy is necessary to assist the sustainability transition. It then shows how 'sustainable education' – change of educational culture towards the realisation of human potential and the interdependence of social, economic and ecological well-being – can lead to transformative learning. The Briefing ends with a discussion of change strategies, emphasising the need for vision and design at all levels of educational systems, and includes action suggestions for both policymakers and practitioners. ISBN 978 1 870098 99 1, 96pp, £7.00 pb.

HOLISTIC EDUCATION
Learning from Schumacher College
by Anne Phillips

Schumacher College, set up as an international centre for ecological and spiritual studies, has developed a worldwide reputation for the quality of the unique learning experience it offers. Individuals and groups come from across the world to learn about subjects relating to environmental and social sustainability. Students are often so inspired that many express a wish to set up similar organisations elsewhere in the world. Educators and trainers ask how the College was set up, what the magic ingredients were, and what students have done after having been there. This book is an attempt to answer those questions, and describes how the College came to be set up by The Dartington Hall Trust in Devon, England. ISBN 978 1 900322 36 2, 144pp with 16pp photos, £9.95 pb.

COMMUNITY, EMPOWERMENT AND SUSTAINABLE DEVELOPMENT
Edited by John Blewitt

"Provides refreshing insights into how diverse communities are engaging with this agenda and taking concrete steps forward. It presents compelling stories which celebrate good practice and which will help inspire changes towards a more sustainable future." – Daniella Tilbury, Professor of Sustainability, University of Gloucestershire

This book explores a compelling range of community-based activities from different cultures and nations which help nurture intercultural understanding and practices of sustainable development. The specially commissioned chapters from practitioners and academics offer a set of interconnected case studies, personal stories, philosophical discussions and critical reflections on direct experiences focusing on co-operative action, creative media innovation and community empowerment connecting individuals, groups, organisations from across our converging world. At the book's core is a central belief that ecological sustainability can only be attained through social learning, community empowerment, participation and a commitment to global justice. ISBN 978 1 900322 31 7, 192pp with photos and diagrams, £14.95 pb.

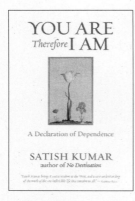

YOU ARE, THEREFORE I AM

A Declaration of Dependence

by Satish Kumar

"Satish Kumar offers us the gift of *So Hum* –'You Are, Therefore I Am'. His mental journey and inspirations need to become everyone's inspiration, to help us to move from violence to non-violence, from greed to compassion, from arrogance to humility."
– Vandana Shiva, author of *Staying Alive*

This book traces the spiritual journey of Satish Kumar – child monk, peace pilgrim, ecological activist and educator. In it he traces the sources of inspiration which formed his understanding of the world as a network of multiple and diverse relationships. Includes memories of discussions with the Indian sage Vinoba Bhave, J. Krishnamurti, Bertrand Russell, Martin Luther King, and E. F. Schumacher. ISBN 978 1 903998 18 2, 320pp, £9.95 pb.

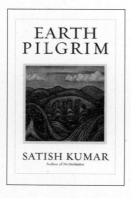

EARTH PILGRIM

by Satish Kumar

In *Earth Pilgrim* Satish Kumar draws on his personal experience and understanding of the spiritual traditions of both East and West. The book takes the form of conversations between Satish and others about the inner and outer aspects of pilgrimage. If we want to tread the pilgrim's path, we need to go beyond ideas of good and evil, and to be dedicated to our quest – to our natural calling. We need to shed not just our unnecessary material possessions, but also our burdens of fear, anxiety, doubt and worry; in this way we can find spiritual renewal and enter on the great adventure into the unknown. Paradoxically, being on a pilgrimage doesn't necessarily mean travelling from one place to another – it means a state of mind, a state of consciousness, a state of fearlessness. Satish believes that at this stage of human history we now need a new kind of pilgrim, unattached to any form of dogma – 'Earth Pilgrims', who are seeking a deep commitment to life in the here and now, upon this earth. We need to realise that we are all connected, and through that connectivity we become pilgrims. ISBN 978 1 900322 57 7, 144pp with drawings by Cecil Collins, £10.95 hb.